Doing Projects and Reports in Engineering

www.thestudyspace.com – the leading study skills website

Study Skills

Academic Success
Academic Writing Skills for International Students
The Business Student's Phrase Book
Cite Them Right (10th edn)
Critical Thinking and Persuasive Writing for
  Postgraduates
Critical Thinking Skills (3rd edn)
Dissertations and Project Reports
Doing Projects and Reports in Engineering
The Employability Journal
Essentials of Essay Writing
The Exam Skills Handbook (2nd edn)
Get Sorted
Great Ways to Learn Anatomy and Physiology
  (2nd edn)
How to Begin Studying English Literature (4th edn)
How to Use Your Reading in Your Essays (3rd edn)
How to Write Better Essays (4th edn)
How to Write Your Undergraduate Dissertation
  (3rd edn)
Improve Your Grammar (2nd edn)
The Mature Student's Handbook
Mindfulness for Students
The Macmillan Student Planner
The Personal Tutor's Handbook
Presentation Skills for Students (3rd edn)
The Principles of Writing in Psychology
Professional Writing (3rd edn)
Skills for Success (3rd edn)
Stand Out from the Crowd
The Student Phrase Book
The Student's Guide to Writing (3rd edn)
Study Skills Connected
The Study Skills Handbook (5th edn)
Study Skills for International Postgraduates
Studying in English
Studying History (4th edn)
Studying Law (4th edn)
Studying Physics
The Study Success Journal
Success in Academic Writing (2nd edn)
Smart Thinking
Teaching Study Skills and Supporting Learning
The Undergraduate Research Handbook (2nd edn)
The Work-Based Learning Student Handbook
  (2nd edn)
Writing for Engineers (4th edn)
Writing History Essays (2nd edn)
Writing for Law
Writing for Nursing and Midwifery Students
  (3rd edn)
Write it Right (2nd edn)
Writing for Science Students

Writing Skills for Education Students
You2Uni: Decide, Prepare, Apply

Pocket Study Skills

14 Days to Exam Success (2nd edn)
Analyzing a Case Study
Blogs, Wikis, Podcasts and More
Brilliant Writing Tips for Students
Completing Your PhD
Doing Research (2nd edn)
Getting Critical (2nd edn)
Managing Stress
Planning Your Dissertation (2nd edn)
Planning Your Essay (2nd edn)
Planning Your PhD
Posters and Presentations
Reading and Making Notes (2nd edn)
Referencing and Understanding Plagiarism
  (2nd edn)
Reflective Writing
Report Writing (2nd edn)
Science Study Skills
Studying with Dyslexia (2nd edn)
Success in Groupwork
Successful Applications
Time Management
Where's Your Argument?
Writing for University (2nd edn)

Research Skills

Authoring a PhD
The Foundations of Research (3rd edn)
Getting to Grips with Doctoral Research
Getting Published
The Good Supervisor (2nd edn)
The Lean PhD
PhD by Published Work
The PhD Viva
The PhD Writing Handbook
Planning Your Postgraduate Research
The Postgraduate Research Handbook (2nd edn)
The Professional Doctorate
Structuring Your Research Thesis

Career Skills

Excel at Graduate Interviews
Graduate CVs and Covering Letters
Graduate Entrepreneurship
How to Succeed at Assessment Centres
Social Media for Your Student and Graduate
  Job Search
The Graduate Career Guidebook
Work Experience, Placements and Internships

For a complete listing of all our titles in this area please visit
www.macmillanihe.com/study-skills

Doing Projects and Reports in Engineering

Samuel Brüning Larsen

First published 2019 by
RED GLOBE PRESS

Red Globe Press in the UK is an imprint of Springer Nature Limited, registered in England, company number 785998, of 4 Crinan Street, London, N1 9XW.

Red Globe Press® is a registered trademark in the United States, the United Kingdom, Europe and other countries.

ISBN 978–1–352–00563–9 paperback

This book is printed on paper suitable for recycling and made from fully managed and sustained forest sources. Logging, pulping and manufacturing processes are expected to conform to the environmental regulations of the country of origin.

A catalogue record for this book is available from the British Library.

A catalog record for this book is available from the Library of Congress.

Contents

Acknowledgements   ix

Introduction   1

Chapter 1 Projects in Engineering   5

Four types of project   6
Characteristics of projects in engineering   7
Types of problems you might be asked to solve   8
The process in engineering projects: analysis, design, and implementation   9

PART 1 The Project Process   11

Chapter 2 The First Phase of a Project   12

Understand the learning objectives of the project   13
The first steps in a free, instructor independent project   13
The problem analysis: your journey from first industrial partner contact
   to problem statement   14
Verify the existence and size of the problem   16
Two specific tools for your problem analysis   18
Choosing your project's problem and analyzing the root causes later in
   the project   19
When your project is a part of a bigger project with your industrial partner 20

Chapter 3 Problem Statements in Engineering Projects   22

Four generic problem types in engineering projects   23
Problem statements for projects that improve an existing entity   24
Problem statements in projects that design new entities   29
Two important characteristics of problem statements: focus and
   quantifiability   30
Avoid mixing the two project problem archetypes   34
Subquestions to your problem statement   35

Chapter 4 Literature, Knowledge, and Expertise in
           Engineering Projects   37

The knowledge foundation embedded in the literature constitutes the
   expertise in your project   39
Making choices about using theories, models, and methods   40
Locating the relevant literature   41
How to use literature in your project   42

When practice-oriented literature does not exist: operationalize theory   48
Without practice-oriented literature or relevant theory: experiment or
   use deductive reasoning   49

Chapter 5 Project Methodology and Planning   51

The philosophy of science in engineering projects   52
Making methodology choices   53
The typical overall structure of engineering projects   54
Standard methods as the backbone of a project's overall structure   59
Argumentation for all important choices, including methodology choices   61
Planning your own project using Gantt charts   62

Chapter 6 Collecting and Analyzing Data   66

Purpose of data collection in engineering projects   67
Locating relevant data   69
When data are not available   70
Data analysis   71
Ensuring valid and reliable data and analysis results   80

Chapter 7 Designing the Project's Solution   84

Solutions in engineering projects   85
Three archetypes of engineering solutions   87
Assessing the effect, ease of implementation, and financial feasibility of
   your solution   92
Quantifying a solution's effect and value   96

Chapter 8 Testing and Implementing the Solution   100

Testing a solution   100
Implementation of solutions   101
Ownership is key to successful implementation   104

PART 2 Collaboration, Supervision, and Stakeholders   107

Chapter 9 Collaboration, Communication, and Supervision   108

Group formation dynamics   109
When the group is formed   109
Trust and psychological safety are key to great collaboration and
   communication   113
Handling conflicts in your team   115
Major conflicts   118
Supervision   119

Chapter 10 Cooperating with Industrial Partners   122

How to "sell" your project to an industrial partner   123
The introductory phase of your industrial partner cooperation   123

Problem statement agreement   125
Continuous cooperation throughout your project period   126
Ensuring timely data collection and industrial partner employee
   availability   128
Ending your industrial partner cooperation   129
The possible pitfalls in industrial partner cooperation   130

Chapter 11 Managing Stakeholders   136

Your key stakeholders   136
The stakeholder analysis   138
Monthly meetings with your contact's boss or (worse) several
   department heads   142

PART 3 The Project Report   143

Chapter 12 The Project Report: Structure and Content   144

The sections of a project report in engineering   145

Chapter 13 Communicating Clearly and Professionally   173

Correct and clear language in engineering reports   173
Sentence construction   176
Numbers in engineering reports   179
Tables, figures, charts, and other graphical displays in engineering
   reports   180

PART 4 The Project Exam   183

Chapter 14 Examination of Engineering Projects   184

Group presentations at your exam   184
"Owning the stage": body language, eye contact, hand gestures,
   and voice   188
Presentation content   189
Poster session exams   190
Individual examination   191
Managing nervousness   192
Dissatisfaction and filing complaints   192
What if I fail?   194

Chapter 15 Getting Top Marks from External Examiners   195

External examiners' expectations of the basics in a project   195
External examiners' official focus when reading the report   196
The relative importance of success criteria for external examiners 197
Examiner assessment of your report's communicative level   198
The "don't do" list   199

PART 5 Technical Research: the Master of Science
(M.Sc.) Project   201

Chapter 16 The Special Requirements of Projects in
Engineering (M.Sc.)   202

The nature of academic research projects   203
Managing both the industrial partner and the university as stakeholders   204
Project structure of academic research projects   204

References   212
Index   213

Acknowledgements

I want to thank my awesome wife, Anne Marie, and my three children, Ida, Bertram and Valdemar, for giving me the time to write this book. I could not have come even close without your support. I also want to extend my thanks to my colleagues for valuable ideas and feedback. In particular, to John Clausen and Per Bigum.

Introduction

Project work within universities comes with different names, as shown in Figure 0.1. Regardless of the name, this handbook will enable you to conduct great engineering projects and write clear and coherent reports.

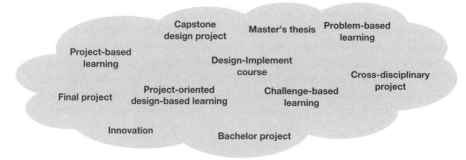

Figure 0.1   Project work comes with different names

This book is for all engineering disciplines, it is useful from the first to the last semester, and focuses on group and single-person projects. It is founded on the principle that *engineers design solutions to problems.* Mechanical engineers design machines, civil engineers design buildings, manufacturing engineers design production systems, electrical engineers design control systems, software engineers design programs, and chemical engineers design chemical processes and products. Great designs of products, buildings, processes, and systems depend on rigorous analyses and are followed by actual implementation. The sequence of analysis, design, and implementation constitutes the core of an engineering project across disciplines.

Figure 0.2   The sequence of the three core activities in an engineering project

Project work within the humanities, social studies, and natural science disciplines, differs quite substantially from engineering fields. Within these disciplines, project work usually means conducting research that investigates unanswered questions and thereby contributes to our common knowledge about the world, human nature, art, and culture.

The purpose of most engineering projects is designing solutions to problems. Designing a solution to a problem differs fundamentally from conducting research that ends with the answer to a research question. This book provides you and your supervisors with concrete advice for conducting each activity in a project and writing a clear and coherent report.

Industrial partner cooperation in engineering projects

A distinct feature of engineering degrees is the direct inclusion of future employers in the educational program; these organizations may include manufacturers, utilities, software developers, or healthcare providers. Universities usually include future employers through internships and project cooperation. In projects, students often work in groups of two to six students and design solutions to specific problems located with an industrial partner.

Industrial partner involvement in engineering education is particularly prevalent in the later stages of a course when students are close to graduating. Some universities even have specific goals for all students to cooperate with industrial partners in their final project. Because industrial partner cooperation is an important characteristic of engineering education projects, this handbook describes the nature of industrial partner cooperation in detail, with guidance on how to locate industrial partners, how to initiate and engage with them in a project, the major interactions throughout the project, and the pitfalls of the cooperation.

Project work terminology in engineering education

Engineering disciplines differ on many parameters, including their terminology for project activities. Universities often use different terms for analysis, design, and implementation. Some disciplines even use different terms for data and theory.

Engineering disciplines reflect the industry that employs their graduates. This applies to the terminology as well. The closer a discipline's relation is with their industry, the more specific is their project work terminology. Examples of engineering disciplines with close ties to their employer industry are civil engineering and software engineering. Other engineering degrees are not industry specific, such as innovation and manufacturing engineering. These degrees use broader terminology for project work.

The knowledge base of the book

The book is based partly on my own experience and partly on numerous interviews, discussions, and conversations with colleagues. My own experience comes from working in consulting, in industry, and at two Danish universities that educate engineers, the Technical University of Denmark and Aalborg University. My experience covers project work from the first semester through to master's theses. I have supervised and examined hundreds of projects.

To ensure a thorough knowledge base for the book, I have conducted interviews and had discussions and conversations with my own colleagues from all major engineering disciplines, professors and lecturers from universities worldwide, and numerous students from many engineering disciplines. Every year, I participate at engineering education conferences. Parts of the research for the book will appear at these conferences (e.g. SEFI, CDIO, and ETALEE).

The book's content

Chapter 1 describes the general nature of engineering projects and how projects fit into an engineering education. Thereafter, Chapters 2–15 are divided into four major themes, as shown in Table 0.1.

Table 0.1 The four themes of the book		
Theme	**Chapters**	**Theme content**
The project process	Chapters 2–8	Part 1 deals with the activities of a project, including problem analysis, formulating the problem statement, using literature and theory, selecting methods, planning and managing the project, collecting and analyzing data, and designing, testing, and implementing solutions
Cooperation, communication, and stakeholders	Chapters 9–11	Part 2 is about cooperation and communication within project groups, managing the project's stakeholders, and the important topic of how to cooperate with the project's most important stakeholder, the industrial partner. The theme also covers project supervision
The project report	Chapters 12 and 13	While Parts 1 and 2 cover the project process, Part 3 deals with the written report. The chapters cover the subjects of report structure, the content, clarity, and coherence of individual sections, and ensuring reader understanding. They also cover language and other means of communication – figures, tables, diagrams, sketches, "box-and-arrow" charts – in a written report
Project examinations	Chapters 14 and 15	Part 4 deals with the examination of projects. The chapters detail how you can deliver effective oral group presentations using slideshows and posters, and how to perform well during individual Q&A examinations. They also deal with grade dissatisfaction and the question of whether to file a formal complaint

Chapter 16 differs from the previous chapters by addressing the requirements of Master of Science projects. At many universities, master's degree students are expected to conduct a *research* project rather than a project that develops a solution to a problem. Research projects explore unanswered questions for the benefit of the world at large, rather than solving a problem for the benefit of *one* industrial partner. Chapter 16 delineates the characteristics of engineering research projects, including the nature of great research questions, how to structure an engineering research project, how to choose the methodology, and how to discuss results and present conclusions.

The book supports the CDIO and PBL engineering education frameworks

More than 150 universities worldwide, including Cambridge (UK), MIT (USA), and Stanford (USA), have adopted the engineering education framework of Conceive, Design, Implement and Operate (CDIO). CDIO is an open concept for design, development, and quality assurance of engineering education. The concept is built on the notion that engineering education should mirror engineering practice. Conceiving, designing, and implementing products and systems are core disciplines in CDIO. Like CDIO, problem-based learning (PBL) is a concept that is applied worldwide. PBL was not developed for engineering education in particular, but has many similarities with CDIO, including a focus on teamwork, collaborative learning, and solving problems. This book supports projects that function as the frame for CDIO and PBL.

Business and other professional skills as integrated components of engineering education

In many countries, engineering courses integrate other professional, non-technical business skills into the curriculum. This book supports this effort by including detailed descriptions of three particular methods:

1 Project planning with Gantt charts (Chapter 5)
2 Evaluating the financial feasibility of a solution (Chapter 7)
3 Analyzing stakeholder interests in a project's outcomes and implementation (Chapter 11).

Projects in Engineering

In this chapter, you will learn:

1 The purpose of project work in engineering education.
2 That project work is among the most effective methods for learning both soft and hard skills.
3 The types and characteristics of projects in engineering education.
4 The two categories of problems for which engineering projects design solutions.
5 The general step-by-step process in engineering projects.

Project work equips you with skills for practicing engineering in your work life after graduation. Time and again, research shows that the so-called "soft skills" are among the most important skills for engineers. Whether you thrive in your work life and provide value to your employer depends as much on your soft skills as your ability to conduct the right calculations correctly (Lippman et al. 2015, cited in Golinkoff and Hirsh-Pasek 2016).

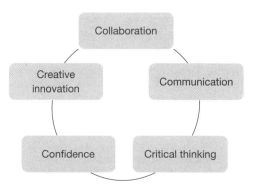

Figure 1.1   Five important soft skills for engineers

Project work is the most prevalent method for learning soft skills in engineering degrees. In particular, free, instructor *independent* projects facilitate effective learning. In these projects, students choose the problem and the methods. Success in free projects requires collaboration within your project group, the critical evaluation of methods and data, and the development of effective and often innovative solutions. These requirements all advance soft skills learning.

From time to time, students are critical of lecturers who are using project work as a learning method. Students often feel that lecturers are not really teaching them anything and they question the purpose of their project work. An experienced biology professor from the University of Wisconsin addressed this question at an engineering education conference in 2015. A student was unhappy with the professor's use of project work. The student asked: "Why don't you teach us biology? That's your job, right?" The professor answered: "No, my job is to help you become biologists." This dialogue demonstrates that the professor's focus is not simply the biology discipline, but students' ability to work as biologists after graduation.

Project work advances your ability to:

1 Identify and understand a problem.
2 Find and use theory and other relevant sources of expertise.
3 Identify causes of problems and solution requirements.
4 Design, specify, and evaluate solutions.
5 Test and implement solutions.

In engineering courses, you, as students, often conduct project work in cooperation with industrial partners. Industrial partners function as project sponsors, provide the frame for the project's problem, and (hopefully) use the solution you design. Examples of industrial partners are manufacturers, software developers, power plants, and building contractors.

Four types of project

Engineering disciplines usually involve four types of project, as shown in Table 1.1.

Table 1.1 The four types of project	
Project type	**Description**
Projects confined to the boundaries of one course	Such projects facilitate deeper and more application-oriented learning than is possible with "from the blackboard" lecturing, in-class group exercises, and fictive desk assignments
Across-course "semester projects"	These projects apply theory and methods from several courses within one project, and can be either fixed assignments given by an instructor or open-ended projects that address a real-life industrial partner problem
Final projects, such as bachelor projects and master's theses	These are the classic final projects conducted by groups of one to three students. At many universities, these projects are likely to concern a real-life industrial partner problem
Interdisciplinary projects	These projects involve students from several engineering fields, such as mechanical engineers, chemical engineers, and software engineers. These projects often concern entrepreneurship or innovation

Characteristics of projects in engineering

The following list presents the characteristics of the typical independent project in engineering:

1 Projects in engineering concern the use of theory and methods in real-life or close to real-life situations.
2 Project groups design solutions to problems that are current and specific, and usually do not concern developing new-to-world knowledge that resolves unanswered questions.
3 Problems in engineering projects are either purely technical in nature or a combination of technical and social, that is, involving changed human behavior.
4 The problems that engineering projects solve are located with industrial partners and must be solved within the industrial partners' specific context.
5 The solution that the project group designs must be implementable with the industrial partner.
6 The project is often conducted by project groups of two to six persons.
7 The project has a minimum of two stakeholders (the university and the industrial partner). Therefore, the project has two sets of target groups, each with its own set of demands.

This list summarizes the characteristics of most typical independent projects, where you as students identify and define the problem and choose the methods for analysis and solution design.

In addition to these independent projects, engineering disciplines also use projects where the course instructor provides the problem and the methods. These projects could be entirely theoretical or perhaps use fictive situations simulating real-life problems. Examples are:

• the design of a fictive production system for an actual product
• the optimization of a chemical process that is located at the university for educational purposes
• the design of a building based on drawings and requirements included in a recent architectural competition.

Projects usually result in a project report and an oral examination. The report usually contains two end results: a conclusion that addresses the problem statement directly, and a set of recommendations for the industrial partner that summarize the project's solution.

Engineering projects differ from projects and larger assignments within the humanities and social sciences. Projects within these disciplines create general knowledge for the world, while engineering projects design solutions to specific problems.

The (fictitious) company FOOD Measurement Systems develops, manufactures, and sells measurement instruments to food manufacturers. The company wants to develop a new instrument for clients in the pharmaceutical industry, and has engaged with a group of engineering students. The project's problem statement concerns developing a version of and existing instrument for use by manufacturers of pharmaceuticals. The project will result in the design of a new version of the measurement instrument. The project group divides their project into two steps:

1   An examination of all the requirements that the new customer group has for measurement instruments and an analysis of how these requirements can be met.

2   A specific design for the new version of the instrument, including physical components, new software, and a user manual for instrument operation.

The project group collects data, including interviews with potential customers and a visit to a pharmaceutical factory where the instrument could be used. The research results in two overall design requirements for the new instrument:

1   The instrument must have different physical dimensions to fit into the processing lines of pharmaceutical manufacturers.

2   The instrument must be able to communicate directly with the other IT systems of the pharmaceutical manufacturer. These IT systems continuously write and print documentation on all produced batches of medicine to ensure product quality and regulatory compliance.

Based on these two design requirements and a list that details the specific measurements that pharmaceutical manufacturers require, the project group design the instrument. The project group draws new outer cabinets and a new instrument base, designs the instrument's interior structure, and draws a set of diagrams for the software that sends reports to other IT systems. When FOOD Measurement Systems implements the solution (constructs and manufactures the new instrument), the instrument will fit directly into pharmaceutical manufacturers' processing lines and communicate with other IT systems.

The project results in a set of recommendations for FOOD Measurement Systems. Among the recommendations are the two design requirements, the drawings of the instrument's physical structure, and the software diagrams.

The example shows that a project group must first understand the problem and write a problem statement. Then, the project group identifies the design requirements and designs the solution. The natural next step is implementing the solution. In the example, the implementation would be beginning a dialogue between the firm's designers and production engineers about how the firm can construct the instrument to ensure effective manufacturing.

Types of problems you might be asked to solve

An engineering project either improves an existing entity or designs a new entity. A project that improves an existing entity could be improving the durability of a machine, and a project that designs a new entity could be a project that designs a new building based on a set of requirements from the construction client. These two types of project constitute the two columns shown in Figure 1.2.

	Improve an existing entity	Design a new entity
Design of a structure	*Examples: improve the durability of a machine or the performance of an engine*	*Examples: design a new building, product or chemical compound*
Design of a process	*Example: reduce the failure rate on a production line*	*Examples: design a new procedure or planning process*

Figure 1.2   Four archetypes of engineering project

The two rows in Figure 1.2 show that an engineering project can design either a structure (a product or a building) or a process (quality assurance procedure or a mathematical algorithm). By combining the two axes, Figure 1.2 shows four archetypes of engineering project.

For projects in the left-hand column, the "problem" is that an existing entity is performing poorly or simply has potential for improvement. The column gives three examples of such projects (a machine with low durability, an engine with poor performance, and a production process with a high failure rate). For projects in the right-hand column, the "problem" is that someone has a need for a currently nonexistent entity. The column gives five examples (a building, a product, a chemical compound, a procedure, and a planning process). The engineering project solves this "it does not exist" problem by designing the entity that is needed. Chapter 3 gives a more detailed description of problems and problem statements in engineering projects.

The process in engineering projects: analysis, design, and implementation

When you have defined your problem and written your problem statement, your project enters its core activities: analysis, solution design, and implementation. Figure 1.3 illustrates this three-step process. Although engineering projects differ with respect to the depth and workload in each activity, they virtually all follow this three-step process.

Figure 1.3   The core activities in an engineering project

The Introduction noted that many universities that educate engineers, Cambridge, MIT, and Stanford, for example, have adopted the CDIO framework for their engineering courses. CDIO indicates that engineering practice follows the four-step process of Conceive, Design, Implement, and Operate. First, the engineer generates an idea (Conceive). Second, the engineer develops the idea into a solution (Design). Third, the engineer implements the solution. Finally, the engineer operates the solution. The two activities in the middle (Design and Implement) match the sequence in Figure 1.3.

Figure 1.3 differs from the CDIO concept by including Analysis and omitting the Operate activity. Although CDIO does not contain an explicit A for Analysis, analysis is a core activity in engineering projects. Operating a solution is, by definition, a different activity from designing the solution. Operating is a continuous, day-to-day activity, whereas a project is a one-time activity with a beginning and an end. Therefore, the term "Operate" is omitted in Figure 1.3. However, solutions must be operational. Including design requirements that enable effective operation is pivotal to any solution. A solution that cannot be operated is useless, so naturally CDIO's last term, "Operate", is important for engineering projects.

Reviewing this chapter's objectives

Tick those objectives you feel you have achieved, and review those you haven't yet accomplished. In this chapter, you have learned:

- ❏ The purpose of project work in engineering education and why instructors often apply project work as a learning methodology.

- ❏ The types and characteristics of projects in engineering education, as well as the two general categories of problems for which engineering projects design solutions.

- ❏ The general step-by-step process of analysis, design, and implementation in engineering projects.

The Project Process

The First Phase of a Project

Project initiation | Problem statement | Literature, knowledge, and expertise | Methodology and planning | Data collection and analysis | Design of solution | Test and implementation of solution

---

In this chapter, you will learn:

1 That the beginning of a project often feels like a chaotic mess.
2 That you become better and better at being confident, cool, and resilient in this chaotic period.
3 That great ideas often emerge in this period.
4 How you and your project team can increase your knowledge and ability to work with the project's topic.
5 How you can conduct a problem analysis that leads to your project's problem statement.
6 That a problem analysis often begins with a need or a wish from your project's industrial partner.
7 How you can keep a critical mindset and ask the right questions when conducting your problem analysis.
8 How to use a problem hierarchy to structure your problem analysis.

The first few weeks of your project are often muddled and chaotic. Whether you conduct a one-person or a group project, no one really knows where you and your team will end up, or the steps you will take on the way. Make sure to keep calm and confident in this situation. The chaotic feeling is entirely normal at the beginning of a project. Even in your working life after graduation, projects will feel confusing in the beginning. The simple reason is that a project only becomes relevant when a task is so complex that no single person can handle it. The good news is that these feelings of confusion and chaos will fade with experience. After three or four projects, you will know much better what to expect in this phase of a project.

Some people thrive in this phase of a project. They may even remember this time during their education as the most exciting time because of its limitless nature. In addition, great ideas often emerge at the beginning of a project that shape the project's content and direction.

Understand the learning objectives of the project

All courses have (or should have) an explicit set of learning objectives. These objectives form the basis for evaluating your performance and receiving your grade. Project-based courses also have learning objectives. The professor responsible for the course has the responsibility to integrate these learning objectives into the project's activities, so that students who deliver a great project will master the objectives.

In projects early in your course, learning objectives are often part of a project description. Project descriptions can be long and complicated. The descriptions specify and operationalize the project's learning objectives to make sure that you understand the project in detail.

Your instructor may plan the project using a set of milestones to help you focus on limited subjects one by one. In the early stages of a project, milestones help you focus on understanding the first tasks only, rather than the whole project at once.

If you or your class peers are in doubt about aspects of the project description, that is, about the specific content of a subset of project activities, then the instructor should provide opportunities for all relevant questions to be answered.

TOP TIPS FOR UNDERSTANDING PROJECT DESCRIPTIONS

1. Insert "Review of project description" as an activity in the agenda for your first three or four project group meetings. Together, you can ensure that you, as a team, have complete command of the project description.
2. Have everyone in your class submit written questions to your professor and persuade him or her to answer these questions on the course website. This way everyone sees all the questions and all the answers.

Some projects do not have written project descriptions, but only a set of overall learning objectives and the instructor's oral description of project goals, requirements, and activities. In these cases, listen carefully, make notes, and ask follow-up questions. Follow-up questions may first arise in the days and weeks after the project's initiation. Ask these questions when they arise. Your professor will expect them.

The first steps in a free, instructor independent project

In a free project, where you as a project team choose a problem and the methods, your own wishes for the project's topic are important. Some of your classmates (perhaps including yourself) are determined young people with ambitious goals for their education and future careers. These students often have clear wishes for a project's topic. Other students, who do not have focused goals for their career, may find many different topics interesting and are often glad that classmates pick a topic on their behalf. When the project's topic is settled, two natural tasks follow:

1 Increase the level of knowledge about the project's topic in your team.
2 Locate and engage with an industrial partner (see Chapter 10 for more specific guidance).

You can increase the level of knowledge in your team by reading literature about your project's content and discussing the topic with your faculty (see Table 2.1).

Table 2.1 Sources for increasing your knowledge level and inspiration	
Source	Details
Textbooks	Borrow textbooks about your project's topic or about an umbrella term that covers your project's topic (perhaps as a distinct textbook chapter)
Textbook references	Scan the reference lists in these textbooks for other books and articles that may be even more relevant
University library	Use rough-cut searches in your university's digital library for books and articles about your topic
Your supervisor	Get your supervisor's "off-the-cuff" thoughts and ideas (your supervisor often has an abundance of experience with projects on your topic as well as related topics)
Other faculty members	Discuss your project informally with other faculty members and pick their brains for ideas, especially those professors who may be more familiar with your topic than your supervisor
Your personal network	Discuss your project with people in your personal network, they might have relevant experience

In this early phase of your project, your focus should be on broad searches and reading of materials. The reading will inspire you to identify potential problems that your project can deal with as well as possible solutions. The knowledge you gain from reading and discussing your topic forms a great foundation for your ability to conduct a problem analysis in your industrial partner's context.

The problem analysis: your journey from first industrial partner contact to problem statement

In a free project, where you as a project team choose the problem and the methods, your first objective is analyzing the problem landscape. The goal is to identify the problem that your project will solve. Figure 2.1 illustrates the problem analysis that gets you from this unknown and often complex problem landscape to a formulated statement of the specific problem that your project will solve.

In projects that improve an existing entity, such as improving the user friendliness of an app or increasing the amount of recyclable materials in a product, the problem

Figure 2.1   Problem analysis

analysis often begins with a *wish* from an industrial partner that your project can fulfill. The firm may be able to state the wish clearly and in detail, or perhaps just vaguely.

1 *Clear wish:* A manufacturer of dough-mixing machines for industrial bakeries tells a project group that they would like them to redesign a machine to reduce production costs. The scope and objective of this project is clear and focused.

2 *Semi-clear wish:* A pharmaceutical manufacturer wants a project group to suggest how they could automate the process that wraps pill packets on pallets. The scope is clear (the wrapping process), but the objective is unclear (is the objective to reduce costs, reduce errors, or speed up the process?).

3 *Vague wish:* A power plant asks a project team to "take a look at" the conveyor belts that transport coal to the plant's ovens from an adjacent lot. The power plant does not provide any objectives, problems, or reasons why the conveyor belts need to be "looked at."

A common starting point of a problem analysis is when the industrial partner points directly at a solution they would like you to design without mentioning the problem that the solution addresses. When the person from your industrial partner who you are in discussions with (your contact) has expressed the firm's wish, your job is to identify the problem that the desired solution addresses. In the discussions, ask the perhaps obvious "why" question: "Why this particular (solution)?" Ideally, the firm's answer to this question is: "It's because we have problems with (your project's problem)" or "We need the solution because (your project's problem)."

Figure 2.2 illustrates an overall four-step sequence from an industrial partner wish to your project's problem. The fourth and final step says: "You verify the problem." The next section details why, how, and when in your project process you have the task of verifying the existence of the problem.

The path from your industrial partner's desired solution to your project's problem is often rocky. It is very common that your industrial partner is unaware what particular problem their desired solution solves. They might even be unaware that the purpose of an engineering project is solving a problem. Ten years down the road from your graduation, *you* may find yourself in a situation asking a student group why they keep asking about a problem rather than just beginning the design of your desired solution. One reason a firm wants a solution might be because a manager

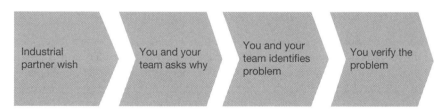

Figure 2.2   The path from industrial partner wish to a verified problem

has seen something fantastic at a conference and wants it. It may also be that the firm simply wants to be nice and help you and your team with a project opportunity.

If your industrial partner is unaware of which problem they want solved, you and your team must ask the questions that lead to the identification of the problem. In addition, you must figure out whether there *is* a problem at all, what the size and consequences of the problem are, and how the desired solution will, in fact, solve the problem.

The dialogue with your industrial partner is not always easy, especially because the personal relations between you and your contact from the firm are new. You are naturally inclined to perceive your contact as a skilled and experienced person. Therefore, you expect your contact to have complete grasp of the problem the firm wants you to solve.

As a student, you might think that the reason you might not understand which problem the firm wants you to solve is your lack of skills and experience. However, this line of reasoning is often not true. So, do not settle for a project without an explicit, focused, and clear problem. You might spend more than one or two meetings and the help of your supervisor to get there, but make sure that you do. Your project examiners expect you to address your industrial partner's wishes with a critical mindset.

TOP TIPS FOR INDUSTRIAL PARTNER CONVERSATIONS

Tip 1: Avoid using the word "Why?" Instead, use the softer: "How come this is the solution you would like us to work with?" For your conversation partner, "How come … ?" feels like you are asking out of interest rather than to check whether things have been properly thought through. "Why … ?" might come across as a bit more critical, making your contact feel as if you think that they have not done their homework for the meeting.

Tip 2: Suggest a possible problem that your industrial partner's desired solution addresses. For example, the formulation "Will the solution impact (suggested problem)?" If your contact says "Yes," then you have your problem. If your contact says "No," then they will be inclined to come up with an alternative reason for asking you to design the solution.

If your contact can define the problem quickly and accurately, then you have a strong indication that the firm has discussed the problem internally prior to your meeting. If your contact "really has no idea," then help them (and yourself) to identify the problem during your conversation (assuming that the problem exists).

Verify the existence and size of the problem

An issue can be more or less problematic for a firm. Problematic issues are, for example, that the capacity of a production line is too small to take in more orders from important customers, or that the launch speed of an app has slowed to a time that is unbearable for users. Less problematic issues are often potential for improvements for something non-critical. It might be that a firm has found that it could utilize more of the value inherent in its product returns; for example, instead of trashing returns, use components as spare parts in the firm's service function.

If the firm is acutely aware of the problem your project addresses, then prior to your meeting the firm will often have collected data that documents the problem, such as monthly or daily records of performance. If the firm has documented the problem, then use that documentation in your project.

If the firm has not verified the existence and size of the problem sufficiently, then you and your project team must do so. If the problem is too little production capacity, then measure the firm's current capacity and tell the reader why the current capacity is a problem. If the problem is the long launch speed of an app, then measure the current launch speed length and tell the reader why the length is a problem.

Often, the firm's data for documenting the problem comes in the form of anecdotal evidence (a story here and there) that indicates the problem's existence and size. If possible, corroborate the stories, either with other data types or through interviews with those at the firm who can explain the stories. Later in your project, conduct your own data collection and measure the size of the problem more thoroughly. See Chapter 6 for details.

You and your team design a solution that addresses the problem. As part of your project, your task is to evaluate the solution's effect on the problem. When evaluating the effect, the size of the problem prior to your project functions as the baseline.

EXAMPLE

A firm produces and distributes products and product components to all the large markets worldwide including China. The firm's global logistics manager has heard a number of stories indicating that the distribution center in China that delivers to all Chinese customers is having trouble delivering products on time. Their on-time delivery (OTD) performance is low. The manager engages with a group of students studying industrial engineering.

The student team examines the current OTD and finds that the OTD is 58%, meaning that 58% of all products are delivered on time, while 42% are delivered late. Competing firms have around 3–7% late deliveries, so the difference between 42% and 3–7% represents the size of the problem.

The student team finds that the reason for the poor delivery performance is that the warehouse personnel, who pick and pack orders, often cannot pack a complete order due to a lack of components. Components take 4–6 weeks to arrive from Europe with great variability. The team designs a solution consisting of two elements:

1   A new policy for reordering components from the firm's factories in Europe that takes delivery times across the globe into account.

2   The team calculates new safety stock levels for each item in the warehouse that reduces the chances of stockouts even if European deliveries vary substantially.

Using the current OTD as the baseline, the project team calculates the effect on the distribution center's OTD. In the team's assessment, solution element 1 will increase OTD by 24% from 58% to 82%. Solution element 2 will increase OTD by an additional 14% from 82% to 96%, which makes the firm's OTD performance comparable to competitors' performance.

Many engineering projects are not about improving something that already exists. Instead, these projects design a new entity. In these projects, the student team does not need to identify the size of a problem. Instead, the team must identify and specify the industrial partner's *solution need*. In your problem analysis, ask the following three questions:

1 Who has the need?
2 What specifically is the need?
3 Why does the need exist?

The sequence in Figure 2.2 about getting from an industrial partner's wish to your project's problem is the same as for projects that improve something that already exists. The only difference is that you should perceive the term "problem" as a *solution need*.

Like this chapter, Chapters 9 and 10 also concern topics that are relevant for the first phase of a project. Chapter 9 describes group formation, group collaboration contracts, and how to build the best foundation for your teamwork. Chapter 10 describes your cooperation with your project's industrial partner (how to locate and engage with the industrial partner).

Two specific tools for your problem analysis

The problem analysis is often an iterative process, where you and your team discuss your project and problem continuously. During this process, you read relevant literature and become smarter and smarter about your project topic. If your industrial partner and your supervisor quickly understand and approve of your suggested problem, then your problem analysis only has one or perhaps two iterations.

During this iterative process, semi-structured interviews work well for collecting information. For structuring your information, you can use a problem tree. These tools are now briefly discussed.

Semi-structured interviews

Semi-structured interviews are interviews that allow for both structured discussions of particular issues and free-flowing conversations for examining unknown terrain. Semi-structured interviews are effective for understanding the nature of the problem landscape with your industrial partner. Your initial industrial partner conversations include getting answers to questions and discussing hypotheses that you have derived from literature, supervisor ideas, or your own reasoning. Your interview guide brings these hypotheses and questions into the conversation one by one. In addition, your interview guide allows for free-flowing unstructured conversations for exploring unknown terrain in your problem landscape.

The problem tree

The problem tree is a tangible tool for structuring all your collected information. The tree is a relationship structure that shows causes and effects. If your project's problem landscape has one simple, one-dimensional cause-and-effect relation, then a short string of "why" questions might be enough for your problem analysis. However, if your problem landscape is more complex and causes have multiple effects, then a problem tree is an effective tool for structuring your information. With a problem tree, you increase your ability to grasp a lot of information simultaneously and judge which information is relevant for your problem analysis. Figure 2.3 illustrates the problem tree.

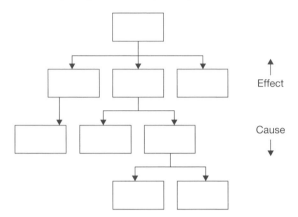

Figure 2.3   The problem tree

The problem tree shows a set of cause-and-effect relationships. A tree can be displayed vertically (as in Figure 2.3), where effects are above and causes below, or horizontally with effects either to the left and causes to the right, or vice versa.

Choosing your project's problem and analyzing the root causes later in the project

You as a project team must choose which box in the problem tree you will consider to be your project's problem and write in your problem statement. Your chosen problem constitutes the starting point for an analysis of the causes of the project's problem

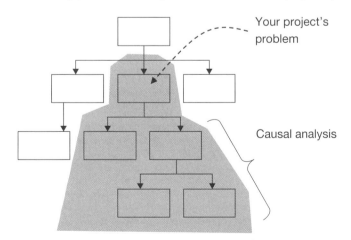

Figure 2.4   The problem in your project is the starting point for your analysis

(as illustrated in Figure 2.4). The gray background represents your project. The box at the top of the gray area is your project's problem and the remaining boxes and arrows below the problem constitute your causal analysis. This causal analysis is your project's analysis, which differs from the problem analysis that you conduct to identify and select your problem. Chapter 6 details the use of the problem tree in your project's analysis.

When your project is a part of a bigger project with your industrial partner

Some projects constitute a smaller part of a bigger project conducted with your industrial partner. These bigger projects, which contain all the smaller projects, are often labelled *program* or *portfolio*. A project portfolio might concern improving a firm's overall production system. Some projects within the project portfolio might concern sales processes, others logistics, and others product assembly.

A firm can have you and your team working on a project within such a portfolio. The firm might even make you *responsible* for a project in the portfolio. In this case, your contact might be the portfolio manager, who is often a higher level manager.

There are advantages and disadvantages of heading a smaller project within a large project portfolio. Even if the firm's personnel are not aware of your particular project, they will quickly identify you when you present yourself as a representative of the overall portfolio – "We are working on X, which is part of the Y program." "Oh, I see." The recognition will allow you access to staff for interviews, IT systems for reports, and other sources of data.

There are two pitfalls if your project is part of a portfolio, and these are detailed in Table 2.2.

Table 2.2 Pitfalls if your project is part of a portfolio	
Pitfall	**Details**
Limited freedom concerning the project's content	You must be allowed to conduct your project without unwanted interference from the portfolio manager. The portfolio manager may want you to include issues that really do not belong in your project and may ruin the coherence of your project. A good project is focused on one problem and does not shift this problem according to your portfolio manager's whims and agenda
Unclear work division between your team and industrial partner employees	Your examiners may find it hard to distinguish between your work and work conducted by employees of your industrial partner. Make sure that your report makes clear when you have used data, analysis, or designs of any kind that your industrial partner (or consultants hired by your industrial partner) have produced. If your examiners have a hard time distinguishing your work from the work of others, then they might not give you credit for parts of your own work, thinking that you have included work you have not conducted yourself

Reviewing this chapter's objectives

Tick those objectives you feel you have achieved, and review those you haven't yet accomplished. In this chapter, you have learned how to:

❑ Remain confident, cool, and resilient during the chaotic period at the beginning of a project.

❑ Conduct a problem analysis and develop a problem statement for your project.

❑ Keep a critical mindset and ask the right questions when conducting your problem analysis.

❑ Use a problem hierarchy to structure your problem analysis.

Problem Statements in Engineering Projects

| Project initiation | Problem statement | Literature, knowledge, and expertise | Methodology and planning | Data collection and analysis | Design of solution | Test and implementation of solution |

In this chapter, you will learn:

1 That an engineering project involves solving a problem.
2 That an engineering project involves improving an existing entity or designing a new entity.
3 How to formulate a clear problem statement.
4 The components of a problem statement.
5 That good problem statements demonstrate focus and quantifiability.
6 How to extract subquestions from the overall problem statement.
7 How to distinguish between acceptable and unacceptable subquestions to the problem statement.

In engineering, a project involves developing a solution to a problem. In an engineering project, the term "problem" differs from the day-to-day use of the term, such as losing your keys or being late for a meeting. In engineering projects, the term "problem" covers the following two issues:

1 An existing entity is underperforming or simply has improvement potential, such as low durability of a product, slow launch speed of an app, or low effectiveness of a chemical process.
2 An entity that someone wants or needs does not exist, such as a building, a product, or an algorithm.

An engineering project solves the problem. For issue 1 above, a project designs a solution that eliminates or reduces the problem. If the problem is low product durability, then the project might redesign the product or select a new material so durability increases. For issue 2 above, the problem is that an entity that someone wants or needs does not exist. This "someone" is often the project's industrial partner. The project solves the problem by first identifying design requirements and then designing the entity. For example, if a manufacturer of exhaust pipes wants a new type of exhaust pipe, then the project identifies the requirements for the new exhaust pipe, and then designs the pipe.

In Chapter 2, you learned how to identify the right problem. In this chapter, you will learn how to formulate the problem *statement*. This statement constitutes the reference point for the whole project. The chapter first describes four generic problem types and details how to formulate a precise and formally correct problem statement. Second, the chapter describes the relation between the problem statement and the project's methodology. Third, the chapter presents the characteristics of great problem statements and describes the development and use of subquestions to the problem statement.

Four generic problem types in engineering projects

Figure 3.1, which is also displayed in Chapter 1, shows a matrix containing four generic problem types in engineering education. The two columns in the matrix represent projects that improve an existing entity and projects that design a new entity. The two rows in the matrix show how an engineering project concerns either a structure or a process.

	Improve an existing entity	**Design a new entity**
Design of a structure	*Examples: improve the durability of a machine or the performance of an engine*	*Examples: design a new building, product or chemical compound*
Design of a process	*Example: reduce the failure rate on a production line*	*Examples: design a new procedure or planning process*

Figure 3.1   Four archetypes of engineering project

Structure refers to the logical construction of an entity. Examples of structures are buildings, machines, components, and products of any kind. A process is a systematic sequence. Examples are production processes, logistical processes, managerial procedures, and so on.

Projects will fall into different quadrants of the matrix depending on their discipline. Electronic engineers often work with improving electronic systems (top left), civil engineers most often design new structures (top right), and manufacturing engineers most often work with improving processes (bottom left).

Improving an existing entity vs. designing a new entity

In the left-hand column of Figure 3.1, an engineering project concerns improving an existing entity. The problem statement must define what in particular the project wants to improve. Examples are the scrap rate from a production line, the thermal emittance of a building façade, the durability of a product, and the idle time of a power plant.

The project analyzes the problem's causes and designs a solution that either eliminates the causes or reduces the effect of the causes. If the problem is low product durability, then possible solutions are a redesign of the product, using different materials, better maintenance instructions, or a combination of solution elements. Depending on a cause analysis, one, two, or all three solutions could contribute to higher product durability.

In the right-hand column of Figure 3.1, an engineering project concerns designing a new entity. The "problem" in such projects is not that an entity needs improvement, but rather that the entity does not exist. If a project concerns the design of a new lamp, building or logistical system, then the problem is the current *nonexistence* of the lamp, building, or logistical system. The solution is to design the entity so that it does exist.

Projects that improve an existing entity and projects that design a new entity differ fundamentally in their methodology and analysis. For an in-depth description of methodology and analysis in either project type, see Chapters 5 and 6. This chapter describes how to formulate problem statements and how the problem statement relates to methodology and analysis. This chapter first describes projects that improve an existing entity and then projects that design a new entity.

Problem statements for projects that improve an existing entity

Table 3.1 shows the problem, methodology, and conclusion for projects that improve an existing entity. Examples could include: a production line that produces too many items that do not pass the quality assurance test; a product that customers return too often with defects; a wind turbine component that needs too many service visits; a component that breaks too quickly; and a machine that is underutilized.

Table 3.1	Projects that improve an existing entity
Problem	The problem is that something is performing poorly or has an unfulfilled improvement potential
Methodology	The project's methodology consists of two overall steps:
	Step 1: An analysis of the cause of the problem. The project team conducts a causal analysis that identifies the problem's cause. The problem may have several causes, of which some have a big effect on the problem and others only a small effect
	Step 2: Design of a solution that eliminates the problem's cause or, as a minimum, reduces the effect of the cause on the problem. For problems with several causes, the project can develop several solution elements that each address one of the causes
Conclusion	The project's conclusion consists of a summary of the project's solution. Often, a project complements the conclusion with a set of recommendations that are easy for the project's industrial partner to understand. If relevant, the recommendation can include an implementation plan

Constructing a problem statement for a project that improves an existing entity

Problem statements in projects that improve an existing entity are usually constructed using a set of predetermined components (see Table 3.2). Here is an example of a problem statement:

> How can Johnson & Wick plc reduce the scrap rate of product AB1280 on production line 12?

When the problem concerns improving an existing entity, the derived problem statement asks *how* to improve the entity. Therefore, the problem statement begins with "How?" Notice that the answer to a "how" question is your project's solution. Below is an example.

EXAMPLE

A project deals with speeding up a chemical separation process for the (fictitious) chemical processing firm ChemTech. The student team has developed a solution that consists of three elements:

1 increasing the temperature of the process

2 having fewer and larger gaps in the separator's outer shell

3 doubling of the number of revolutions per minute of the process.

The project's problem statement:

> How can ChemTech increase the speed of separating liquids?

Equals

The answer to the problem statement:

> Increase the temperature, have a separator with fewer but larger gaps in the outer shell, and double the number of revolutions per minute of the process.

Following the interrogative *how* in your project statement is the actor that has the problem and can implement the solution. This is usually the industrial partner (in the example: "Johnson & Wick plc"). The actor could also be a business unit or department within the industrial partner's organization.

Following the name of the actor is the action that your project will do to solve the problem. The action is usually *reduce* or *increase* (e.g. reduce costs or increase quality). Following the action is the name of the variable that the project wants to improve. Depending on the engineering discipline, this variable could be durability, delivery speed, volume, launch speed, memory, flow, traceability, viscosity, weight, utilization, accuracy, cost, capacity, and so on.

Following the variable name, the problem statement usually contains a set of circumstantial specifications that limit the problem. The Johnson & Wick plc example contains two of these specifications: "of product AB1280" and "on production line 12." Other examples are "of the API process" (in chemical engineering), "of the measurement instrument's engine" (in mechanical engineering), and "of the drone battery" (in electrical engineering).

The variable you want to improve connects logically to other variables (e.g. strength often relates to weight). In your problem statement, you can specify any requirements regarding these logically related variables. Here is an example for a project that wants to improve the durability of a product: "… while keeping the product's manufacturing costs steady."

Requirements within a problem statement can also concern methods. A problem statement can include the formulation "by (name of method)." For example, a project wants to reduce the material costs of a product by selecting a different material. With this requirement, the student team indicates that the project will reduce material costs by selecting a new material, and not by redesigning the product to reduce the material needed per product or by reducing any material waste in the product's production.

Table 3.2 summarizes the set of predetermined components in a problem statement in engineering projects.

Table 3.2 Problem statement components in projects that improve an existing entity

Component	Description
Interrogative	The interrogative in these projects is usually *How*
Actor	The industrial partner (perhaps a department or business unit)
Action	One of the verbs *reduce* or *increase*
Variable	The variable your project will improve
Circumstantial specifications	When, where, and what the project is about
Relations to other variables	Links to other logically linked variables
Methodological requirements	Limits the project to apply a particular method

Here is another example of a problem statement constructed from the set of predetermined components in Table 3.2:

> How can Wind & Co. reduce the service needs of electrical converters in AB1400 wind turbines without reductions in converter durability and functionality?

In the example, Wind & Co. is the actor. The problem that Wind & Co. wants to reduce is a too high service need. The project is limited by the circumstantial specification "of electrical converters in AB1400 wind turbines." In addition, the project must solve the problem without reductions of the two logically related variables of durability (the number of years the converter can operate) and functionality (the number of functions the converter is able to perform).

The problem statement could include a methodological requirement, such as "thorough redesign of the converter." You could consider writing this requirement into a delimitation section that usually follows the problem statement in your report. If your problem statement becomes a bit too dense, then consider moving some of the problem statement components into the delimitation section. See Chapter 12 for details about this section.

The two rows in Figure 3.1 divide engineering projects into two categories that concern the design of a structure and the design of a process, respectively. A structure is a logically constructed entity, such as a product or a building. A process is a step-by-step sequence, such as a production process or a quality assurance procedure. In projects that design a structure, the actor's name may not be relevant in the problem statement because the project's pivotal elements do not concern the operation or development of the firm's processes. Instead, the pivotal element is the structure itself. Problem statements that focus on a structure therefore often omit the name of the industrial partner. Here are two examples of structure-oriented problem statements:

1   How can the weight of a handheld camera be reduced without changing functionality and use conditions?
2   How can the measurement speed of the AU3000 instrument be increased?

Once you and your project team have selected and formulated your problem statement, all your future choices must reflect this problem statement. Your examiners will assess all your choices with reference to your problem statement. That is why formulating a meaningful and correct problem statement is so important for your project.

Changing your problem statement during your project period

Most supervisors would say that as you increase your knowledge about your problem landscape, you can increase the specificity of your problem statement. You will naturally be much more knowledgeable about your project three months into the project than two weeks after you initiate your project.

However, there is a serious pitfall you need to avoid. Falling into this pitfall can keep you in the project's problem analysis phase way too long and may well prevent you from having the time to design a proper, high-quality solution. The pitfall centers around three terms:

1 The problem
2 "The real problem"
3 The problem's cause.

The pitfall you can fall into is perceiving the cause of your problem as "the real problem." When you have found "the real problem," you swiftly change your problem statement to reflect this new problem. Then you examine the causes of the new problem. You find a cause and, again, you consider this cause as yet another "real problem" and change your problem statement. This spiral may well keep going for several iterations while your project's timescale slowly but surely diminishes and your panic level rises. Figure 3.2 illustrates the pitfall.

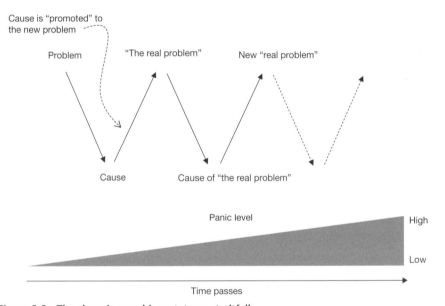

Figure 3.2   The changing problem statement pitfall

The advice is simply to stick with your original problem and perceive the cause of your problem as the cause and not as the new "real problem."

EXAMPLE OF FALLING INTO THE CHANGING PROBLEM STATEMENT PITFALL

The firm CUP Inc. manufactures a series of modern plastic cups. The firm sells its cups in large order quantities to distributors and large retailers. To produce cups, the firm uses molds. The durability of the molds is too low and the firm needs to purchase new molds too often. The problem statement therefore is:

How can CUP Inc. increase the durability of the molds used for the production of plastic cups?

The student team analyzes the causes of the molds' low durability and finds as follows:

1 The firm produces cups in large quantities (many orders are in the 4–8,000 cup range).

2 The firm produces cups when it receives an order.

3 When the firm begins to run an order, the production does not stop until the whole order is produced.

4 For each order, the firm uses the same mold regardless of order size.

5 The molds have a maximum capacity.

6 The firm's production planners do not take the maximum capacity into account when planning.

7 The mold cannot endure production runs of larger orders.

8 The production planning does not apply fixed rules, but runs on an ad hoc basis.

The student team wants to change the project's problem from low mold durability to poor production planning. The team therefore changes their problem statement and begins looking for reasons why the production planning runs poorly. Half the project period is now over and the team's panic level has increased.

In the CUP Inc. example, the team should stick with the problem of low mold durability and consider the poor production planning as the cause of cracking molds. Once the team has documented the poor (bordering on nonexistent) production planning procedures, then the team can design a production planning policy as the solution. The policy should include a rule that ensures sticking within the molds' maximum endurance limits.

Good reasons for changing a problem statement do exist. However, changing your problem statement should occur for reasons other than promoting a problem cause to the project's problem. If you want to change your problem statement, remember to consult your supervisor.

Problem statements in projects that design new entities

Table 3.3 shows the problem, methodology, and conclusion for projects that design new entities, such as a roof for a high-rise building or software for a hospital's staff scheduling. A new entity does not mean "new to the world."

In projects that design new entities, the problem is a defined need. Usually, the project's industrial partner is the "someone" who has the need. The problem statement defines the need. If the problem statement defines a high-rise roof as the need, then the project's solution are drawings of the roof and a set of selected materials. If the need is an app for a hospital's staff scheduling, then the solution is a set of diagrams that show the construction of the app, use cases, and perhaps code that illustrates a few key functions.

Table 3.3	Projects that design new entities
Problem	The project develops a new entity. This could be a chemical process, an algorithm, a machine component, or a planning procedure. The problem is not that an existing entity performs poorly, but simply that someone, often your industrial partner, has a need for a solution that is not developed (yet). If your projects designs a new entity, your job is to describe the need your industrial partner has as clearly as possible
Methodology	The project's methodology consists of two overall steps:
	Step 1: Determine all the requirements for your solution. Some of these requirements will stem from the need you have defined in your problem statement. Other requirements apply simply because of the solution type, such as product safety regulations, industrial standards for power outlets, and so on. The set of requirements should also include "soft" requirements, for example that a building's façade should satisfy the construction client's aesthetic wishes *Step 2:* Design of the solution, that is, technical drawings of a machine component, diagrams of an algorithm, recipe of a chemical product, and so on. The solution must meet all requirements identified in Step 1
Conclusion	The project's conclusion consists of a summary of the designed solution. The summary might be complemented by an implementation plan where you suggest how the industrial partner could implement the solution – build the building, code the app, have employees follow a new procedure, and so on

The problem statement in this type of project is a specified need for the solution that your industrial partner wants. Prior to defining the need, you should ask questions while applying a critical mindset. Examine why the firm has this need, and why this particular need. The answers might lead to a different need than the need the firm originally stated or perhaps a problem with an existing entity. Chapter 2 details the process of the problem analysis that occurs prior to formulating your problem statement.

A key ingredient in a great engineering solution in projects that design a new entity is to identify all the relevant design requirements for your solution. Through a thorough analysis, you will get to know the solution's use scenarios, how the solution integrates technically with its surroundings, and which laws, norms, technical regulations, and industry standards your solution must adhere to. See Chapters 4, 6, and 7 for details on conducting this analysis and using the results in your solution design.

Two important characteristics of problem statements: focus and quantifiability

A problem statement in an engineering project should be focused and concern quantifiable variables. The following sections describe what focus means in an engineering project and how to work with quantifiable variables.

Focus

Irrespective of whether your project designs a structure or a process, your project should have *one* focus. Students often hear their supervisors mention the word "focus." One supervisor even mentioned "the 3 Fs" of a project – "focus, focus, focus."

For projects that improve an existing entity, focus means that you should improve one (and only one) variable. A lecturer from mechanical engineering once gave the following statement about problem statements in engineering projects:

> Students often tell me that their project will optimize something. That's not focused enough. I tell the students to return to their chambers and think harder about their project. I want them to return with one variable that needs to be either maximized or minimized, and under which circumstances and requirements.

The quote uses the terms "maximize" and "minimize." A softer version is "reduce" and "increase." Whether the variable should be reduced or increased depends on the variable. While productivity and quality should usually be increased, costs and speed should usually be reduced.

Often, your industrial partner wants you to optimize a product or a process. Although this is a great baseline for your problem analysis, it is not specific or focused enough for your problem statement. Your job in the problem analysis, which you conduct prior to formulating the problem statement, is to identify that *one*, right variable that your project will improve.

The archenemy of focus is the word "and." Every time you allow *and* to sneak its way into your problem statement, the focus of your project is reduced because you want to improve two things simultaneously. Notice that none of the examples of problem statements given in this book include *and*. Two (or more) variables is not focused and this lack of focus reduces your ability to conduct and communicate a well-reasoned, high-quality project. Dealing with several issues simultaneously makes it harder for you to limit your search for the relevant literature, identify the right data types and sources, conduct coherent analyses, and communicate your findings and solution clearly.

Should you improve just one variable?

You might find that your supervisor does not agree that your project should try to improve only one variable. The reason might be that your problem statement and the body of your project (analysis and solutions design) are located on different levels of your problem tree.

EXAMPLE

A student team works on improving a product. The industrial partner is losing market share because competing products sell at cheaper prices. The firm's cost price of producing the product does not permit reducing the sales price without losing money, so the industrial partner cannot reduce its prices. The problem statement therefore says:

How can the firm reduce the cost price of the product?

The problem statement has one variable: the *product's cost price*, measured in "£ per product."

During a supervision meeting, you tell your supervisor how this book says that a project should only deal with one variable. Your supervisor thinks and counter-argues as follows:

One variable? Hmm … no, that's a misunderstanding by (the book's author). An engineering project rarely works with just one variable. Take *your* project, you work on weight reduction, new materials, and shape redesign, all at the same time.

Your supervisor is certainly correct that you do work with several subjects simultaneously. However, remember that the reason you work with these three particular subjects is that they all allow the industrial partner to reduce the cost price (your one variable).

The problem in your problem statement and the main body of the project work on two problem tree levels. This explains how a project can deal with both one variable and several issues simultaneously, as shown in the figure below.

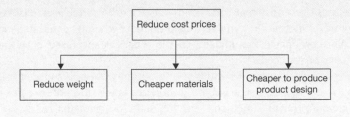

The earlier quote by the mechanical engineering lecturer finishes with a statement about the circumstances and requirements under which the project will improve their variable. In your project report, your job is to state these circumstances and requirements clearly. Often, identifying requirements and understanding their impact on your project is an ongoing activity throughout your project, and you may need to add a requirement to your problem statement at a later stage in your project. See the following example.

EXAMPLE

The project concerns reducing a product's weight without reducing functionality or increasing the purchasing costs of raw materials. The project team examines material choices and finds a new, lighter material that meets the functionality and purchasing cost requirements. However, an interview with a production engineer reveals that the selected material will hugely increase production costs. The project team has found one more variable that logically connects to the problem variable of product weight. The project team therefore adds to their project the requirement that production costs must remain steady.

Multi-criteria variables in the problem statement

Some engineering disciplines apply multi-criteria variables that integrate several individual variables into one variable. When using multi-criteria variables, a project can have several variables within the same problem statement. For example, a project can deal with product durability, product weight, and product performance within the same variable. The project assigns weights to each individual variable that reflect the relative importance, and then integrates the three variables into one variable.

Multi-criteria variables work well in work situations and it is certainly standard operating procedure for most engineers to work on improving the performance of an entity on several variables during the same period. However, in educational projects, using multi-criteria variables brings along roughly the same set of pitfalls as having two or more variables in your problem statement. If a project deals with durability, weight, and performance in the same project, then this poses much greater challenges for identifying the relevant literature, relevant data sources, and analytical work. In addition, communicating your project clearly in your project report becomes a greater challenge because readers will have to juggle information about three issues simultaneously.

If the use of multi-criteria variables is standard practice within your discipline, then your engineering field will have developed methods for handling several variables and examiners will expect the added complexity of your project. If you study a course where multi-criteria variables are not normal practice, remember to consult your supervisor for advice.

Quantifiability

The variable that your project improves should be quantifiable and measurable. A few examples are: durability can be measured in years or months, capacity in output per day, and scrap rate as a percentage.

During your first few weeks, you might find yourself working with a variable without an obvious unit of measurement, for example quality or efficiency. These vaguely defined variables are fine to begin with, but be sure to define them clearly with a unit of measurement as soon as possible. For example, replace the vaguely defined variable "quality" with "number of approved products per hour" or "daily number of approved products vs. all produced products."

If you are lucky, your industrial partner already measures the performance of the variable. It might even be the poor performance on this variable that made the firm engage with you in the first place. If the variable is already measured, then stick with the current measurement method and unit, so you can assess the effect of your project's solution on the performance of the variable.

If the variable is neither precisely defined, quantified, nor measured, then your job is to define, quantify, and measure. Quantifying and measuring the current performance on the problem variable is often the very first part of your project's analysis. For example, if your industrial partner thinks that they can reduce their inventory costs based on anecdotal evidence, then your job is, first, to define the variable "inventory cost" (including a unit of measurement) and, second, to measure these costs. The odds are that you *can* in fact reduce these costs, but without a real measurement, who knows? Maybe these costs are already as low as they can get and the firm's anecdotal evidence is just coincidental.

Having a clear measurement of the current performance of the problem variable allows for a clear assessment of your solution.

EXAMPLE

A student team has designed a new inventory policy for inventory cost reduction. The team has measured the current performance on the variable "inventory cost," and found that the firm currently has inventory costs of €3.4 million. The team assesses their policy's effect on the firm's inventory costs and finds that their policy will lead to future inventory costs of €1.2 million. Because the team has measured current inventory costs, the team can now rightly claim that their solution will reduce costs by €2.4 million.

Some supervisors like their students to include an objective in their problem statements. For example, a project might have the problem statement: "How can Eugene & Berry Inc. reduce material waste by 20%." If you insert an objective, make sure to argue why you have selected the number you have. For the Eugene & Berry example, one could ask: Why not 40% or 2%?

Avoid mixing the two project problem archetypes

This chapter describes problem statements for the two types of engineering projects. These are projects that improve an existing entity and projects that design a new entity. Although not advisable, mixing the two archetypes within the same project is entirely possible.

EXAMPLE

A project team works with a producer of payment terminals. The team has identified the problem they wish to work with. The problem is the slow speed of VISA payment transactions. The team has measured the average speed to be 8.24 seconds. This project aims to improve an existing entity (the payment terminal).

During the project, the student team's contact at the firm comes up with the idea that the terminal should also be able to show the customer their current account balance. Your contact person asks you to include this new function in your project. Suddenly, your project improves an entity (the payment terminal) and develops a new entity (the account balance function) within the same project.

Mixing the archetypes erodes your project's focus. When reading your report, your examiners may well ask themselves what your project is really about. Mixing archetypes makes your project's problem unclear to your examiners because your project concerns several issues simultaneously. Ideally, you should choose to either improve something that already exists or design a new entity. If you do decide to mix the archetypes, remember to consult your supervisor.

Industrial partners often like to include new issues and tasks into a project. In your working life, you will find that including all manner of issues into the same project (coherent or not) is quite common. Therefore, your contact often sees no problem at all asking you to include an additional subject into your project. This is one of the classic pitfalls of working with industrial partners (see more about these pitfalls and how to handle them in Chapter 10).

Subquestions to your problem statement

Formulating a set of subquestions to your problem statement is often a great idea. Formulating these questions breaks your problem statement into more easily handled chunks of work and gives you clarity about which literature, theory, and information your project needs. However, not all questions can function as subquestions to your problem statement.

The principle that decides whether a question can "lawfully" function as a subquestion to your problem statement is whether the question *must* be answered before you can answer your problem statement. Some lecturers like to say that subquestions "unfold the problem statement."

Acceptable subquestions deal with issues that are already part of the problem statement. In the example in Table 3.4, the subquestions concern, among others, product availability and inventory reduction. Answering the acceptable subquestions makes you understand the elements in your problem statement and their interrelations. Answering these questions is a prerequisite to answering the overall problem statement. In the FISH&CHIPS example, the project team cannot answer the problem statement without knowing what product availability is or how to calculate an average inventory.

Table 3.4   Example of subquestions to the problem statement

Problem statement	
"How can FISH&CHIPS plc reduce the average inventory of fish fillets without reducing the availability of fish fillets for purchasing customers?"	
Acceptable subquestion	**Unacceptable subquestions**
Who is FISH&CHIPS plc?	Can FISH&CHIPS benefit from outsourcing their inventory?
What is an inventory?	Could FISH&CHIPS reduce their production lead time?
How is an average inventory calculated?	How does FISH&CHIPS' top management view their inventory of fish fillets?
What is the availability of products?	Can FISH&CHIPS sell types of seafood other than fish fillets?
How does the size of inventory influence the availability of products?	Can FISH&CHIPS use suppliers to help them keep their availability steady?
How can inventory be reduced (in general)?	Are FISH&CHIPS' sales numbers increasing or decreasing?
How can the inventory at FISH&CHIPS be reduced?	Could FISH&CHIPS use new types of packaging materials?
What is the current availability of products for FISH&CHIPS' customers?	Could the inventory be better categorized?

Some subquestions are simple and often readers of your report will know intuitively that you will answer them regardless of whether you mention them as explicit subquestions. For the FISH&CHIPS example, a simple subquestion is: "What is an inventory?" None of the subquestions are as complex as the problem statement itself. The problem statement juggles all elements from all subquestions in the same question.

The unacceptable subquestions bring into play *new* elements that are not already in the problem statement. In the FISH&CHIPS case, examples are outsourcing, production lead times, and packaging materials. These elements can absolutely be part of the project's analysis and solution, but they do not belong among the subquestions to the problem statement. Although some readers might know from experience or sheer logic that the new elements in the subquestions are relevant to solving the problem, the reader does not know (formally) that the new elements are relevant at this point in the report. Readers who are unfamiliar with the report's topic will perceive a new element in a subquestion like a bolt from the blue.

Bringing in new elements is relevant at later stages of your project. Chapter 4 describes the project's knowledge foundation of literature. Literature brings new elements into play in the project; for example, elements that can function as components in your project's solution. However, it is much too early to bring in new elements when you are formulating your problem statement.

Reviewing this chapter's objectives

Tick those objectives you feel you have achieved, and review those you haven't yet accomplished. In this chapter, you have learned how to:

- ❏ Formulate a clear problem statement and understand the components of a problem statement.
- ❏ Understand how problem statements demonstrate focus and quantifiability.
- ❏ Extract subquestions from the overall problem statement.

4

Literature, Knowledge, and Expertise in Engineering Projects

In this chapter, you will learn:

1 What constitutes the knowledge foundation in engineering projects.
2 That engineering students utilize both practice-oriented literature (standards, guidelines, instructions) and academic literature (textbooks and papers published in scientific journals).
3 How to locate the relevant literature and other knowledge sources for an engineering project.
4 Sources of relevant literature and other knowledge.
5 How and where in the project to utilize the literature and other knowledge sources.
6 How to utilize the literature to define the project's central variables, ensure a rigorous analysis, and design an effective solution.
7 How to operationalize theory when practice-oriented literature is missing.
8 What to do if the knowledge you need does not exist: experimentation and logical reasoning.

An engineering project builds on the knowledge embedded in practice-oriented and academic literature. Practice-oriented literature is that which practicing engineers apply, while academic literature comprises university textbooks and papers published in scientific journals.

EXAMPLES OF TYPES OF PRACTICE-ORIENTED LITERATURE

- Construction codes and regulations (e.g. Eurocodes and public building regulations)
- EU directives (e.g. the WEEE directive on the reuse and recycling of electronic equipment)
- Programming rules (e.g. syntax rules in Java programming)
- Standards for correct technical drawings (e.g. Geometrical Product Specifications for tolerances)
- Principles for effective manufacturing (e.g. the lean principles)
- Guidelines (e.g. Kotter's eight steps for successful organizational change)
- Industry-specific guidelines (e.g. planning guidelines for installing wind turbines)
- Regulations for patenting and immaterial property rights (e.g. EU patenting regulations)
- Rules for conducting investment analysis in accounting
- Elaborate to-do lists (e.g. Business Model Canvas for a complete business model)

The knowledge embedded in practice-oriented literature is built on the experience of an engineering discipline's community and on the research that is often referred to as *applied science*. Academia likes to differentiate between the applied sciences, which research subjects closer to practice, and the basic sciences. Figure 4.1 shows the relationship between the types of practice-oriented literature and the foundation of applied sciences and basic sciences.

The boxes at the top of Figure 4.1 represent the different types of practice-oriented literature. The practice-oriented literature is built on the applied sciences, which in turn are built on the basic sciences.

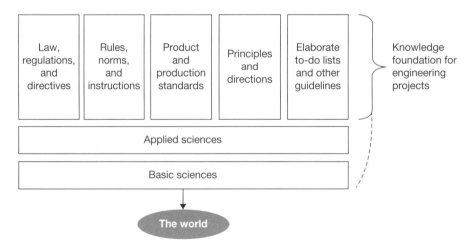

Figure 4.1   The knowledge foundation of engineering projects

1 An engineering project develops a new type of energy-efficient window. The team of engineers uses a construction code for constructing the window. The code says an energy-efficient window should have three panes of glass and there should be a gas, such as argon, between the panes. These two guidelines are based on the applied science that researches how heat moves through materials. This applied science is built on the laws of thermodynamics from the basic sciences.

2 A project develops a software program. To develop the program, the engineers apply a programming language that contains a set of syntax rules. These rules are developed in computer science (an applied science). Computer science is built on, among other disciplines algebra in the basic sciences.

Since antiquity, basic and applied sciences have published theories, models, mathematical expressions, and methods. These research results are usually first published in academic papers. Later, when a theory or research result is recognized as important, the theory or research result is included in a textbook or academic handbook, which makes science more widely accessible and easy to understand.

The right-hand side of Figure 4.1 shows a curly bracket and a dotted line representing the full knowledge foundation for engineering projects. The practice-oriented literature genres are the main source of literature-based knowledge in engineering projects. However, all engineers learn the basic sciences of physics, mathematics, materials science, electrical science, and often economics as well. In engineering projects, examiners expect you to utilize knowledge from both applied and basic sciences when necessary. Examples of theories or models from basic sciences are Ohm's law of electrical resistance, Bernoulli's principle in fluid dynamics, Newton's laws in physics, and Kirchhoff's laws of electrical circuits.

Often, you need to operationalize a theory or a model to apply the model directly in your project. A later section in this chapter describes how to operationalize a theory or model for direct use.

The knowledge foundation embedded in the literature constitutes the expertise in your project

The first sentence in the chapter's introduction says that engineering projects build on the knowledge embedded in practice-oriented and academic literature. When you conduct your project's activities, you use the literature for numerous tasks; for example, to qualify choices, conduct correct calculations and analyses, ensure proper datasets for your analyses, and design effective solutions.

The knowledge embedded in the literature constitutes *the expertise* in your project. You may be inclined to think that your industrial partner contact and your supervisor are the experts of your project. Your industrial partner contact is often a graduate from the same engineering discipline you are currently studying and your supervisor is a university professor. These two people are certainly skilled, but you should remember that these two well-qualified individuals do not work most/all of their time on your project and their skill set is built on the very same literature you have at your disposal.

Selecting the relevant literature for an engineering project

There is a vast amount of literature to choose from, and your job is to locate and select that which is precisely relevant for your particular project. Your problem statement provides the foundation for making your literature choices. The problem statement contains one or more words that tell you which literature is necessary in your project.

EXAMPLE

The project is to design an energy-efficient window. The project team has formulated their problem statement and wants to locate and select the literature that is relevant for their design task. Because the problem statement concerns the design of an energy-efficient window, the project team has extracted the following four questions for which the literature contains the answers:

1   What is an energy-efficient window?

2   Which general, technical requirements must windows meet – safety, heat containment, etc.?

3   Which functions can an energy-efficient window have – ability to open, ventilation, etc.?

4   How should an energy-efficient window be designed to ensure functionality and durability?

The project team collects the literature that deals with these four questions. This comprises industry standards, rules and guidelines, and regulations for window design. By reading this literature, the project group finds that the energy-efficient window needs three panes of glass (triple glazing) and two sets of rubber strips to minimize air leakage. The project team also discovers:

●   how the window design can fix the glass panes in the window frames

●   the requirements for the mechanical structure of the frame

●   how the window maintains the gas between the glass panes

●   which types of rubber strips ensure a minimum of air leakage.

The next step is to ensure the understanding and inclusion of all the design requirements of the industrial partner (a window producer) and their group of customers. With a complete requirement specification, the project group is ready to begin designing the new energy-efficient window.

Making choices about using theories, models, and methods

The literature contains theories, models, methods, and many other necessities for an engineering project. Often, the use of a particular model or method is obvious to all relevant parties in and around your project. The choice of a model might be so obvious that if you were to select a different model, your examiners might think that you did not make it past your first semester. In these cases, examiners do not expect you to provide explicit arguments for your choice of theory.

However, choosing a method or model might be a choice between two or more *real* alternatives. In these cases, you must argue for your choice. It may be that you have a great argument right off the bat. For example: "The project uses Geometrical Product Specifications for indicating tolerances because this is the standard applied in the firm's industry." However, having such spot-on arguments is not always the case. The more important and ambiguous a choice is, the more thought you should invest in arguing for your choice.

Arguing for your choice means answering the question: "Why have you chosen (name of method)?" A good answer to this question satisfies your examiners. Adding to the strength of your argument as well as the clarity of your report is explaining to the reader how you plan to apply the method. An easy rule of thumb to remember is the phrase WHY+APPLY – indicating WHY you have selected the method and how you plan to APPLY it. Answering the WHY+APPLY questions ties your selected method or model into the overall coherent flow of your project. Answering WHY explains how your chosen method or model fits with the earlier parts of your project, the problem statement in particular. Answering APPLY explains how your chosen method or model fits into the later parts of the project – in particular, your analysis and solution design. Figure 4.2 illustrates the WHY+APPLY questions.

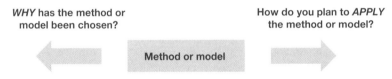

WHY has the method or model been chosen?

How do you plan to **APPLY** the method or model?

Method or model

Figure 4.2   The WHY+APPLY questions

Chapter 12 provides more detail about how to describe theories, methods, and models in your project report.

Locating the relevant literature

In projects where your lecturers specify your problem and methods, they will have predetermined the relevant literature and usually listed it in the project course's curriculum. Using specified methods and models is usually an integral component of reaching the project course's learning objectives.

In free projects, where you make all the important choices, the tasks of defining, locating, and selecting the relevant literature is yours. The top tips box overleaf lists methods for locating the literature that is relevant for your particular project.

The key to finding the right theory, method, or model is having a clear set of information needs. The example about designing energy-efficient windows shows how you extract a set of information needs from a problem statement. A focused problem statement is in itself an effective tool for limiting your search for relevant sources, but the more specific you can be about what you are looking for, the easier your search. The example shows how a great starting point for your literature search is the element that your project designs (a bridge, an automated process, an app, etc.) or the variable that your project seeks to improve (e.g. durability, software speed, or power plant downtime).

TOP TIPS FOR LOCATING RELEVANT LITERATURE

- Ask your supervisor or other faculty members at your university
- Ask your industrial partner contact and colleagues
- Ask the librarian at your university library
- Search in your university library's physical and digital selections
- Search other digital sources, such as industry organization websites
- Check your textbook references for more specifically relevant papers and other textbooks
- Use Google and Google Scholar searches about your project's topic and specific information needs
- Check out Wikipedia articles' list of sources, but do avoid using the Wikipedia article itself as a reference

The literature in your course curriculum is often *not* the most relevant

It might be that the most relevant literature for your particular project is part of the curriculum in one of the courses of your degree. You should remember, though, that the further on you are in your degree, the less likelihood there is that the literature your instructor has chosen for a course happens to "fit like a glove" with your particular knowledge needs. Your project often needs more specific literature than the papers and texts in your curriculum.

Searching textbook reference lists is often a great place to begin your literature search. Borrow or download the literature you find from examining textbook references and see if they work. If not, continue the strategy and look in these new sources' reference lists. This method of examining references (sometimes called *snowballing*) is effective. Do remember that every time you "roll the snowball," the literature gets older, and that practice-oriented literature is not always part of textbook references.

If a book is not digitally available, then borrow a physical copy from your university library. Amazon is a great resource for identifying textbooks for specialist subjects. If you find a book on Amazon, then borrow the book through your university library. Remember also that Google Scholar has many, many books digitally available, and even more if you access the site through your university library.

How to use literature in your project

An engineering project uses literature throughout the project. This chapter details how to use the literature for the following three distinct purposes: to define the project's important terms; as the foundation for a thorough analysis; and as a tool for designing the project's solution.

Purpose 1: To define the project's important terms

Chapter 3 states that an engineering project can improve an existing entity or design a new entity. For projects that improve an existing entity, the problem statement contains at least one term that needs accurate definition. That term is the project's problem variable; for example, too short product durability of a machine, too high levels of CO_2 emissions from a production system, or too much heat radiation from a building. To ensure a clear understanding of your problem variable as well as other central variables, use the literature to find the right definition.

In some projects, ensuring clear variable definitions is straightforward. For example, in a project to increase the speed of a measurement instrument, the team can easily define the speed as "number of minutes between conducting the measurement until the instrument delivers a measurement result." In other projects, you need to define the problem variable and perhaps other key terms as well. The literature can help you find the right definitions.

EXAMPLE

A project team cooperates with a distributor of kitchen cabinets and tabletops. The firm has a large finished goods inventory. Using forklifts, staff pick items for customer orders from the finished goods inventory and deliver them to a designated area in the building where orders are assembled, packed, and shipped.

The student team wants to increase the inventory personnel's *order picking productivity*. The team therefore needs a clear definition of this term. To define the term, the project team borrows a set of logistics and inventory management textbooks and finds appropriate definitions of *order picking productivity* as well as the related term *finished goods inventory.*

It is quite common that technical fields with a long history have developed a set of standard terms, and that everyone who works in or studies the field is familiar with these terms and their exact meaning. Examples of such fields are construction and electrical engineering. Construction builds on the sciences of mechanics, materials science, and Newtonian physics founded hundreds of years ago. If you are working within these fields, the need to define terms often just means selecting the units of measurement that your project will use; for example, kW/m^2 for heat consumption and *liter/minute* for measuring liquid flow through a pipe (e.g. at a power plant or soda factory).

Explained: complex terms are often built from simpler terms

Terms are usually defined using simpler terms. For example, acceleration is defined as m/s^2 (meters per second squared). Meter and second are simpler and more broadly known than acceleration.

If your project applies technically complex terms that you expect your reader may not know, then make sure to specify them explicitly. Some terms can be quite abstract and tough to grasp.

You may experience that your reader misinterprets a term that you find straightforward and intuitively easy to understand. Take, for example, the term *quality*. Does quality mean that a product works as intended or that the manufacturer produces very few defective products? The right definition depends on the project. Make sure to select a definition that suits your problem and describe the definition explicitly in your report.

If you work with a problem where standard terms are scarce, then you can define your own term. Be careful to define such a term clearly. If at all possible, base your definitions on existing literature. If you want to define quality, then borrow several quality assurance or quality management textbooks. Get to know these textbook definitions of quality. Then, define your own quality term either by using a textbook definition verbatim, or by incorporating elements from textbook definitions into your own definition. If textbooks do not help you, define a term of your own without textbook assistance.

If you define your own term for something that your field already has a well-known definition for, the risk is that your reader will think about the term with the traditional definition when reading your report. For example, if you define cost as "€ per order" and your examiners are used to thinking about cost as "€ per item," make sure to repeat your own definition a number of times throughout your project to ensure your reader remembers that you are applying a definition that differs from the traditional definition.

> **TOP TIP**
>
> Avoid using general dictionaries for defining your terms. Dictionary authors are usually not experts within your particular field. The authoritative book *The Craft of Research* (Booth et al. 2008) states that if a definition is needed, then a dictionary will not suffice. Instead, make an effort to use your field's literature to define your key terms rather than using a (random) dictionary's definition. In addition, avoid using random internet definitions. Examiners are not fans of the "Google – I'm feeling lucky" approach to defining key terms in engineering projects.

In addition to naming the variable, be sure to indicate the unit of measurement. A unit of measurement may apply specifically to your project. For example, one project measures density as *ton/m³* and another project uses *kg/liter*. Knowing the unit of measurement is important for ensuring correct calculations as well as clarity.

When you have defined your project's central variables, your reader has a complete understanding of your project's problem and objective. In principle, once your reader has acquired this understanding, they can understand and evaluate your project's methodology. Methodology is described in Chapter 5.

Purpose 2: As the foundation for your project's analysis

The literature increases your ability to conduct a thorough analysis. Projects that design a new entity can use literature to identify the general design requirements that apply to the type of entity your project is designing (e.g. regulations for the built environment and safety regulations for machinery and appliances). Chapter 6 deals with identifying these requirements. For projects that improve an existing entity, the analysis has the objective of examining causes and opportunities (see Table 4.1).

Table 4.1 The analysis works with both causes and opportunities for improvement	
Causes	Opportunities
The analysis seeks to identify the cause for your project's problem. A project's problem may have multiple causes, each impacting the problem with different effects and severity	The analysis seeks to identify whether generically available opportunities for eliminating your problem are applied by your industrial partner

The analysis seeks to identify the cause of your project's problem. In your analysis, an unused opportunity constitutes a cause (see the top tip box on p. 47). For a project that improves an existing entity, Chapter 3 states that the problem is that the entity is performing inadequately or simply has an unfulfilled improvement potential. For example, if a product requires too much servicing, then the project's analysis will seek to identify the cause for the required services.

In addition to uncovering the cause of the project's problem, the analysis examines whether generically available opportunities for eliminating the problem are currently applied by your industrial partner. For example, if a project seeks to increase the speed of a chemical separation of two liquids, the project team can examine whether extant opportunities for increasing the speed are already implemented.

To effectively examine causes and opportunities, you should take advantage of the knowledge about your project's problem in the literature. To support your search for relevant literature, ask these two questions:

1 What are the generic causes for the existence of the type of problem your project works with?
2 What are the generic opportunities for eliminating or reducing the problem your project works with?

The adjective "generic" is related to "general." In this context, generic means theoretically possible. In other words, a generic cause is a cause that *could be* a reality in your project. Your later analysis will examine whether generic causes are actual causes. The answers to the two questions are two lists of generic causes and generic opportunities. Table 4.2 shows an example for a project that seeks to increase the monthly output rate from a production machine.

Table 4.2 Generic causes and opportunities for low output

Generic causes for low output	Generic opportunities for low output
1. Operators spend too much time setting up machines to run orders	1. Material needs and shortages can be anticipated through planning procedures and forecasting
2. Machines ready to run an order wait for materials to process	2. Breakdowns and other sudden maintenance needs can be reduced through productivity-based preventive maintenance processes
3. Machines break down and need unscheduled here-and-now maintenance	3. Clear instruction manuals ensure more effective machine operation
4. Machines run slower than necessary due to worn tools and fixtures	4. Effective operator training can support high-efficiency operation and maximum output per utilized hour
5. Machines are not operated correctly, resulting in unnecessarily long order run-times	
6. Machines that may be utilized enough do not produce to maximum hourly capacity	
7. Unclear operator manuals may lead to incorrect machine operation	

Once you have written down the two lists of generic causes and opportunities for your particular project, your next step is organizing these causes and opportunities in a *generic, hierarchical problem tree.* This problem tree constitutes the result of your work with the literature prior to your analysis. Figure 4.3 shows an example of a problem tree for the same project as Table 4.2 about increasing the output of a production machine (measured as output per month).

The problem tree in Figure 4.3 has organized Table 4.2's seven causes and four opportunities in a hierarchical problem tree. The problem tree has four levels (ranging from left to right). Level 1 is the project's problem. Level 2 divides causes into two categories "Low machine utilization" and "Low output per utilized hour." All other

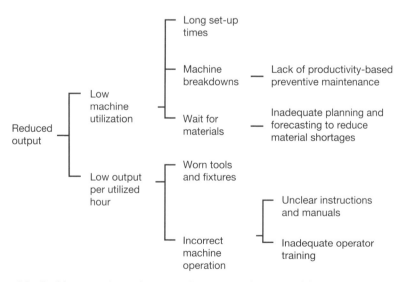

Figure 4.3   Problem tree (organizes generic causes and opportunities)

causes are organized within one of these two categories. The project team has organized the causes logically. For example, breakdowns in level 3 relate to maintenance in level 4.

TOP TIP

The problem tree in Figure 4.3 shows how the generic causes and opportunities are organized. A rule when developing problem trees is that:

An unused opportunity = a cause

Figure 4.3 shows the problem tree for a production machine with a low monthly output rate. The student team has read the relevant literature and found that *productivity-based preventive maintenance* can reduce the frequency of sudden machine breakdowns. In the project's analysis of the firm's maintenance, the student team examines whether the firm does indeed use the maintenance method. If the firm does not use the method, then this unused opportunity is a cause for the project's problem (provided that implementing and operating the method are physically and practically possible).

While the problem tree in Figure 4.3 contains generic causes, your later analysis will use the problem tree to identify whether the generic causes are *actual* causes in your project. Your problem tree defines which analyses are relevant for your project to conduct. Figure 4.4 shows the exact same problem tree as Figure 4.3, with the addition of the analyses that are relevant for the project on the right. If long set-up times are a generic cause for your project's problem, then your analysis needs to examine whether set-up times are in fact long and reducible in your particular case.

Remember that a generic problem tree is limited to the literature you have read and your own prior knowledge of the field. Your industrial partner may well have circumstances that make other issues the actual causes. So, make sure to be open to explanations other than your generic causes for your project's problem.

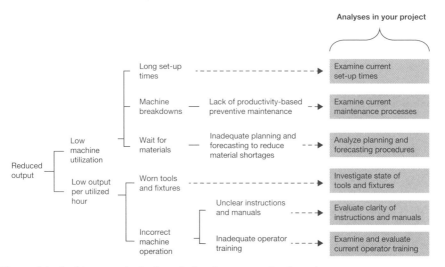

Figure 4.4   Problem tree is the foundation for your project's analyses

If you have spent time developing a thorough problem tree, your analysis will be that much better. Remember, a thorough analysis is a prerequisite for designing an effective solution.

Purpose 3: As tools for designing your project's solution

One example in this chapter describes a project to develop a new energy-efficient window. The project team has found that the energy-efficient window needs three panes of glass, that there should be gas between the panes, and that two or three sets of rubber strips ensure minimal air leakage between the window and the outer frame. The project team is now getting ready to design their energy-efficient window. The team needs to know how to fix the panes of glass in the window frames, maintain the gas between the glass panes, and place the rubber strips on the frame. The necessary knowledge is embedded in design guidelines and construction codes; for example, the relationship between glass pane weight and the mechanical structure of the window frame.

When practice-oriented literature does not exist: operationalize theory

The beginning of this chapter describes how the literature available to engineers consists of both practice-oriented literature (instructions, standards, codes, etc.) and academic literature (textbooks and papers). The practice-oriented literature is by nature more directly useful to practitioners. The literature is *operational*.

If operational literature does not exist or is unattainable for a particular task, then you need to apply theory from the applied and basic sciences. This theory is more abstract and therefore less operational for your project. To operationalize theory means making the theory directly applicable to your project. The term is frequently used in the social sciences where, for example, abstract economic theory is applied in projects that analyze current market situations (e.g. stocks or real estate bonds).

Among the specifics of operationalization is identifying and extracting the relevant variables in a theory and embedding them in a set of questions. These questions are the foundation for your data collection and analysis.

EXAMPLES

Example 1: Design of a load-bearing steel structure in a floor

A project team designs the load-bearing steel structure in a floor between basement and ground floor in an office building. So, the student team finds and reads the literature about the characteristics of steel and load-bearing steel structures. The project team identifies the variable "thickness" in the theory about steel structure. "Thickness" refers to how thick a steel beam must be in the load-bearing structure. The team embeds the variable in a question that needs answering:

How thick should the load-bearing steel beams in the floor structure be?

Extracting the variable "thickness" from the theory and embedding the variable in one or more questions constitutes theory operationalizing. This question prompts other questions about the steel type, beam profile, and distance between the load-bearing walls.

Example 2: Reducing the costs of operating a raw materials inventory

A project team works to reduce a manufacturer's costs of operating the firm's raw materials inventory. The student team locates and reads the theory about inventory costs and finds the variable "quantity per order" (the quantity in which the firm orders a raw material at every purchase, e.g. 300 kg). The team finds that this order size impacts the inventory size and therefore the costs of holding the inventory. The team needs to find the order size that results in the lowest inventory costs without raising other costs. The team operationalizes the theory by inserting the variable in a question that the team needs to answer:

Which order size results in the lowest inventory costs?

Without practice-oriented literature or relevant theory: experiment or use deductive reasoning

Engineering projects do not always have access to a neat set of guidelines or theory to operationalize. For example, a student team needs to calculate the maximum bending moment for an H-beam (a steel beam with an H-shaped cross-section). The team finds a model for this calculation in a construction standard. However, the architect wants to twist the beam around its own axis three times (for aesthetic reasons). Now the construction standard cannot help. In this case, the team needs to conduct an experiment that shows the maximum bending moment, or deduce a method for calculation. For an experiment, the team might have their industrial partner help them twist a steel beam in the industrial partner's workshop. The test can find the beam's maximum bending moment. Or they could conduct the test on a smaller version of a steel beam and extrapolate to a larger beam.

   Examiners (and society) expect engineers to use their ingenuity to develop project-specific knowledge if necessary. You can develop project-specific knowledge by drawing logical conclusions from known facts and verified theories to your situation. This process is known as *deduction*. Conducting an experiment and drawing conclusions from a single experiment to a larger population or context constitutes *induction*. Deduction and induction are the two most common principles for generating knowledge.

Explained: deduction and induction

Deduction

Deduction means drawing logically correct conclusions from a set of premises. The set of premises consists of knowledge, theory, or models that all relevant parties consider true. Simply put, deduce means drawing a conclusion with the form: "if A and B are true, then C *must* be true." For example: "if rain makes things wet and it's been raining for hours, then things are wet" or "if a = 2 and b = 4, then a + b must be 6." In an engineering project, a deduction could be:

> If the construction standard says 60 mm of insulation in Scandinavia, that must mean 40 mm in Mediterranean Europe because winter temperatures are 7.8 degrees lower than in Scandinavia.

No one will question the two simple deduction examples about rain or a+b. However, deductions in engineering projects are often more complex and harder to grasp. You might have to argue for why you claim that a conclusion drawn from a set of premises is actually logically correct. From time to time, you might even have to argue whether your premises are in fact true.

Induction

Induction means drawing logical conclusions from a single or a small set of observations to a larger population. An example from the pharmaceutical industry could be:

> This medicine works on 80% of a representative sample of 200 patients. Therefore, the medicine will work on 80% of all future patients.

Engineering projects use inductive reasoning when a project team has conducted a series of tests. Here are two examples:

1   A study tests the number of unscheduled stops of a machine over a three-month period when using a new maintenance policy. The number of unscheduled stops is 30% lower compared to those with the old maintenance policy. Therefore, the 30% reduction in unscheduled stops will apply in the future as well.

2   A study examines the effect of a new assembly instruction on the number of finished products that fail their final functionality test. The study tests 250 products and finds that the failure rate is reduced by 46%. Therefore, the 46% reduction will apply to future products as well.

Reviewing this chapter's objectives

Tick those objectives you feel you have achieved, and review those you haven't yet accomplished. In this chapter, you have learned how to:

❐ Locate the relevant literature and other knowledge sources for your project.

❐ Utilize literature for defining the project's central variables, for ensuring a rigorous analysis, and for designing an effective solution.

❐ Operationalize theory when practice-oriented literature is missing.

❐ Use experimentation and logical reasoning when the knowledge you need does not exist.

Project Methodology and Planning

| Project initiation | Problem statement | Literature, knowledge, and expertise | Methodology and planning | Data collection and analysis | Design of solution | Test and implementation of solution |

In this chapter, you will learn:

1 The meaning of the term *methodology*.
2 The philosophy of science in engineering projects and why engineering projects do not usually contain explicit discussions of philosophy in science.
3 How your project ensures coherence throughout your project's activities.
4 That your project's methodology consists of both the overall sequence of steps in which you organize your project and the selected methods, tools, and techniques for specific project activities.
5 The typical overall structure of engineering projects that improve an existing entity or design a new entity.
6 For which purposes your project applies methods, tools, and techniques.
7 The categories of choices that you make throughout your project and the types of arguments that can persuade a reader that your methodological choices are sound.
8 How you as a project team can plan your own project using Gantt charts.

The term "methodology" comes from the Greek *met-hodos* meaning "the way along which." For an engineering project, the methodology means the way along which your project solves the problem in your problem statement. You can select the methodology that is best suited for your project when you have a clearly formulated problem statement. The right methodology depends entirely on the problem you want to solve. When the reader has read your methodology section, they should have a clear picture of how your project flows from problem statement through analysis and solution design to conclusions and recommendations for your industrial partner.

The philosophy of science in engineering projects

With few exceptions, the philosophy of science of engineering projects consists of these three components:

1 Engineering is rooted in a positivistic, "natural science" worldview.
2 Reasons for events are explained through classic, cause-and-effect relationships.
3 Engineering concerns learning *problem solving* and designing solutions for specific problems rather than knowledge creation for society and the world at large.

Engineering projects rarely contain explicit discussions of the philosophy of science. The positivistic worldview and the objective of problem solving rather than knowledge creation for the world at large means that engineering projects do not need discussions of the philosophy of science. All parties to an engineering project consider the laws of nature and the derived laws of engineering as true and therefore implicitly indisputable.

Engineering projects differ from projects within the humanities and social sciences. In these fields, students make great efforts to select and describe a specific "lens" through which the project perceives the problem. These lenses are often called "perspectives" or "paradigms." The simple fact that there *are* options to choose from makes humanities and social sciences different from natural sciences and engineering.

Engineering reports do not include discussions concerning the choice of perspective; for example, a discussion about which perspective would best suit the analysis of whether a zinc-based surface treatment is more effective against corrosion than a surface treatment with a zinc-lead alloy. In the humanities and social sciences, this discussion concerning perspective is of paramount importance.

EXAMPLE

A sociology project examines why long-term unemployment is a social problem. The student team must choose a perspective (a philosophy of science) for their project. Two possible perspectives are positivism and social constructivism.

If the student team chooses positivism, the study would find that long-term unemployment leads to lower quality of life and premature death. In other words, long-term unemployment is a social problem due to its consequences. If the student team chooses social constructivism, then the results would be very different. With social constructivism, the study would find that long-term unemployment has become a social problem due to a long public debate between NGOs, politicians, academics, and celebrities. As a result of this decades-long debate, all parties now perceive long-term unemployment as a social problem.

This example shows that the reason long-term unemployment is perceived to be a social problem differs substantially between studies. Whether the reason is "premature death" or "debate" depends entirely on the choice of perspective, and therefore the choice of perspective requires a big effort on the part of the student team.

The three components in the philosophy of science of engineering, detailed above, apply to most engineering disciplines. However, there are exceptions, for example projects that integrate technical and social disciplines. These could be projects about innovation that consider technology as the result of a social construction process, and projects about changed human behavior (e.g. from customers or employees).

Engineering projects *implicitly* use a number of terms that are often part of philosophy of science classes. Examples are deduction/induction and quantitative/qualitative. Methodology sections in engineering projects, however, do not focus on discussing the philosophical foundation of the project. Instead, they focus on the methodology specifics and on argumentation as to why the chosen methodology will lead to an effective solution and a great set of recommendations for the project's industrial partner.

Making methodology choices

Engineering students often ask their supervisor two questions: "What's a methodology section?" and "How do we choose the right methodology?" The description and choice of methodology are often unclear activities, and the weight your faculty puts on this choice differs hugely between disciplines and universities.

So what is methodology? The answer is actually quite simple. For all projects – instructor-devised or independent – the methodology is the answer to the question of *how* you conduct your project to reach a solution to your project's problem. When you have written your problem statement and clearly defined all the important variables in your project, you are ready to answer this question. The answer to this "how" question is your methodology. A more specific version of the question is: "Which activities will you conduct in your project and in which sequence?" The answer is always a sequence of activities – "first we will do X, then Y, and finally Z." This sequence of activities is your project's methodology.

Often, a project can be conducted using two or three different methodologies. In these cases, your methodology is a choice.

EXAMPLE

An engineering project concerns increasing a manufacturer's ability to deliver orders on time. The student team examines how to conduct the project and finds they have three alternative methodologies:

1 Follow a series of customer orders to identify the reasons why they are delayed. Then, develop a solution that eliminates the causes for delays.

2 Interview staff to identify the reasons why the orders are delayed. Then, develop a solution that eliminates the causes.

3 Divide the firm's product portfolio into groups to identify the product group that is usually late. Then, develop a solution that concerns these product groups.

The student team should select a methodology and argue why their selected methodology will result in an effective solution that reduces the number of late orders. The project team could apply two methods simultaneously to ensure stronger conclusions and solutions.

In general, your choice of methodology is closely connected with the validity of your conclusion. A bulletproof methodology leads to a bulletproof conclusion. In engineering projects, the conclusion is usually a summary of the developed solution to the project's problem. Therefore, conclusion validity equals solution effectiveness. As a project team, you should ask yourself: "Which methodology will lead to an effective solution?"

In your report, you should describe your methodology and include arguments for its usefulness in your project. The reader should feel convinced that your methodology will in fact result in a great solution. See details about how to describe the methodology in Chapter 12.

The typical overall structure of engineering projects

The methodology in a project consists of two elements:

1 The overall project structure (the sequence of "big steps" in the project).
2 The specific methods, tools, and techniques that you apply *within* each of the big steps in your project structure (e.g. finite element methods for mechanical design or value stream mapping for production analysis).

The overall structure of engineering projects shares some characteristics across disciplines. The structure does, however, differ greatly from the structure of a traditional academic research project. Traditional research begins with an introduction, which includes the project's purpose and/or explicit research questions. Second, traditional research selects theory, methods, and materials. Third, the study is conducted and results are presented. Finally, traditional research discusses findings and presents conclusions. Figure 5.1 illustrates this structure of a traditional academic research project. This structure is often abbreviated as IMRAD for Introduction, Methods and materials, Results, And Discussion.

Figure 5.1   The structure of traditional research projects

The structure of an engineering project differs substantially from the traditional academic research project because there are fundamental differences between conducting research that answers questions and conducting a project that solves a problem.

Academic research answers questions. These research questions are usually complicated questions that are immensely relevant to science and society at large. For example, a student project within geography examines how the increasing prevalence of cumulus clouds influences the earth's absorption of sunlight. Deriving a robust answer to such a question requires thorough research and a rigorous method. However, the answer to this question is not a solution to a problem.

Solving problems is a different genre of project. Therefore, the structure differs from the structure of traditional research projects. Figure 5.2 shows the typical structure of an engineering project, which is explained as follows:

1 The project team introduces the project.
2 The team formulates the problem statement.
3 The team defines the key terms and variables, and chooses and specifies the project's methodology.
4 The team conducts the project's analysis. The analysis differs between projects that improve an existing entity and projects that design a new entity. If the project improves an existing entity, the analysis identifies the cause(s) of the project's problem. If the project designs a new entity, the analysis identifies the solution's design requirements and subsystems (see details later in the chapter).
5 When the analysis is finished, the team designs the solution.
6 The team tests and implements the solution.
7 Conclusions and recommendations are presented.

Figure 5.2   The typical structure of an engineering project

This is the classic structure of an engineering project. The structure is the same as the figure at the beginning of Chapters 2–8. At some universities, the final semesters of a five-year degree include more research-oriented projects that answer unanswered questions rather than design solutions to problems. Chapter 16 covers how to conduct engineering research projects.

Although Figure 5.2 captures the overall structure of engineering projects, there are differences between projects that improve an existing entity and projects that design a new entity. The typical methodology of each of these two project archetypes is now discussed.

Typical structure of a project that improves an existing entity

Figure 5.3 shows a typical structure for an engineering project that improves an existing entity. The figure shows four boxes each containing one or more activities. The first box contains the project's problem statement about variable X with inadequate performance (e.g. low product durability or a high production quality failure rate). The second box shows the project's analysis of causes as to why current performance is inadequate. The causal analysis answers a series of why questions leading to the root causes that the project can address with solutions. Each why question constitutes a causal trajectory between problem (inadequate performance on variable X) and cause. In Figure 5.3, the problem has five independent causes that each impact the problem with differing effects and severity.

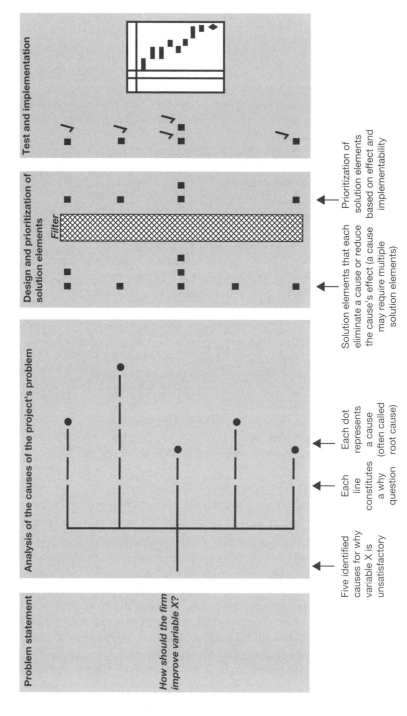

Figure 5.3   The typical structure of a project that improves an existing entity

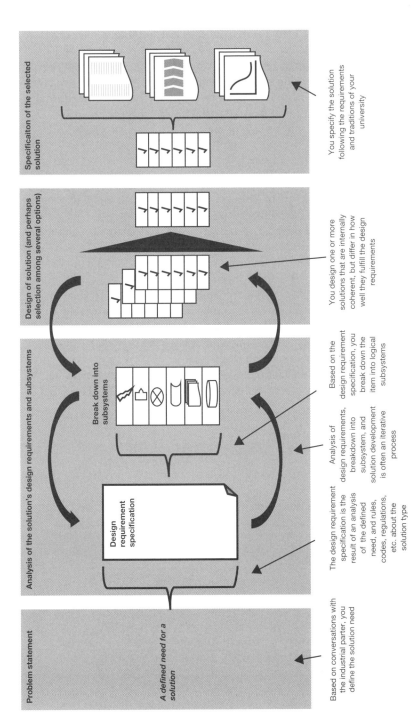

Figure 5.4 The typical structure of a project that designs a new entity from scratch

Once the causes are identified and specified, the project team designs solutions that eliminate the causes or reduce their effect. The solution often consists of a set of independent elements (that together form the project's overall solution). These solution elements may appear unconnected, but they all constitute solutions to causes of the same problem.

Often, a project needs to prioritize among the possible solution elements. The prioritization criteria should include a solution element's effect on the problem and the ease of implementing the solution element (usually with the project's industrial partner). In the final box, the project team tests and implements the prioritized solution elements. The details of each step in the project structure are found in Chapters 6, 7 and 8.

Typical structure of a project that designs a new entity

Figure 5.4 shows a typical structure of a project that designs a new entity (e.g. a new product, a new app, or a new building).

The problem in this type of project is a *specified need* for a solution. Usually, your industrial partner or your industrial partner's customers have this need. Through your initial conversations and problem analysis, you specify the need. Through a closer analysis of the solution need, you develop a design requirement specification (colloquially called "the spec"). Some design requirements will apply to your *particular* solution, while other requirements apply to the *type* of solution (e.g. building codes for a building and quality assurance regulations for a manufacturing system). For projects that design a new entity, the analysis involves identifying all the requirements that specify the solution.

The success criteria for the analysis of design requirements is *a complete and accurate interpretation of all requirements from all relevant actors as well as laws and*

EXAMPLE

A project seeks to develop an app for a pharmaceutical company. The company wants to collect data from patients to monitor a drug's effect and patient behavior. In their analysis of how patients will use the app and the data types the app will collect and store, the project team defines design requirements within the following areas:

- app–user interface
- functions and data collection
- patient hardware (devices)
- storage of data in the firm's data storage facilities
- cybersecurity.

Some of these requirements stem from the particular app needs of the firm and other requirements stem from the type of item, that is, a data collection and storage app; for example, that the app needs to adhere to regulations concerning storing sensitive personal information.

regulations. Often, your industrial partner has already written a design requirement spec. If this is the case in your project, remember to review the spec critically. Perhaps your industrial partner has overlooked a critical function, included two conflicting requirements, or misinterpreted a user demand.

Based on the design requirements spec, the analysis breaks down the item into its logical subsystems. For example, a project seeks to develop a measurement instrument for a heated area of an oil refinery. The instrument's logical subsystems include: power supply; sensor technology; outer cabinet; control unit; and a moving function that moves the sensor back and forth between making measurements and being out of the way of the refinery's operations. The solution you design must be technically realizable and functional both on a subsystems level and in its totality. Individual subsystems must function together.

A project often runs as an iterative process where you revisit design requirements, subsystem breakdown, and solution design when necessary. Figure 5.4 illustrates the iterative process with the arrows. There are two reasons for conducting the project as an iterative process:

1   You as the designers and your industrial partner become wiser as you go through the design process (e.g. multiple iterations are an effective way of designing large software programs successfully).
2   The design process is orchestrated as a set of ever more detailed iterations (e.g. this is the modern way of developing construction designs).

When design requirements and subsystems are analyzed, the design of the solution begins. Within some fields, the tradition is to develop two or more solutions at a conceptual level. Figure 5.4 shows three of these conceptual solutions, an arrow, and then one selected solution. The next step in the project then specifies the solution following your course's traditions and formal requirements.

A project that has designed a new entity might include implementation. However, whether implementation is expected from a student project differs across faculties. More often than not, implementation is left to the industrial partner. If implementation is part of the project, then imagine the final box from Figure 5.3 hooked on the right-hand side of Figure 5.4.

Standard methods as the backbone of a project's overall structure

Each engineering discipline has its own set of standard methods for developing solutions. These methods usually contain a fixed set of steps that the project team will conduct in a specified sequence. Examples of such methods are DMAIC (Define, Measure, Analyze, Improve, and Control) and business process reengineering in process optimization, the V-model in software development, and rapid prototyping in mechanical design.

Following these methods ensures that your project does not overlook an important activity. DMAIC is a classic method for process optimization. The method divides a project into the five logical steps in the method's name. These five steps begin with defining the problem and end with controlling the solution's long-term sustainability (that it works in the long run).

Some standard methods are industry specific. Software engineering often uses the Unified Process, which contains a series of steps (e.g. defining design requirements and designing the solution). Disciplines that prepare their students for a specific industry usually apply a project structure and terminology that mirrors the project structures that are applied in industrial practice.

Regardless of industry, all disciplines use a structure where the three main activities are analysis, design, and implementation. Although the weighting of the main activities differs across disciplines, the design of the solution is the core of the project. The team conducts their analysis as the foundation for the solution design and implementation enables the solution's use.

The timing of methodology choices

The methodology in a project consists of the project's overall structure (the sequence of "big steps" in the project), and the specific methods, tools, and techniques that you apply *within* each of the big steps in your project structure. Defining and sequencing the steps in the overall structure and choosing specific tools and techniques are your project's methodology choices.

You are ready to work on your project structure once you have formulated your problem statement and defined the key terms in the statement. See Chapters 3 and 4 for details on problem statements and definition of key terms. The specific tools and techniques are often selected when needed and throughout your project. There are situations where you cannot choose specific methods, tools, and techniques this early in your project. See the example below.

EXAMPLE

A project group examines an increase in the failure rate of a quality control process for a hydraulic component. The causal analysis finds that one-third of components going through the quality control process fail the process because they are missing one or more gaskets. The question becomes why products are assembled without all necessary gaskets. The student team finds that assembly instructions are clear and that gaskets are always available. However, the student team also finds that assembly staff often forget a gasket here and there, and that their work motivation is low in general.

Now the student team needs to understand the drivers of the low motivation and how to instill quality as a more decisive work value. For this purpose, the team reads literature on workforce motivation and finds a method for analyzing motivation and work values. The resulting analysis reveals that a newly hired department head has changed the management style from the previous manager's to a more micromanaging style that has hurt workforce morale and ownership of high-quality products.

This example shows that when making the project's overall methodological choices, the student team could not predict which methods and tools their analysis would end up needing. Engineering projects often choose methods, tools, and techniques at various points in the project and much later than the time when the overall project structure is defined and sequenced.

Argumentation for all important choices, including methodology choices

Every choice you make that affects how you conduct your project influences the validity of your project's solution, conclusions, and industrial partner recommendations. Therefore, you should argue for your choices so your reader is convinced that your choices are the right ones. A typical pitfall is being unaware of the choices you make. The following list provides examples of activities that constitute choices:

1   Defining a term is a choice because selecting one definition is implicitly a deselection of other possible definitions.
2   The use of a theory, method, or model is a choice because you have deselected other possible theories or models.
3   A specific analysis technique may be a choice depending on whether realistic alternatives exist.
4   A certain measurement instrument or sensor may be a choice.
5   Decisions about which individual from your industrial partner to include in a workshop, or user test group are choices (explain to the reader why you have chosen certain people).

Argumentation types

An argument is an explanation of why you have chosen what you have. Among the good arguments for a method is the purpose – "Because the objective of the study is X, the project chooses Y as method." You might also argue that particular circumstances have influenced your choice of method – "The study data are not sufficient for a valid result. Therefore, the study uses an estimation technique."

You can base arguments for choices related to your solution in the design requirements that you have defined previously in your project. For example: "The structure and the selected materials for the roof construction ensure that the construction can carry the 70 cm of dense snow that the solution's design requirements specify." Making arguments based in your project's earlier analyses is great because your reader will interpret these intra-project connections as coherence. Remember to write clearly that the foundation for your argument is in fact from within your own project (use an explicit reference to an earlier section and include a page number).

Choices that deviate from traditions (nontraditional choices)

Make sure to argue for choices that fall outside the realm of tradition in your field. You might have chosen a method that works well in your project, but is unusual in your field. This will make readers think: "Why do they need to choose this method and not a traditional method?" or "How does this project differ from other projects to justify the use of this unusual method?" Going outside the norm means inviting additional uncertainty, which usually comes at a cost. Remember that the reason a method is considered the right method in a field is because the method has a proven track record. If you use a nontraditional method, make the case that your method is better than the traditional methods for your particular project.

EXAMPLE

A group of software engineering students choose a method for designing a program. In software development, the current norm is to use an agile design process conducted through several iterations. The student team chooses the older, waterfall method that consists of just one, large sequence of activities. This method requires a complete understanding of all user requirements prior to designing the program.

Because this choice is outside the current norm, the student team should explain why they are using the waterfall method. An argument could be the method's simplicity. The group should include arguments for why the method will credibly identify all design requirements in one single activity rather than through several iterations.

Planning your own project using Gantt charts

When you have formulated your problem statement, you can begin planning your project. A project plan is a practical tool that shows when you as a team should perform the individual activities of your project. Often, your supervisor requests a project plan soon after your project has begun. Such a request prompts you to think about:

- which activities are part of your project
- in which sequence you should conduct them
- how long they take
- when in the project you should conduct them
- how you divide the responsibility for conducting activities within your team.

A Gantt chart is a useful tool to organize the component parts of your project. You can use Gantt charts regardless of the complexity of your project. Figure 5.5 shows a Gantt chart.

To develop a Gantt chart that covers your project, you can follow these steps:

1 Identify your project's activities.
2 Place your identified activities in a logical sequence.

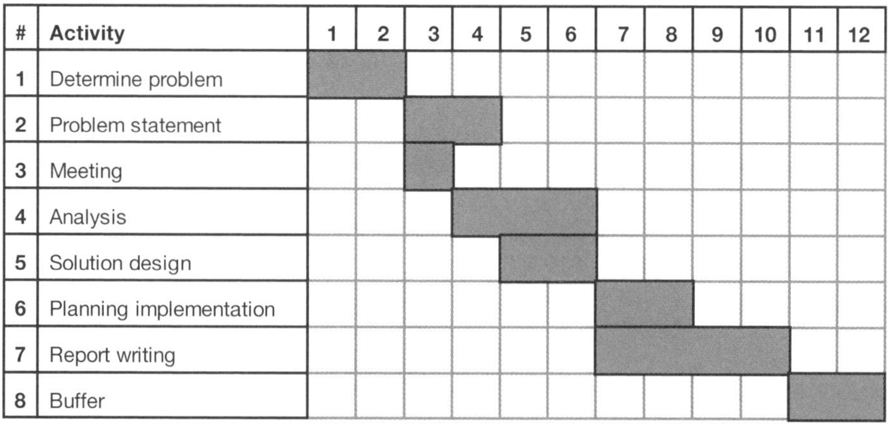

#	Activity	1	2	3	4	5	6	7	8	9	10	11	12
1	Determine problem	■	■										
2	Problem statement			■									
3	Meeting			■									
4	Analysis				■	■							
5	Solution design						■						
6	Planning implementation							■	■				
7	Report writing							■	■	■	■		
8	Buffer											■	■

Figure 5.5   Example of a Gantt chart

3 Identify each activity's predecessors.
4 Estimate the duration of each activity.
5 For each activity, decide who in your team will be responsible.
6 Fill in the Gantt chart.

To identify your project's activities, look to your selected methodology. First, look at the big steps in your project: your analysis, solution design, and implementation. Break these three activities down into smaller bits and pieces. Make a list of all these activities.

Because you conduct your project as a learning activity, knowing the number, nature, and sequence of all project activities is near impossible. However, do not despair. The instructors know very well that you are in the class to learn, and that your first draft of a project plan therefore is a shot from the hip. Luckily, a Gantt chart is fluid and you can update the chart every time you learn new things that affect your various activities, their length, predecessors, and so on. You must develop your very first Gantt chart knowing full well that the chart is built on lots of good guesses.

TOP TIPS FOR DEVELOPING YOUR GANTT CHART	
Brainstorm using sticky notes:	A practical method for sequencing your activities is writing each activity on a sticky note. Then, place all sticky notes on the wall so all your group can see all the activities. Then, place the activities in the sequence that you consider the right one. Again, your first sequence is based on your incomplete project knowledge and you should expect changes in the plan as you become wiser.

Quick-and-dirty estimation of duration:	Estimating duration is difficult because you often do not know the specific content of an activity. However, you can begin with a general rule of thumb: easy and small activities take one or two days, difficult activities take six–eight days, and activities in the middle take three–four days.
Utilize your resources:	Make sure to utilize your team's full set of resources. If your group comprises six people, then develop a plan that has scheduled three activities every day of the project period. To know whether you have three activities on schedule every day, look at the columns in your Gant chart. In Figure 5.5, each column is one week. Each column should have three shaded squares corresponding to three activities.
Use the "triangle below the waterfall":	Take advantage of the "triangle below the waterfall." In Figure 5.5, the set of activities resemble a waterfall flowing from left to right. Under the waterfall is a lot of empty space. Divide activities into a preparation part and a finishing part. You can often conduct the preparation part of an activity prior to finishing the predecessor activities. For example, design an Excel model for an activity during the preparation part and fill in the needed numbers when predecessor activities are completed. Place preparation parts of activities earlier in your plan when your plan shows days with only few daily activities.
Use one end-of-project buffer:	Estimate the duration of your individual activities without "just in case" buffers. Delaying until the last minute is a natural tendency for most people. If an activity take three days, but you plan five days to take account of unexpected events, then the activity will take five days with or without unexpected events. In project management theory, this tendency is referred to as "Parkinson's law." Instead of inserting buffers into all individual activities, insert one, large buffer at the end of the overall project. With one large end-of-project buffer, you will have a buffer while avoiding the natural tendency of delaying until the last minute.
Have one project planner:	Make one person responsible for the plan. This person is your project planner. Have your project planner insert "Project plan follow-up" as a fixed agenda point for all your regular project meetings.

Reviewing this chapter's objectives

Tick those objectives you feel you have achieved, and review those you haven't yet accomplished. In this chapter, you have learned how to:

❏ Ensure coherence throughout your project's activities.

❏ Design the overall sequence of steps in which you organize your project and select the methods, tools, and techniques for specific project activities.

❏ Develop arguments that convince readers of the rigor of your methodological choices.

❏ Plan your own project using a Gantt chart.

Collecting and Analyzing Data

Project initiation	Problem statement	Literature, knowledge, and expertise	Methodology and planning	Data collection and analysis	Design of solution	Test and implementation of solution

In this chapter, you will learn:

1 The nature of data in engineering projects.

2 The purpose of data collection in engineering projects.

3 How to localize data and data sources.

4 The nature of an engineering project's analysis.

5 How to identify the causes of the problem in your project.

6 How to identify the design requirements for your solution.

7 How to break your solution down into logical subsystems.

8 How to ensure that you collect valid and reliable data for your analysis.

9 The relationship between data analysis and the solution design.

The term "data" might seem rather straightforward, but this is not the case. For example: when studying theology, data comprise biblical scriptures and texts written in antiquity and medieval times; when studying psychology, data comprise client interviews; and when studying economics, data comprise national and international statistics. In other words, the term "data" has many meanings and covers a diverse set of materials.

Theology, psychology, and economics are single disciplines, which means that data usually are of the same kind. Naturally, a discipline and its data type match. Engineering differs from single disciplines in many ways and one of those ways is *data type diversity*. Engineering projects apply numerous data types within the same project. The following list exemplifies the diverse data used in engineering projects:

- Informal conversations, such as those with industrial partner staff
- Emails from digital correspondence
- Technical descriptions and drawings
- Formal interviews with the use of interview guides
- Reports from the industrial partner's IT systems

- Information from the industrial partner's website and intranet
- Your own observations of people, products, machines, building plots, and so on
- Your own tests and experiments
- Macroeconomic facts from national and international databases
- Requests from materials databases.

This list is not exhaustive, and indicates the diversity in engineering projects' data types. Which data are relevant for a particular project depends on the theme and problem of the project.

A project seeks to develop the outer casing for a dental drill. The student team collects specifications about the drill's electronic and mechanical content, writes and runs requests in materials databases, and conducts interviews with dentists, who are the future dental drill users.

A project with the objective of reducing work hours in a warehouse collects IT system reports about order sizes and stock-keeping units, conducts time studies of current work patterns, and has a range of formal and informal conversations with warehouse managers, warehouse operators, and suppliers of warehouse technology.

The fact that conversations, interviews, and emails constitute data often comes as a surprise to engineering students. Many fields consider only lists of numbers as data. However, remember that lists of numbers are insufficient for identifying design requirements, analyzing causes, identifying an entity's logical subsystems, and designing an effective solution. As Chapter 3 stated, an engineering project's problem statement is usually a how question. How questions cannot be answered with, say, "45%" or "23,000 pieces." Numbers are answers to *how much* questions, which do not usually function as problem statements in engineering projects.

The data that are relevant to your project are quite simply the data you require to solve the problem in your problem statement. In the sections below, first, the purpose of data collection is outlined, followed by where to collect the relevant data, what to do when data are not available, and finally how to analyze your collected data.

Purpose of data collection in engineering projects

Chapter 5 explains how the structure of engineering projects differs from the classic structure for research. One of the main differences lies in the purpose for collecting data.

Traditional research projects answer research questions for the world at large and way beyond one industrial partner. Based on the research question, the researchers select a methodology that, among other issues, defines what data the study needs and how to collect these data. The study then collects data to analyze them to answer the research question. The important point here is that traditional research projects collect data *once for one purpose*.

Engineering projects, on the other hand, collect data *several times for several purposes*. Figure 6.1 illustrates where in the process the project collects data.

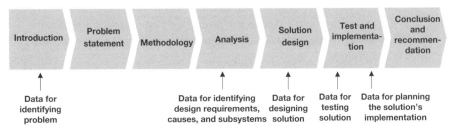

Figure 6.1   Continuous collection of data throughout the project

Figure 6.1 shows that an engineering project collects data throughout the project for five distinct purposes. The following list describes each purpose:

1   A project often begins with an idea, a need, or a problem that is not yet specified to the degree necessary for a problem statement. Your task as the project team is to understand the problem landscape so well that you can formulate a focused problem statement. Reaching the problem statement requires a thorough understanding of the situation. For this purpose, you collect data. These data are often in the form of informal conversations and semi-structured interviews conducted either face to face or on the phone (see Chapter 2 for details).

2   The traditional purpose of collecting data is for a study's analysis. Reports usually describe this particular data collection process in a more formal fashion than other data collections. For example, reports describe preplanned efforts to ensure data validity and reliability when collecting data. Later sections of this chapter describe data collection for the analysis in detail.

3   When you have conducted your analysis, the design of the solution begins. Solution design requires data collection because the data for solution design often differ from the data for your analysis. The example that follows exemplifies how projects collect data for analysis and solution design.

4   When the solution is designed, your next step is to test the solution. You might be able to test your solutions in simulation software or perhaps directly in your development kit. Other solutions require real-life testing, which requires data from real situations; for example, a project that designs a new quality assurance policy. You can measure the policy's effect on a selected production process over a period. For this purpose, you must collect data (e.g. the production process failure rate).

5   To plan the implementation of the solution, you need data about the potential implementation project team, manager, steering group, and which activities need to be part of the implementation plan. These data are usually the last data a project needs.

Engineering disciplines differ with respect to these five purposes. Some engineering courses do not expect their students to collect data for solution testing and implementation. The industrial partner is expected to handle these activities after the students have finished their project. Other projects have a design requirement specification from their industrial partner and therefore jump straight to solution design. For these projects, data collection has to do with solution design only.

A project team wants to reduce the size of a handheld device used in ambulances for measuring blood pressure. The project team wants to reduce the size because space (m^3) in the ambulance is limited.

Data collection for the project's analysis

The analysis develops the design requirement specification. For this purpose, the team collects data about:

- the room for maneuvering in the ambulance
- the location of the device in the ambulance
- how and how often the device is used
- how often the device is dropped on the floor or is otherwise exposed to rough conditions.

The team collects these data using observations of an ambulance, informal conversations, and interviews.

Data collection for the project's solution design: one example

The next step is designing the device. This particular handheld device heats up during use, so the team needs to assess the necessary space inside the device for a cooling mechanism that keeps the device from overheating. The team therefore needs to gather new data about the types of cooling systems available on the market, and the cooling effect each mechanism will have on the device's heat-generating elements. The team gathers these data by searching for manufacturers of cooling mechanisms and conversations with manufacturers' sales and technical staff.

This example shows how the data types and collection methods differ between a project's analysis and solution design.

Locating relevant data

Once you have identified your data need, the next issue is locating the data. The most common data sources for an engineering project are:

- The employees and managers of your industrial partner. These data are usually collected through interviews and informal conversations
- The digital systems and databases at your industrial partner, such as financial and planning systems or product databases
- At your industrial partner but where no individual person has the information, you collect these data through personal observations and by being present at the firm

- Generally available statistics databases
- Websites of manufacturers of mechanical or electrical components, building materials, and so on
- General reference databases and books you can access either digitally or by borrowing a reference book. This could be a materials database
- Organizations other than your industrial partner. This could be customers or suppliers (current as well as previous), and industrial organizations. You collect these data through interviews and internet searches.

Some data are available for you to collect. For example, if you need a statistic from a firm's IT system, you can request a particular file from your industrial partner's planning system. If one or two members of your project team are familiar with the IT systems of your industrial partner, then these members can collect the data directly by generating system reports themselves. Usually, however, you will need to get these data by asking an employee at your industrial partner to generate a system report for you. You will receive the report as raw numbers and will need to process the data so you can use them. In some cases, your industrial partner has analytics programs that can process the data, so you receive them in a more readily usable format, such as diagrams or tables.

When data are not available

Often, there are no data available for you to request, or the data the firm does have are unsuitable for your particular data need. The general rule is that if there are no data available, you must generate the data.

TOP TIPS WHEN DATA ARE NOT AVAILABLE

This list presents methods for generating your own datasets. The relevance of each method depends on the particular data type you need:

1. Run tests of a solution to check for viability.
2. Conduct experiments and extrapolate to a larger population.
3. Conduct observational studies using your eyes and ears, or equipment – stop watches, recording devices, vibration sensors, and so on.
4. Begin logging data by installing your own sensors in a device.
5. Use simulation or calculation verification.

If these methods are beyond the scope of your study or are unavailable for other reasons, then the question of continuing your project without adequate data becomes relevant. Consider the following shortcuts, but be sure to consult with your supervisor:

1. Work with assumptions that are accepted by all parties as being reasonable.
2. Use qualified guesses and pressure test your guesses with experts.
3. Discuss your data need with one or more experts, such as a professor at your university or an industry "guru."

4. Quantify qualitative statements and interview results (see Chapter 7 for specific advice about quantification).

5. Use intervals and conduct calculations for interval boundaries; for example, for a transportation project measuring tunnel traffic, you work with "between 1,600 and 2,000 trucks per 24-hour cycle," rather than spending weeks measuring actual traffic.

Generating data comes with its own pitfalls, reliability challenges, and often quite a substantial extra workload, which you might not have planned for. Discuss your particular data needs with your supervisor.

Data analysis

As noted in earlier chapters, engineering projects solve problems. Chapter 3 describes how solving a problem means either improving an existing entity (e.g. increase a product's durability) or designing a new entity (e.g. a new building or app). The nature of a project's analysis depends on whether the project improves an existing entity or designs a new entity.

If the project aims to improve an existing entity, then the purpose of the analysis is to identify the cause of the project's problem (e.g. why the durability of the product is as low as it is). The cause, which may be single or plural, is the foundation for the solution design. For example, if the cause for a product's limited durability is a cabinet that cracks open years before the planned end of the product's operation, then the solution is a new and stronger design or a different material for the cabinet. On the other hand, if the cause is that the user uses the product in an unconsciously destructive way, then the solution is a clearer user manual and user training.

If the project is to design a new entity, the analysis is not a matter of identifying causes, but identifying the design requirements for the item and the subsystems that constitute the item. The following sections first detail the analysis for projects that improve an existing entity and then for projects that design a new entity.

The analysis for projects that improve an existing entity

The purpose of the analysis is to identify the cause(s) of the project's problem. The analysis is a causal analysis. However, before you identify the causes, you might need to spend time assessing the size of the project's problem.

Measuring the size of your project's problem

The size of your project's problem is important to find. Problem size expresses the extent of your problem. For example, a baked goods manufacturer bakes cinnamon buns in a large industrial oven. The problem is that some of the buns burn, making them unsellable. The fraction of burnt buns expresses the size of the problem (e.g. 20% or 80%).

Only if you know the problem's size are you able to assess the effect (and the derived financial value) of your solution to a reasonably precise degree. For the cinnamon bun example, you might know that your solution will reduce the fraction of charred buns to just 5% per run. Is that good, great, or absolutely spectacular? The effect of your solution depends on the size of the problem prior to implementing your solution. If the problem size was 20% burnt buns, then your solution reduces the problem by 15%. If the problem size was 80% burnt buns, then your solution reduces the problem by a staggering 75%.

If your industrial partner has easily accessible and convincing data that document your problem's size, then report the size in your project's introduction and illustrate it with a chart if possible. If there are no convincing data that show the problem's size, then generating the data to measure the size is your job. Ideally, aim for collecting quantitative data, so you can express the problem size with a number. If the perfect quantitative dataset is nonexistent, then try one of the following alternatives:

1 Conduct a small set of your own measurements and extrapolate.
2 Conduct a series of interviews to examine how two or three informants experience the problem (if relevant, include in your interview informants from several hierarchical layers and different functions).
3 Look at other data types that give indications of your project's problem.

EXAMPLE: WHEN THE IDEAL DATASET IS MISSING

A student team works with a chemical manufacturer. The manufacturer runs (among other things) a process that separates a solid substance from a liquid. The team's contact with the industrial partner says that each run of the separation process should extract around 40 kg of solid substance. The project's problem is that the process extracts much lower amounts. The firm does not measure the amount of extracted substance per run, so there is no precise assessment of the problem's size. If the extracted amount is 25 kg, then the problem size is 15 kg. If the extracted amount is 35 kg, then the problem size is 5 kg. The team therefore needs to measure the problem's size. The firm has the following datasets:

1 The number of runs over a 12-month period.

2 The separation process is the first of two processes in the same production line. The extracted substance from the separation process is the raw material for the second machine in the line. The firm knows how much substance this second machine has consumed over the same 12 months.

3 Separation machine operators' experience with how much the separation process extracts.

Using these three datasets (two sets of numbers and one set of interview data), the student team obtains a reasonably precise picture of the project's problem. The team divides the second machine's 12-month consumption with the number of runs in the same period and discusses variance with the separation process operator. The team finds that the separation process currently extracts 23–30 kg of substance. This is not an exact number, but the interval does express the problem's existence and that the problem is substantial.

This interval constitutes the reference when the project team assesses the effect of their solution. Depending on the causes for the ineffective separation process, a solution could be a redesigned separator centrifuge, different process temperatures, or a different centrifuge speed. Later in the project, the team assesses how their solution results in an increased amount of extracted substance (e.g. an interval of 30–32 kg).

Identifying the causes of the problem

The main activity in your analysis is the identification of the cause(s) of your project's problem. When beginning the analysis, your starting point is the project's problem. For example, if the problem is a production system's high rate of products that fail their quality test, then the analysis seeks to identify why products fail the quality test. When the analysis has identified the causes, then you are able to design a solution. If there are multiple causes, then the solution will consist of several individual solution elements that together form the total solution. The solution will either eliminate the causes altogether or reduce their effect on the problem.

To identify the causes, you work your way through a set of *causal trajectories*. These causal trajectories begin with your project's problem and end with a root cause.

EXAMPLE OF CAUSAL ANALYSIS

The firm Bing & Co. produces measurement instruments for hospitals and labs. The instruments are assembled, quality tested, and shipped to customers. Too many instruments fail their quality test. The firm wants to reduce the failure rate from 23% to 3%. For this purpose, the firm has engaged a group of engineering students. The problem statement is: "How can Bing & Co. reduce the failure rate for its products from 23% to 3%?" The students begin analyzing products that have failed their test to identify the causes for the high failure rate.

Figure 6.2 shows the student team's analysis. The analysis begins with the project's problem on the left-hand side ("Failed tests"). The analysis finds that instruments that fail their test either fail the pressure test or show wrong results when conducting test measurements. For each of these two causes, the student team asks "Why?" The team keeps asking these questions until the team reaches the root causes. A root cause is a cause that the team can address with a solution.

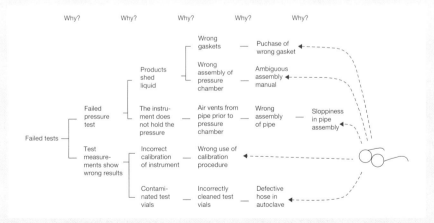

Figure 6.2   The project's analysis

Through the glasses in the figure's right-hand side, the team can see the root causes. The problem has five root causes: purchase of wrong gaskets; an ambiguous assembly manual; sloppiness in the pipe assembly; wrong use of a calibration procedure; and a defective hose in the autoclave process.

The team can now design a solution that addresses these five root causes. The solution will consist of a number of solution elements, each addressing their own root cause.

The analysis keeps asking why until it has identified the root causes that can be addressed with solutions. It's entirely possible to continue asking why and go way past the root cause and reach some sort of original cause. Such an original cause usually has to do with the nature of man or the world. For example, you might ask why operators misunderstand assembly instructions. The answer probably has to do with how humans perceive visual signals. For an engineering project, addressing the way humans perceive signals is not realistic (yet).

Continually asking why is sometimes called the "5 Whys" method. Figure 6.2 shows that asking five times is not always necessary. In other cases, you might have to ask six or seven times before arriving at your root cause.

An alternative to the 5 Whys method is the fishbone diagram, illustrated in Figure 6.3. It begins with the project's problem on the right-hand side. From there, the analysis moves towards the left seeking the cause of the problem. The cause (singular or plural) may lie in methods, machines, man (meaning staff), management, materials, or measurements. All potential cause categories conveniently begin with an M.

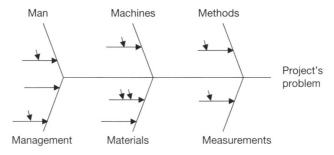

Figure 6.3   The fishbone diagram

These six cause categories function well as inspiration for brainstorming and discussion. The smaller arrows indicate the next steps in the analysis. If a project finds a cause in, say, machines, the team asks why and identifies the machine-related cause. Using the fishbone diagram as a first step in your analysis is an effective method. However, make sure to end with a problem tree (as in the earlier example about Bing & Co.'s failed measurement instrument tests). The problem tree works without categories and facilitates your work better.

When you conduct your analysis, make sure to include in your analysis all categories that an informed reader can think of. You can rule out many of these causes immediately because unlike your reader you are much more familiar with your particular project and industrial partner. Do remember to show your dismissal of causes explicitly in your report, so your reader can follow your reasoning. If you omit causes that a reader would expect you to include, they might assume that your analysis is incomplete because you forgot the cause.

To begin your analysis, you might consider using broad categories of causes. Then, in the subsequent step, identify all the individual causes within that category. Make sure that your cause categories are mutually exclusive, so your analysis is logically constructed and you avoid misunderstandings.

How to use a generic problem tree in your analysis

Working your way along the causal trajectories is not an easy task. Your help lies in your literature, supervisor, industrial partner staff, and your own ingenuity.

Chapter 4 presents a method that guides your search for relevant literature and helps you organize your literature findings in a problem tree of generic (theoretically possible) causes. This literature-based problem tree can serve as your analysis's foundation. Depending on whether your particular problem is well researched, your problem tree is either a voluminous tree with many branches or a simple set of literature-based conjectures. When using a generic problem tree in your analysis, you have two distinct tasks:

1 Examine whether the generic causes in the problem tree are actual causes for your specific problem.
2 Grow the tree to include causal trajectories that your literature and generic problem tree did not include.

Figure 6.4 illustrates a problem tree. The thick blue line illustrates a causal trajectory between the project's problem and a root cause. It passes through several boxes as well as relations between boxes. Your analysis examines whether these interbox relations actually exist in your project. If the relation exists, then keep that branch in your tree. If not, delete the branch. Through your analysis, step by step you replace the generic problem tree with the actual problem tree.

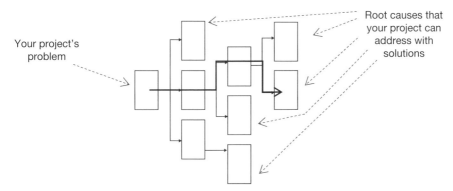

Figure 6.4   Problem tree and a causal trajectory

Quantification of the identified causes' importance

When your analysis has identified the causes of your project's problem, your next task is to assess which of these causes have the greatest effect on the problem. You want to find each cause's relative impact on the problem.

The example of Bing & Co. identified five causes for the high rate of failed measurement instrument tests. The question is: Which of these causes results in most failed tests? There might be considerable difference between each cause's impact on the problem. Your analysis should identify each cause's relative importance so that you can prioritize which causes you should develop solutions for. A much used technique for visualizing an analysis of the relative importance among causes is the Pareto chart, which is based on the Pareto principle (also known as "the 80/20 rule").

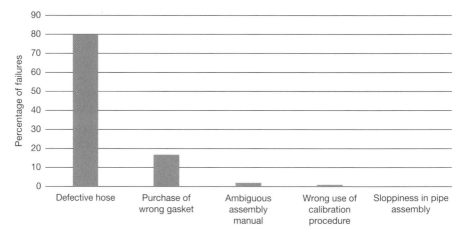

Figure 6.5   Pareto chart representing the relative impact of each cause

Figure 6.5 shows a Pareto chart for the five causes given in Figure 6.2. Figure 6.5 shows that 80% of the failed tests are caused by the defective autoclave hose and that only 0.005% of the failed tests are caused by sloppiness in the pipe assembly. Such a result is quite common. The 80/20 rule has its name because more often than not 80% of the effect is caused by 20% of the causes.

Whether you can use a Pareto chart depends on the data you have available. A Pareto chart requires many observations usually going back in time. Often, you are not able to get enough observations through your own study. You need historical data collected by the firm itself prior to your arrival. Perhaps the firm has not collected these data or perhaps it has collected tons of data, but not noted the causes you happened to identify. In both cases, using a Pareto chart is not possible.

Without data comprehensive enough for reliable conclusions, you should use a different method for assessing each cause's relative impact. Instead of the Pareto chart, divide your causes into more general categories; for example, the two categories "important" and "unimportant". Categorize your causes based on your own observations and interviews. Few observations are incomprehensive, but combined with other (perhaps qualitative) data types you can draw reasonably reliable conclusions. In complex analyses, your dataset may well be a patchwork of many heterogeneous data types that together form the basis for categorizing causes as important or unimportant.

When you have identified the important causes, you are ready to design a solution that eliminates these important causes (or reduces their effect on the problem). See Chapter 7 about solution design.

The analysis for projects that design a new entity

In projects that design new entities (e.g. a building or an app), the problem is not that an existing entity is performing poorly, but that someone has a need. This "someone" is often your industrial partner or a customer or client of your industrial partner. The analysis is therefore not a matter of identifying causes, but identifying design requirements and often also the subsystems of the entity. The subsystems for a building are, among others, the foundation, the plumbing system, and the electric system. For a machine, subsystems are, among others, power, controls, and user interface.

To identify design requirements, your job is to examine:

- use situations and patterns
- implicit and explicit user expectations
- the regulations and laws that regulate the construction and use of the solution
- any industrial codes and standards that apply to the solution.

Identifying a comprehensive set of design requirements is the cornerstone of a project, regardless of whether the entity is a building, a bridge, an app, an instrument, an algorithm, a chemical compound, or a production system.

Make sure to involve your industrial partner and your supervisor in the analysis. The involvement of your industrial partner creates ownership, which increases the chance of your solution's implementation. Ownership also creates an easier path for you and your team because if the firm has accepted the conclusions of your analysis, then it will be more inclined to support your solution design activities. Discussing your results with your supervisor minimizes the risk of having your examiners point to design requirements that you have omitted in your report, but that your examiners consider to be "obvious inclusions."

The most common design requirements for an engineering solution

A chemical compound differs vastly from an app or a building. However, there are a number of common requirement categories that apply to most solutions. Figure 6.6 provides an overview of these typical design requirement categories.

Figure 6.6 shows the design requirements arising from very different sources. Usually, your most work-heavy analysis activity is understanding your users' needs. Users require functionality and a solution they can operate and maintain at a reasonable cost. In addition, some solutions are products that your industrial partner will produce in the thousands. In these cases, your industrial partner will require a product that can be manufactured efficiently.

In addition to user requirements, engineering solutions are subject to numerous codes, regulations, and industrial standards. These requirements often concern safety, the environment, and how the solution interacts with its adjacent systems (e.g. the size of a power outlet).

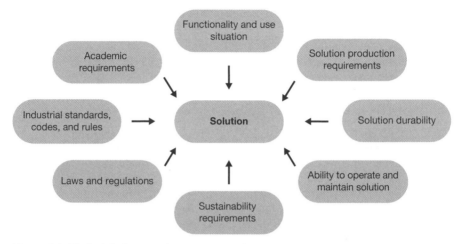

Figure 6.6   Typical design requirement categories

Absolute design requirements and "as good as possible" requirements

Once you have specified all the design requirements, consider which requirements are absolute demands that must be met and which requirements need a solution that is "as good as possible" (AGAP). See the example below. For each design requirement, make sure to identify whether the requirement is absolute or AGAP.

EXAMPLE

A project team designs a wheelbarrow. An absolute requirement is that the wheelbarrow must have a load-bearing capacity of 140 kg. An AGAP requirement is that the wheelbarrow's material must be as cheap as possible. In this example, load-bearing capacity is an absolute demand, while material cost is an AGAP requirement. Absolute vs. AGAP could be reversed. Perhaps the wheelbarrow's material must be cheaper than €10 per kg, and the wheelbarrow must be able to carry as much as possible.

The process of identifying design requirements

The success criteria for identifying design requirements is to identify all relevant requirements. The best foundation for this task is to increase your group's combined knowledge about the problem and the solution. You increase your knowledge level through a process of reading the literature about your problem and solution, and then interpreting these findings in the context of your project.

Here are few practical tips to begin this process:

- borrow a stack of books about your subject from the university library
- skim your textbooks for relevant content
- search for relevant literature at your university library database
- conduct informal conversations with employees of your industrial partner
- discuss your findings with your supervisor.

You should continuously make notes about identified design requirements.

EXAMPLE: THE DESIGN REQUIREMENT IDENTIFICATION PROCESS

Chapter 4 describes an example of a project about designing the floor structure that separates the basement and the ground floor in a building. The project team begins reading literature about such a floor structure. The team finds literature about the load-bearing construction within the floor structure, ceiling and floor types, how the floor structure integrates with the surrounding walls that carry the floor structure, and potential materials for all elements of the floor structure. Based on the literature, the team now knows which types of data they need from the architect and the construction client to define the specific set of design requirements.

The team collects data through interviews and informal conversations with the building's architect, the construction client, engineering advisors, and employees with potential contractors. In addition, the team conducts a series of searches in a materials database.

The team finds that the load-bearing construction in the floor structure must be built from steel, the floors must be wooden, the soundproofing between the two floors will be separate layers of mineral wool and plaster, and the ceiling must have a sound-reducing surface. The team studies the building's drawings and calculates the right floor structure dimensions. Finally, the team studies building codes and construction guidelines.

Based on all this information, the team writes a comprehensive set of design requirements for the floor structure.

You can achieve quite a lot by brainstorming. Discuss design requirements in your group and write down a list with all your ideas for relevant design requirements. In this phase, your ideas need not be specific. You can begin by generating a list of areas in which you think there will be design requirements. Once you have written down the list of your first ideas, the next step is to expand and detail this list. When conducting this second step, you work in two dimensions.

1 Ensure that you have included all relevant design requirements.
2 Specify all relevant requirements to an operational degree (directly useful in your solution design).

You can use the design requirement categories shown in Figure 6.6. It includes requirements that the literature may not express clearly, but that your examiners expect you to include. However, do remember that Figure 6.6 is not exhaustive for every type of engineering solution, so avoid using it as a *complete* checklist.

Once you have identified all requirements and described them to an operational degree, write them all down in a document. This document is your solution's design requirement specification, often just called the spec.

The process of breaking down requirements

Some requirements are important yet abstract and non-operational. For example: "The building must have bathrooms with adequate space." What does "adequate space" really mean? To operationalize an abstract requirement, break the requirement down into several operational requirements. For the bathroom example, include the following three operational requirements: "at least 10 square meters," "a shower and a bathtub," and "at least 2.5 meters from sink to exit." Figure 6.7 provides an illustration. Remember to consult with your industrial partner and perhaps construction client when breaking down requirements.

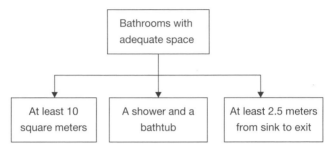

Figure 6.7 **Example of how requirements are broken down into operational requirements**

Between design requirements and solution design

The engineering solution that you design usually consists of subsystems, each with their own function. For example, a building has foundations, insulation, plumbing, and electricity throughout the building. Machines have, among other things, power, cabinet, controls, and sensors. Software applications, production systems, and chemicals also have subsystems. For example, a drug has an active ingredient and a set of substances that complement the active ingredient to form a complete pill.

Once you have formulated all requirements to an operational degree, you are able to identify the item's subsystems. In addition to identifying the subsystems, you are able to find the potential technical solutions for each subsystem. Figure 6.8 shows a matrix from mechanical engineering with the machine's subsystems down the columns and the potential categories of technical solutions across the rows (the matrix is also referred to as a "morphological diagram"). Within the boxes, you are able to describe the specific technical solutions. Some boxes will naturally not have any content and other boxes will have several options.

Developing the matrix in Figure 6.8 concludes your analyses. The next step is to make a set of coherent decisions that together form your solution. When you start making decisions about your solution, your solution design has begun.

In some fields, analysis and solution design are parallel activities happening in iterative cycles. For example, in civil engineering, the design of a building or a bridge happens in steps that delve further and further into the details of the building, beginning with the outer dimensions and building orientation, and ending with choosing the color of power outlets and doorknobs.

Ensuring valid and reliable data and analysis results

The data you collect for your project must be reliable and you must be able to get real, meaningful, and useful analysis results from analyzing your data. The two most common quality criteria for a dataset are validity and reliability, and they are now described.

	Mechanical	Electrical	Pneumatic	Hydraulic	Software	Magnetic
Power						
Foundation						
Cabinet						
Lift						
Open/close						
Sensors						
Controls						

Potential technical solutions

Figure 6.8   Matrix of subsystems and potential technical solutions

Validity in engineering projects

Valid data are data that you can use to answer the questions your analysis poses (e.g. what is the cause of the project's problem?). You might ask yourself why anyone would want to collect data that they cannot use. The answer is that ensuring data validity is often difficult.

Example 1

A student team conducts a project with their industrial partner, Fast Process Inc. The team has designed a new production process involving an industrial robot. The team is currently evaluating the financial feasibility of replacing the firm's current manual process with the robot. Thus, the team examines the cost price of a product produced with the current manual process and another produced with the industrial robot. Both the manual process and the robot take time to produce a product. The more time, the higher the product's cost price. The firm knows the time the current process takes, so the team must assess the time spent per product by the robot.

Through the robot supplier, Robotics plc, the student team gains access to a factory with the firm Slow Process Inc., where the robot currently operates. The team decides to use the production times from Slow Process Inc. for their assessment. The team conducts multiple measurements and ends up with a very reliable dataset. However, the team finds out later that Slow Process Inc.'s robot operation differs in two subtle but important ways with respect to time taken:

1   At Slow Process Inc. the robot lifts heavier items, which makes the lifting process slower.

2   The robot operates at different speeds due to changing temperatures in the production facility.

Thus the time usage data from Slow Process Inc. is reliable but non-valid because the team cannot use the data for their purpose.

Example 2

A project team examines the causes for why a manufacturer has a large product return rate. Potential causes for the high return rate are that customers change their mind, products are defective, or products fail to meet customer expectations. The student team examines return causes using an employee survey, where the team asks a series of closed and open-ended questions.

The team receives very reliable answers that present employees' perceptions of return causes very well. The dataset is reliable but non-valid because the team wants to examine the actual causes of high return rates and not employee perceptions of causes. Luckily, discussion with their supervisor exposes the validity problem, and the team conducts their own investigation on 50 returned products.

A common way that validity problems surface in a project is through discussions either within your group or with your supervisor (or with your examiners at the exam). For example 2 above about product returns, your supervisor might (with a perplexed facial expression) ask: "Doesn't your data only say something about employee perceptions rather the actual return causes?"

Reliability in engineering projects

Intuitively, reliability is often easier to understand than validity. Reliable data are simply data that are precise and trustworthy. Precision is relevant when you conduct measurements by yourself. For example, if you were to test drive the robot from example 1 in the previous box by yourself, you could run a batch of 200 products with the robot. However, if a number of random incidents interrupt your 200 runs, then your average run-times are not precise and therefore your data are not reliable.

If you do not conduct your own measurements, but instead rely on measurements conducted by other parties, you should be cautious about both precision and trustworthiness. Let us assume that you get run-time data from the robot supplier or a department with your industrial partner that is rewarded for successfully installing new technology. Because both of these parties have a vested interest in exchanging the manual process with the robot, their data may well be biased. They might (consciously or unconsciously) deliver precise run-time data, but omit the time taken to set up the robot for each batch and the time taken for daily robot maintenance. See more about handling potentially biased stakeholders in Chapter 11.

Validity and reliability are both important in engineering projects

A project might have data that are 100% reliable, but 0% valid. These are precise and trustworthy data that do not match your data needs (i.e. you cannot use them to answer your questions). A project can also have 0% reliable but 100% valid data. These data fit perfectly with your data needs, but are neither precise nor trustworthy.

Remember that data in engineering projects go well beyond technical drawings and long lists of numbers. Data include interview statements, emails, and informal conversations. The sources for these data types could be operators and engineers, but also senior managers and department heads with their own agendas. You should keep a critical mindset regardless of the data type or data source. In addition, keep a critical mindset about both data reliability and validity. Ask these three questions about your data:

1 Are your data precise?
2 Is the source trustworthy (or biased)?
3 Do the data meet your analysis's data needs?

You collect much of your data from your industrial partner. From time to time, a student project can be a part of a power struggle between, say, two department heads, or simply lead to changes that a person finds threatening to their job content or job security. Therefore, your data sources may be biased. Imagine that you are interviewing a person about a solution suggestion and the answer is: "That won't work, why don't you try (different suggestions)." Maybe your suggestion will not work. However, maybe your solution *will* work, but your informant finds your solution threatening. Ask follow-up questions to see if there is a rational explanation for their dismissal. Keep a professional tone, but do not be afraid to ask specific questions and ask for specific reasons. If your interview does not lead to a rational explanation, then verify your informant's claims through other sources. For example, ask other informants or your contact at the firm.

Reviewing this chapter's objectives

Tick those objectives you feel you have achieved, and review those you haven't yet accomplished. In this chapter, you have learned how to:

❐ Localize data and data sources.

❐ Identify the causes of the problem in your project and the design requirements for your solution.

❐ Break your solution down into logical subsystems.

❐ Ensure that you collect valid and reliable data for your analysis.

❐ Ensure coherence between data analysis and the solution design.

Designing the Project's Solution

Project initiation	Problem statement	Literature, knowledge, and expertise	Methodology and planning	Data collection and analysis	Design of solution	Test and implemen-tation of solution

In this chapter, you will learn:

1 The basic nature of solutions in engineering projects.
2 The general requirements of a good solution.
3 Three generic archetypes of solutions in engineering projects (the single solution, the either/or solution, and the multiple elements solution).
4 How to select one solution among several potential solutions in either/or solutions.
5 How to select which elements to include in the solution in multiple elements solutions.
6 How to assess a solution's effect and ease of implementation.
7 How to quantify the financial value of the solution's effect on the project's problem.
8 The coherence between the project's analysis and solution design on the one hand, and the coherence between the solution and the project's conclusion and industrial partner recommendations on the other.

This chapter is about the core of an engineering project: designing the solution to the problem in your problem statement. It may sound a bit strange that an engineering project is about designing a solution. The term "design" may lead you to think about designer clothing or designer furniture, and the term "solution" might make you think about what software companies develop. It is important to know that engineering projects develop solutions to problems regardless of engineering discipline. If a project designs a house, develops an algorithm, or constructs a liquid separation process, then the house drawings, the finished algorithm, and the developed liquid separation process each constitute the project's solution. To draw the house, develop the algorithm, and construct the separation process *is* to design a solution.

Solutions in engineering projects

To design a solution means to make a number of decisions that together form a decision hierarchy. The term "hierarchy" means that some decisions are superior to other decisions, as shown in Figure 7.1.

Figure 7.1   A decision hierarchy

The superior decisions, which concern overall issues, are taken early on in the project and naturally limit the decision space for the subordinate decisions that concern more detailed issues. For example, if building a house, the architect's first decisions concern the outer dimensions of the house, which limit the decisions concerning ground plan and staircases. Ground plan and staircase decisions are superior to decisions concerning the interior design of kitchen, living room, and bathrooms, and so on. The decisions lowest in the hierarchy concern the most detailed choices about the house, e.g. power outlets, ceiling material, bathtub design, and so on.

Solutions in engineering projects are either purely technical (e.g. a new wind turbine component) or a combination of technical and social (e.g. a changed procedure for operator maintenance of a machine). Table 7.1 provides some examples of solutions in various engineering fields.

Common to all solutions in Table 7.1 is that they solve the problem stated in the project's problem statement. In Table 7.1, one electrical engineering example mentions an electrical substation with fewer failures. The electrical substation is the solution designed by a student team in cooperation with a power distribution company. The electrical substation constitutes the project's solution because the substation solves the project's problem, which is too many failures in the current substation. The project group analyzes the causes for the failures in the currently operating substation and then designs a substation that can operate with fewer failures.

The analysis is the basis for solution design

Projects that improve an existing entity analyze the root causes of the project's problem. The solution then either eliminates the root causes or reduces their impact on the problem. The analysis in projects that design a new entity does not find root causes, but instead identifies all relevant design requirements for the solution and the subsystems of the entity and possible technical solutions for subsystems. With a clear and operational design requirement specification and a set of possible subsystems solutions, you can design a solution that meets the design requirements. Chapter 6 provides details for analysis of root causes, design requirements, and subsystems.

Field	Solution examples
Table 7.1	**Examples of solutions to problems in various engineering fields**
Civil engineering	A small town waste water system for better handling of storm surges A new type of roof that can open and close windows for utilization of direct solar heat A bridge that can open/close lanes depending on traffic patterns
Mechanical engineering	A mechanical component that is easier to maintain An electrical engine that better fits into a machine A robot arm that can lift heavy items in a packaging process
Industrial engineering	A quality management procedure for faster changes in pharmaceutical manufacturing A distribution system that better meets customer requirements A maintenance procedure that allows for better utilization of processing equipment
Chemical engineering	A recipe for an excipient for a new type of detergent A chemical production process that mixes two liquids more quickly A quality assurance procedure that allows for faster release of batches of pharmaceutical products
Electrical engineering	An intelligent house control system that delivers more precise failure detection information for faster failure handling and less idle time A ventilation system for larger buildings that utilizes geothermal heating An electrical substation with fewer failures
Software engineering	A program for cars that automatically collects real-time data from publicly available traffic databases An app that collects user data to individualize user experiences

When designing the solution, you should utilize all the expertise at your disposal. Here are a number of sources you can use for inspiration and expertise for your solution design:

- Theory from the textbooks in your university library
- The available design guidelines, codes, rules, industry standards, and so on
- Searches in academic journal databases
- The staff at your project's industrial partner
- Your own ability to generate and develop ideas and concepts
- Ideas from your supervisor
- Ideas from other lecturers, instructors, and professors beyond your main supervisor
- Inspiration from other companies (within and outside the industry of the project's industrial partner).

The first step is usually to have a group brainstorming session. The brainstorming generates ideas for the solution itself and ideas for sources of inspiration and expertise. You can achieve a fair bit using just your own brain power. The ideas from the brainstorm constitute the basis for a dialogue with your industrial partner and your supervisor, and for locating the relevant literature.

General requirements for a good engineering solution

Almost all solutions in engineering must:

1 Be based on the results of the project's analysis.
2 Meet the requirements of the industrial partner.
3 Be implementable both technically and practically.
4 Be financially feasible to implement for your industrial partner.
5 Solve the problem of the project.

In addition, the solution can be beautiful, exciting, innovative, and perhaps a bit surprising. These are, however, only "nice-to-have" requirements.

Three archetypes of engineering solutions

Most engineering projects design one of the following archetypes: the single solution, the either/or solution, or the multiple elements solution, as shown in Figure 7.2.

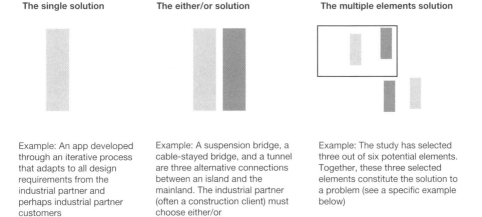

The single solution	The either/or solution	The multiple elements solution
Example: An app developed through an iterative process that adapts to all design requirements from the industrial partner and perhaps industrial partner customers	Example: A suspension bridge, a cable-stayed bridge, and a tunnel are three alternative connections between an island and the mainland. The industrial partner (often a construction client) must choose either/or	Example: The study has selected three out of six potential elements. Together, these three selected elements constitute the solution to a problem (see a specific example below)

Figure 7.2   Typology of solution archetypes

The single solution is constituted by a single, comprehensive entity. A single, comprehensive entity could be a bridge, a machine, or an app. The either/or solution first develops two or more single entities that (each) function as a solution, but with varying degrees of requirement fulfillment, effectiveness, and ease of implementation. The multiple elements solution consists of several *solution elements* that each address a cause of the project's problem. For example: a project deals with a high failure rate from a production process. The project has analyzed the root causes and identified a set of solution elements that together vastly reduce the number of failures. The elements are clearer assembly instructions, a stricter component control procedure, and a higher frequency of production equipment maintenance. These three archetype solutions are each discussed in detail now.

The single solution

The single solution emerges from a design process where the student team first identifies the design requirements and then develops a solution that fits with the requirements. The design process can be either sequential or iterative where the student team specifies design requirements and develops the solution through a number of *cycles*.

The design requirements are often technical (e.g. "The machine must endure 24-hour use"), legal (e.g. "The filling machine in the pharmaceutical industry must provide documentation for each batch"), or derived from users or customers (e.g. "The building must be heated with a heat pump").

The single solution is often applied in software development and the development of mechanical products, machines, or components. In software development, the success criteria of an app relate to how well the app meets the design requirements (often stemming from future users of the app).

The single solution fits well if the project's problem is the design of a new entity. The single solution is evaluated by how well the solution meets the design requirements and its ease of implementation. The solution is usually implemented in one piece rather than bit by bit. A later section describes how to evaluate a single solution's financial feasibility.

The either/or solution

In some engineering disciplines, the tradition is to develop a set of alternative solutions. Each solution must be technically realizable. Your industrial partner or perhaps a customer of your industrial partner will then select one of the solutions. The success criteria for the selection include how well the solution meets the design requirements, as well as "soft" criteria, for example a building's aesthetic qualities. In civil engineering, student teams often develop two or three conceptual solutions for a building. Subsequently, the construction client makes a decision.

Choosing a solution in either/or solutions

If you develop two or more alternative solutions in your project, then either you, your industrial partner, or a customer must choose the best alternative. "Best" means how well a solution meets the design requirements.

Assessing which solution best meets the often long list of design requirements can be a complex task. A simple yet effective method is the *weighted factor method*. This method breaks the complex assessment of a solution down into several, less complex assessments. You can apply the method in MS Excel using the following steps:

1 List all design requirements – write the requirement names in the first column.
2 Distribute weights to all requirements based on the relative importance of each requirement. Distribute percentages (a total of 100%) across all requirements and note the percentages in the second column.
3 For each solution, insert a scoring column. For each requirement, score how well the solution meets the requirement (e.g. 1–10).
4 For each solution, insert a result column. In each cell, multiply weight with solution score, resulting in the weighted scores.
5 For each solution, sum up all the weighted scores and compare solutions.

EXAMPLE

A project team studying construction engineering have designed three alternative traffic connections between two islands. The connections must handle both road and rail traffic. The three alternatives are a tunnel, a suspension bridge, and a combination of cable-stayed bridge for road traffic and a tunnel for rail traffic. The project team assesses which of the three connections best meets the design requirements.

Design requirement	Weight	Solution scores			Weighted scores		
		Tunnel	Susp. bridge	Combi.	Tunnel	Susp. Bridge	Combi.
Budget of €2 bn* max.	Abs	No	Yes	Yes	–	+	+
Capacity (vehicles per hour)	34		10	8		340	272
Capacity (trains per hour)	23		7	10		161	230
Energy use when operating	12		6	4		72	48
Built by local craftsmen	22		8	5		176	110
Aesthetic qualities	9		10	8		90	72
Total	100				–	839	732

* The budget is an absolute "must-have" requirement

The design requirements are listed in the first column. Observe how the budget requirement is an absolute requirement (noted as "Abs" in the Weight column). The tunnel (for both road and rail) does not meet the budget requirement and therefore the remaining analysis only scores the suspension bridge and the combination of cable-stayed bridge and rail tunnel. The figures in the weighted scores columns are the result of multiplying weight with solution score (e.g. the weight 34 is multiplied with score of 10 for the suspension bridge's vehicle capacity). The suspension bridge receives a total weighted score of 839, surpassing the combination of cable-stayed bridge and rail tunnel by 107 points.

When using the weighted factor method, you assign weights to all design requirements. The weights represent the relative importance of each design requirement. In the example given above, the weights were given without further explanation. In your project, make sure to present arguments for your weighting.

Giving weights to design requirements is often a complex task that can feel like comparing apples and oranges. A method of making the weighting easier is by breaking your weighting into a larger set of less complex decisions. A simple version of the method is now explained.

The matrix in Table 7.2 shows seven design requirements for a solution. The design requirements figure in both columns and rows. In each cell of the matrix, your job is to decide whether the requirement in the row or the column is more important. If the requirement in the row is more important, then write a 1 into the cell, if not, a 0. The total number of points in the matrix is 21. In Table 7.2, requirement 1 received six points, corresponding to 29% of the 21 total points. Requirement 3 got one point, corresponding to 5% of the 21 total points. These percentages are the requirements' weights.

Table 7.2 Determining the importance among design requirements								
	Req. 1	Req. 2	Req. 3	Req. 4	Req. 5	Req. 6	Req. 7	Relative importance
Req. 1		1	1	1	1	1	1	6
Req. 2	0		1	1	1	1	1	5
Req. 3	0	0		0	1	0	0	1
Req. 4	0	0	1		1	1	0	3
Req. 5	0	0	0	0		0	0	0
Req. 6	0	0	1	0	1		0	2
Req. 7	0	0	1	1	1	1		4

Think critically about your results because the method does not guarantee the perfect weighting. Requirement 1 got six points and 29%, which is the maximum weight. However, maybe requirement 1 is even more important compared to the other requirements than 29%. Table 7.2 also indicates that requirement 1 is just a tiny bit more important than requirement 2. Perhaps requirement 1 is much more important and not just a tiny bit.

To include all design requirements (in an often long specification) can be a huge and unnecessarily complex task. A simpler yet still effective method for assessing solutions is to aggregate the requirements into a smaller set of solution *success criteria*. Then, evaluate each solution against this smaller set of success criteria.

Multiple elements solutions

Earlier, a student project designed to reduce the amount of failures in an electrical substation was described. The analysis for the failure causes shows that the substation cannot handle the voltage in the hours of peak power consumption. The student team designs a solution to the problem. The team finds two solutions: redesign the substation to handle higher voltages, or develop a power consumption policy that results in more even power consumption. Either one might function as the whole solution, but the team decides to include *both* a redesigned substation *and* a power consumption policy as two elements of one solution.

Having several solution elements in the same solution is traditional in many engineering fields. For example, a mechanical engineering project aims to reduce the maintenance time for a component in a ship's engine by redesigning both the component and the maintenance procedure. In business engineering, a student team works to increase sales of wind turbines to the Chinese market. The team's solution includes both a new turbine service concept that Chinese customers value and a new type of promotion that better fits the norms of Chinese business culture.

Prioritizing solution elements in multiple elements solutions

The individual solution elements are designed as if they were single, whole solutions. As with the alternative solutions in the either/or solution, the student team specifies each solution element in the multiple elements solution to a degree that makes prioritization among solution elements possible. Therefore, solution elements are specified to a quite rough-cut degree. If you were to specify each solution element in detail, you would end up spending unnecessary time on elements that you do not later prioritize as part of your complete solution.

Once you have designed all the solution elements, your task is to find the right combination of solution elements. Elements are often prioritized using two selection criteria:

1 The solution element's effect on your project's problem.
2 The ease of implementing the solution element with your industrial partner.

A prioritization matrix (see Figure 7.3) is a practical tool for this purpose. The horizontal axis shows each solution element's effect and the vertical axis its ease of implementation. A later section shows how to assess effect and ease of implementation.

Once you have assessed each solution element on both selection criteria, place the solution elements in the matrix shown in Figure 7.3. Elements in the top-right square go directly into the complete solution, elements in the bottom-left square are immediately excluded, and elements in the top-left and bottom-right squares need a closer look.

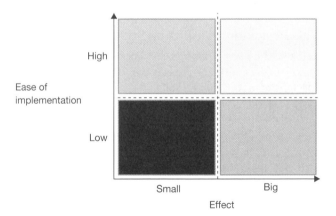

Figure 7.3 Prioritization matrix

When you make the selection, check for interdependencies between solutions elements. It might be that a solution element in the top-right square cannot be implemented before an element in the bottom-left square is implemented first. In this case, see if you can assess the ease of implementation and effect for both elements in combination. Then, place the combination in the matrix and see in which corner the combination lands.

Specifying your solution after the selection

Once you have selected a solution in the either/or solution, or prioritized solution elements in the multiple elements solution, your subsequent task is a closer specification of the selected, total solution. In civil and mechanical engineering, students draw detailed technical drawings, and student teams in manufacturing engineering develop production layout and flow charts. The specific documentation depends on your particular discipline and its traditions.

Assessing the effect, ease of implementation, and financial feasibility of your solution

All engineering disciplines require that a project assess the solution's effect on the problem. In addition, many faculties and supervisors expect a project to conduct an explicit analysis of the solution's financial feasibility, that is, whether the solution is financially feasible to implement. In total, evaluate your solution on the following three parameters:

1 The effect on your project's problem.
2 The ease of implementing the solution with your industrial partner.
3 Your solution's financial feasibility.

Some solutions carry significant risk with them. If you design a solution with technical risk, business risk, or other relevant risk type, then include a risk assessment in your project, in addition to the three assessments in the list above.

The following sections will first describe each of these three assessments, and then outline how to deal with the (often tough) task of quantifying the relevant variables.

Assessment of the solution's effect on your project's problem

The term "effect" differs between projects that improve an existing entity and projects that design a new entity. For projects that design new entities (e.g. a building or a machine component), the solution's effect is usually how well the solution matches its design requirements derived from, among others, the future users. For projects that improve an existing entity (e.g. the durability of a product), the effect of the solution is the size of the improvement that the solution produces (e.g. another five years of product durability).

The purpose of designing the solution is the solution's effect on your project's problem. If a project concerns reducing the scrap rate in a production line, the effect of the solution is a reduced scrap rate, for example a reduction from 30% to 10%.

Depending on the specific solution and the assessment techniques at your disposal, an effect assessment can be a measurement, a calculation, or a qualitative estimate. The challenge in effect assessments is to ensure a reasonable degree of precision. Some industries, such as the construction industry, and their corresponding engineering disciplines, have methods for assessing a solution's effect. Such methods are usually perceived as reasonably precise and are accepted by all parties.

The effect assessment is more difficult if you work with a problem where the engineering field's methods cannot be directly used or perhaps do not exist at all. In these cases, effect assessments are harder to conduct and results are more uncertain. The following box presents two effect assessment examples: one with a directly applicable method and one where the student team develops an effect assessment technique for their particular project.

TWO EXAMPLES OF EFFECT ASSESSMENTS

Heat radiation from a building's façade

A project team works with reducing the heat radiation from the façade of a type of tract home (predesigned house). The team has developed five individual solution elements that each reduce the heat radiation. The team now wants to assess each element's effect to fill their prioritization matrix. Three of the solution elements are:

1 Increase the façade insulation by 2 cm.

2 Change windows from double to triple glazed energy-efficient windows.

3 Keep the window type but remove two windows from the house plans.

The team uses the construction codes and industrial guidelines to conduct specific calculations that result in three numbers expressing the reduction in heat radiation for each solution element.

Increased usage of publicly available electric bikes

A student team wants to increase the usage of publicly available electric bikes for tourists. The student team wants to increase bike usage by increasing the functionality and user satisfaction of the app with which users control the bike (unlock the bike, pay for its use, and use as GPS during bike rides).

With the objective of increasing functionality and user satisfaction, the student team interviews a number of potential users, including tourists from six different countries. The interviews and following analysis result in eight different ideas for changing the app. The question is how big an effect each of these ideas will have on functionality and user satisfaction, and ultimately on bike usage. The team cannot apply a standard method directly, so the students need to develop their own assessment technique.

The team would like to express the effect of idea 1 as: "Idea 1 will increase bike usage by 2–6%." Idea 1 has to do with unlocking a bike using the app. The team decides to conduct a statistical test of how many potential users give up due to the current app's lack of functionality and user friendliness in unlocking bikes. The team assesses that 25% of potential users give up. Now the team can more precisely assess how many of these 25% would actually use the bike if idea 1 were implemented.

Assessment of ease of implementation

A solution's ease of implementation is a more intangible measure than the solution's effect. The term is difficult to quantify. To measure ease of implementation, break the term down into more easily measurable factors that are relevant for your solution. For example:

1 The amount of capital required to implement the solution.
2 Whether the necessary amount of technical expertise is available.
3 The amount of organizational resistance that the implementation must likely handle.

First, give each solution element a score from 1–10 on each of these factors. To place the solution elements on the ease of implementation axis (the Y-axis) of the prioritization matrix in Figure 7.3, you need one number for each element. To get from 1–10 assessments on three separate factors to one number, aggregate the three measures for each solution element into one number. See the example in the box below.

EXAMPLE: ASSESSING EASE OF IMPLEMENTATION

A student team works with a manufacturer of syringes used in hospitals and clinics. The project's objective is to reduce the scrap rate from a syringe production line. The student team has designed three solution elements (A, B, and C) and wants to assess the ease of implementation for each element. In the table below, a high number means high ease, that is, easy to implement.

	Solution element A	Solution element B	Solution element C
Required capital	5	2	9
Necessary technical expertise	8	3	8
Organizational resistance	2	8	3
Ease of implementation	**15**	**13**	**20**

The table shows that solution element C is the easiest to implement and element B the hardest. Using these numbers, you can place each element on the prioritization matrix's Y-axis.

Assessment of the solution's financial feasibility

The financial feasibility of a solution depends on the financial value of the solution and the cost of implementing and operating the solution. Engineering solutions are very diverse and the value of a solution can constitute many different things, as shown in Table 7.3.

For solutions that improve an existing entity, Figure 7.4 shows the relationship between solution and value. The solution has an effect and the effect has a value.

Both Table 7.3 and Figure 7.4 deal only with the value of a solution and not the costs. Implementing a solution has costs. A solution's financial feasibility is calculated by subtracting costs from value. These costs of a solution have two components: the *investment* the firm makes to implement the solution, and the *costs of operating* the

Table 7.3   Examples of solution values

Solution	Solution value
A new app	Selling the app gives the firm revenue, which constitutes the solution's value. Note that the cost of selling and supporting the app is not subtracted yet. When subtracting the costs from the value, you reach the financial feasibility of the solution
Reduced inventory	A reduced inventory means lower inventory costs. The firm's costs (theft, obsolescence, forklifts, rent, etc.) are reduced. The cost reduction is the value of the solution
Increased product durability	Increased product durability makes the product more valuable to the firm's target customers. Therefore, the firm can increase its prices. The added revenue resulting from the price rise constitutes the solution's value. If the firm does not increase the product's price, its sales will increase. In this case, the net profit from the increased number of products sold is the solution's value
A new bridge	A bridge is paid for by the construction client (e.g. a state or municipality). For the construction firm, the price of the bridge is the solution's value. Note that the costs of constructing the bridge are not subtracted yet. When subtracting the costs from the bridge's price, the result is the solution's financial feasibility
Increased traffic across a bridge	A solution that adapts the number of lanes across a bridge with traffic patterns increases the bridge's capacity. More capacity means less queuing and less queuing means that more commuters and other travelers will use the bridge. If the bridge owner charges for using the bridge, more usage creates more revenue. This added revenue is the solution's value
Faster product delivery	Delivering a product faster means a better ability to compete for orders from those customer segments that value delivery speed, and therefore higher revenue. In addition, the solution means that customer payments arrive faster. Faster payments means that the firm has lower costs of financing its outlay to produce the product (raw materials, salaries, rent, etc.)
Lower liquid viscosity in medicine production	Lower liquid viscosity means faster liquid flow. If the solution can have lower viscosity without reducing other liquid characteristics relevant for the production or product quality, then higher speed results in higher system capacity and lower fixed costs per unit of finished product. The reduction in unit cost is the value of the solution

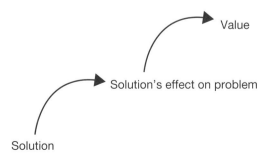

Figure 7.4   Solution effect and value

solution once implemented. Engineering solutions differ across disciplines including how much investment is needed for implementing a solution. These are a few examples:

1 For a building, investment is needed for purchasing materials and paying craftsmen.
2 For improving a process, investment is needed for worker training, running the implementation project, and perhaps a new machine.
3 For a new drug component, investment is needed for running tests of the drug component, getting governmental approval, and perhaps a new machine in the production line.

All solutions have *operating costs*. They might not be large, but they are there. If a team of software engineers were to develop a new app for use by healthcare professionals, then operating costs would be delivering continuous support for users.

Figure 7.5 illustrates a solution's value, investment, and operating costs. The arrow expresses time beginning from year 0, where the investment is made, and ending at year *n*. The size of the vertical lines expresses the size of the investment, the solution's value, and the solution's operating costs.

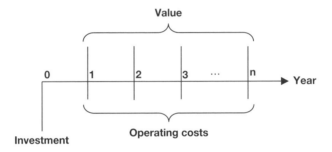

Figure 7.5   The solution's value, investment, and operating costs

Figure 7.5 is often used to illustrate the net present value method (also called discounted cash flow analysis). The method calculates the net present value of an investment taking future cash flows into account. Describing the method in detail is outside the scope of this book, but it is a core discipline in all investment analysis and corporate finance, so you can find detailed descriptions of it by borrowing a textbook in one of these disciplines. Other more rough-cut investment analyses include the payback time method and the break-even method.

Quantifying a solution's effect and value

Whether a solution has an effect on a problem is often a matter of logic. For example, increased durability of a product leads to a perception of higher product quality by customers, which in turn leads to higher sales (assuming that the price is kept steady). The challenge is usually not a matter of arguing *whether* the solution has an effect, but rather *the extent* of the effect.

As a project team, you often lack quantitative data to calculate the effect of a solution. You may instead have a set of qualitative data available; for example, a relevant employee stating that the solution will have "a huge impact." To conduct an analysis of the financial feasibility of a solution, you often need to quantify these qualitative data. The two numbers that are often difficult to quantify are:

1 The solution's effect on your project's problem.
2 The financial value of the effect.

Example 1: Challenge in quantifying a solution's effect

A team of students works with the firm DataDrive, a developer of software for public organizations. DataDrive has recently sold a program to the social departments of around 50 municipalities. The software replaces homemade solutions that the municipalities have built themselves (e.g. different combinations of spreadsheets and databases). DataDrive's software is much smoother and more effective than the homemade solutions. The firm's problem is that although the social departments have purchased the software, they do not use the software as much as intended, and DataDrive's payments from the municipalities depend on the usage. Many employees in the social departments stick with their original homemade solutions. Currently, only 13 of the 50 social departments apply all functions of the software, 27 use some of the functions, and the remaining 10 do not apply the software at all.

The student team's objective is to develop the software's user interface to increase the use of functions. Following all the right guidelines for a user participation study, the student team has conducted a field study with 10 social departments. The study has resulted in a series of suggestions for user interface modifications including some shortcuts that reduce the time taken to use the program. The user interface modifications and shortcuts constitute the project's solution.

The team has collected a series of statements from software users about the solution that leaves no doubt that the solution will indeed make life much easier for users. The solution even makes learning to use the program much easier. One workshop participant said: "With these shortcuts, I'll absolutely use the software." The question is therefore not *whether* the solution will have an effect, but *how much* of an effect. How does the team of students quantify their qualitative statements? See advice for quantification later in this section.

Example 2: Challenge in quantifying the value of a solution's effect

The firm Kitchens & Kitchens produces custom-made tabletops for kitchens and bathrooms. The firm's customers are kitchen firms that sell whole kitchens and bathroom furniture to homeowners and construction companies. The firm has long had trouble keeping its delivery promises. At present, the firm only delivers 62% of orders on time (so 38% are late). The firm also receives almost daily complaints and recently one of its largest contracts was cancelled.

A team of students conduct a project to reduce the amount of late orders. The team has designed a solution consisting of four elements: a new planning procedure; a new policy for inventory management; a set of updates to the firm's IT system; and more thorough logistics training for new staff. The team has assessed that the solution will reduce late orders from 38% down to a mere 3–5%. Future customers can look forward to getting their orders on time.

The next question is how valuable the reduction from 38% to 3–5% really is. The firm assumes that the solution will increase customer retention and also attract customers that are dissatisfied with competitors' late deliveries. In addition, the solution will relieve some of the firm's staff with the task of dealing with complaining customers. There is no doubt that the solution has significant value, but how big is it?

There are a number of methods for quantification. Here are four commonly used methods:

1 *Generalizing from few to many observations*: For example, from one work station to all work stations or from one customer to all customers.
2 *Using correlating variables*: For example, if beer sales are forecasted to increase by 10%, it is reasonable to assume that beer bottle sales will increase by about 10% as well.
3 *Transference of results from similar cases*: For example, if a competing shipping company reduces oil consumption per container by 0.45% when travelling at slower speeds, it is fair to assume that this 0.45% will apply elsewhere as well.
4 *The "turning qualitative to quantitative" strategy*: Gather as much qualitative evidence as you can from multiple and preferably diverse sources. Have your informants make estimates independently of one another, and finally present the result as an interval (e.g. "the solution will reduce costs by 20–40%").

For the example about software usage, the immediate strategy would be to ask the software firm about its prior experience of bestselling products, and then transfer this experience to the software for the municipalities' social departments. A "Plan B" could be to look more generally at how fast process changes can be implemented in municipalities. The "turning qualitative to quantitative" strategy could be used as well, perhaps as a fallback strategy.

Supervisor opinion

The research done for this book revealed that supervisors have different opinions about whether to quantify variables that are difficult to quantify. You have three generic options:

1 Quantify those values that you can quantify with high certainty. Those variables that you cannot quantify with high certainty, you just describe qualitatively. The firm will then have to make decisions about implementation on the basis of both quantitative and qualitative variables.
2 Quantify those values that you can quantify with high certainty. In addition, for those variables that you cannot quantify with high certainty, describe how the firm can achieve certainty by conducting additional analyses.

3 Quantify all variables and describe the size and nature of uncertainties. With this quantitative analysis, the firm can make implementation decisions knowing all uncertainties well.

The advantage of options 1 and 2 is that all quantifications are robust. The disadvantage is a limited usefulness of the analysis of financial feasibility. Often, industrial partners expect a feasibility study where one number expresses whether implementation is financially feasible or not. The advantage of option 3 is that the option provides this one number, but with lots of uncertainty.

If you decide to quantify uncertain numbers, you take the risk that your examiners may find the uncertainty of your results problematic. On the other hand, if you choose not to quantify, but describe variables with text, you take the risk that your examiners find your study useless. So, discuss which option your supervisor finds most "professional" and remember to provide arguments for the legitimacy of your quantification methods.

Reviewing this chapter's objectives

Tick those objectives you feel you have achieved, and review those you haven't yet accomplished. In this chapter, you have learned how to:

❒ Identify the general requirements of a good solution.

❒ Distinguish between the single solution, the either/or solution, and the multiple elements solution.

❒ Select one solution among several potential solutions (for the either/or archetype) and select which elements to include in the solution (for the multiple elements archetype).

❒ Assess a solution's effect and ease of implementation.

❒ Quantify the financial value of the solution's effect on the project's problem.

Testing and Implementing the Solution

| Project initiation | Problem statement | Literature, knowledge, and expertise | Methodology and planning | Data collection and analysis | Design of solution | Test and implementation of solution |

In this chapter, you will learn:

1 How the test of a solution fits into a project's coherent flow.
2 How to involve your industrial partner in a test.
3 The meaning of the term "implementation" across engineering disciplines.
4 How to plan the implementation of a solution.
5 How the implementation plan should take into account both the practical step-by-step implementation process as well as potential resistance among your industrial partner's employees (and perhaps even managers).
6 That the key to successful implementation is ownership of the solution among the future solution users with your industrial partner.
7 How to create a sense of ownership among key employees and managers through the continuous inclusion of key people throughout the whole project.

Engineering projects design a solution (a building, a machine, an algorithm, a chemical process, etc.). Within many disciplines, testing and implementing solutions are either specific expectations among examiners or just "nice-to-have" components of your project. The chapter first describes how to test a solution and then how to implement it.

Testing a solution

Because solutions differ greatly among engineering disciplines, testing solutions differs as well. Testing a solution might be a pivotal component of a project that examiners expect. If a project has developed an algorithm, then the project team must test whether the algorithm returns the right results. If a project develops a new purchasing and inventory policy that will reduce inventories, then the project team should test whether the policy does, in fact, reduce inventories in practice.

Some solutions are difficult and expensive to test authentically (e.g. the structure of a high-rise roof). In such cases, you might be able to test your solution using simulation software. Some solutions can be tested using a live-action format, for example a new quality assurance procedure. Such a procedure could be tested using a workshop that includes staff from the relevant departments (e.g. production, logistics, and quality assurance). The workshop introduction might go as follows: "Today, our job is to test the new procedure. Your roles are as follows: Bob's production crew submits deviations from quality standards and then we (the quality department) register the deviation. Then, Paul and Beth fill out a report and finally Sheila approves the report."

Involving your industrial partner in the test

Testing solutions in a realistic setting often involves employees of your industrial partner. Therefore, make sure to plan your solution test well in advance, so the relevant employees can book the time in their calendars. Book employees around one month in advance using a meeting request with the headline: "Test of (solution name)." Include in your meeting request a sentence saying: "We will send a specific agenda prior to the meeting." Chapter 10 details how you can handle industrial partner employees with very busy schedules.

Implementation of solutions

The term "implementation" has different meanings across engineering disciplines. The term does, however, always cover the activities following the solution design:

1 In civil engineering, implementation means constructing the building, bridge, crossing, railway stretch, and so on.
2 In mechanical and product design engineering, implementation means a dialogue with the firm's production engineers about how to manufacture the product in large quantities.
3 In production engineering, implementation means beginning the use of a new procedure or process.
4 In software engineering, implementation means programming code and embedding the code in an instrument's overall program.

Figure 8.1 illustrates these examples.

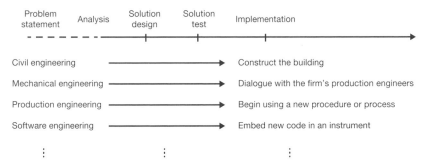

Figure 8.1   Perceptions of the term "implementation" across engineering disciplines

Although the perception of the term "implementation" differs across engineering disciplines, implementation always means a series of steps conducted by an actor – a person, a department, an organization, or several organizations.

Whether a solution is implemented is usually outside the control of your project team. Implementation usually means that managers located high up in the hierarchy of your industrial partner must commit resources and perhaps involve suppliers or customers. In your project, implementation therefore usually means *planning* the implementation rather than actually executing the implementation.

The two steps of implementation: planning and execution

Generally, implementation has the two steps of planning the implementation and executing the plan. As previously stated, examiners usually expect a plan to come from your project. A plan for implementing a solution consists of three elements. For each element, your team, as the implementation planners, needs to consider a number of component parts:

1 *A project plan:*
   a The activities the industrial partner will conduct.
   b The sequence in which activities are conducted.
2 *A project organization:*
   a The project manager responsible for executing the implementation project.
   b The managers and technical experts in the project's steering group.
   c Decisions about whether to allocate full-time employees or, say, 25% of employees' working hours.
   d A process for how to keep the steering group involved, in particular the steering group chairperson.
3 *A plan for dealing with organizational resistance to implementing your solution:*
   a Identification of groups and alliances that you can expect to show resistance to the implementation of your solution (see Chapter 11 for a specific method).
   b A plan for how the project organization can communicate appropriately to the relevant groups of employees and managers that are affected by the implementation. This plan includes how to communicate, what to communicate (e.g. early successes), and when to communicate.
   c A plan for sustaining changes resulting from the implementation (e.g. altering the firm's incentive structures and promotion prerequisites).

The next three sections detail the project plan, project organization and dealing with resistance. Parts of the following discussion are most relevant to solutions that require changes in behavior (e.g. from industrial partner employees or managers, from customers or suppliers).

Project plan for the implementation

You can develop the project plan as a Gantt chart (see Chapter 5). The implementation plan is usually a rough version of a project plan compared to the plan this book suggests you develop for your own project.

If your solution is a multiple elements solution, then consider suggesting implementing the elements in smaller groups (sometimes called "waves"). For example, if a project suggests implementing six solution elements, you can suggest implementing the elements in two waves, each consisting of three elements. Your plan could suggest implementing the elements in wave 1 first, and when these elements are implemented (hopefully with success), continue to the three elements in wave 2. You can use the "prioritization matrix" described in Chapter 7 (Figure 7.3) to assess how to group elements in waves.

The following list contains four subjects that are worth considering when planning your implementation of several solution elements:

1 Consider implementing elements that are easy to implement first (the "low-hanging fruit"). These elements will likely prove their effect quickly and you can use this success story as leverage for getting approval and resources committed to the elements that are tougher to implement.
2 As mentioned above, consider grouping elements in smaller waves that are easier to grasp and manage.
3 If your set of solution elements contains elements without heavy investment needs, then consider placing these in the first wave. Management will be less likely to prohibit the implementation of investment-free solutions.
4 There might be interdependencies among solution elements that require some elements to precede others. Make sure to integrate this logic into your plan.

Project organization for the implementation

As part of your implementation plan, consider including a suggestion for how to organize the implementation. Organization means deciding who runs the implementation project, who supervises and approves (the steering committee), and who works on and supports the implementation project.

For a project about the implementation of a production process and launch of a new product, a project organization might consist of a project manager, project participants, a steering group, and a group of external consultants and suppliers, as shown in Figure 8.2. The steering group could consist of the firm's product development head, the operations manager, and the sales manager.

Figure 8.2   Example of project organization

The following list, based on the work of Kotter (2007) and Sirkin et al. (2005), describes four important rules of thumb for project organization:

1 The steering group must have enough power in the organization to make all critical decisions about the implementation of the solution.
2 The person leading the project must have the skill set and experience that will convince the organization that this implementation will indeed happen.
3 Project participants should, as far as possible, work full time on the implementation. The alternative, having employees work, say, 20% on the project while maintaining their current tasks, often results in delays and other problems.
4 Plan for frequent steering group meetings (ideally one per month) to keep the implementation running.

Managing resistance to change

If the implementation of your solution or solution elements requires changes in human behavior, then the complexity greatly increases. To suggest activities that can deal with resistance to change, you need to improve your knowledge about managing change and dealing with organizational resistance. Read the literature on the topic. With the right grounding, you are then able to suggest how the implementation project can manage potential resistance to behavioral change. One idea is to involve key employees early in the process to identify pockets of resistance and employees' reasons for resisting.

Your implementation might be resisted by future users of the solution. This type of resistance is often best dealt with through early and appropriate communication and the involvement of key persons from the group of future users. Consider involving key future users in your project's early phases, including your analysis and solution design.

Your implementation plan should consider potential resistance not just from future users, but also from powerful actors in the organization. An effective tool for gaining insight into often complex informal power structures is the stakeholder analysis (see Chapter 11). This analysis provides insight into:

- those people and groups with a stake in the implementation
- whether these people or groups will promote or inhibit successful implementation
- whether these people or groups have sufficient power to prove problematic.

Ownership is key to successful implementation

Great engineering projects result in implementable solutions. The key to whether the industrial partner will, in fact, implement your solution is *ownership*. If your industrial partner feels a strong sense of ownership of the solutions you have developed, the chances of having your solution implemented are that much better than if the firm felt that your solutions "fell out of clear sky."

The key to ensuring ownership is to involve key industrial partner employees and managers early on and then throughout your project. An industrial partner may well exhibit tons of interest in your project at first, but forget the project five minutes later. To counter this, be sure to involve the industrial partner continuously; for example, by dropping by the office/desk of important employees to "give them a brief update."

One opportunity for more in-depth industrial partner involvement is using workshops with key employees as participants. Chapter 10 describes three particular workshops where your project team act as workshop hosts and the industrial partner employees are invited participants. Briefly, they are:

1 *The analysis workshop*: The purpose is to ensure consensus about your analysis results. In the best-case scenario, the industrial partner employees agree completely with your results. Then, your results constitute the foundation for your solution design.

2 *The solution workshop*: One purpose is to ensure that your industrial partner has ownership of your solution. To this end, develop a set of rough ideas and outlines of solutions. Use the workshop to detail and refine your ideas and solution outlines. If your industrial partner employees can clearly see their own imprint on your solutions, their sense of ownership increases quite dramatically.

3 *The implementation workshop*: The purpose is to ensure, among other things, a realistic project plan, develop guidelines for communication, and a plan for sustaining the use of the solution. During the workshop, industrial partner employees and managers might get ideas for how to implement your solution and how to handle potential resistance. Your job is to facilitate discussions about potential implementation barriers and how to handle them. Consider using the lists in this chapter as themes and discussion points for the implementation workshop.

Reviewing this chapter's objectives

Tick those objectives you feel you have achieved, and review those you haven't yet accomplished. In this chapter, you have learned how to:

❐ Test a solution using simulation software, live-action events, and by testing just a few critical individual solution elements.

❐ Include industrial partner employees in your solution test and arrange for their participation well in advance.

❐ Ensure that the implementation plan includes both the step-by-step implementation process as well as plans for handling potential resistance to implementation.

❐ Create a sense of ownership among key employees and managers through continuous inclusion throughout the whole project.

Collaboration, Supervision, and Stakeholders

Collaboration, Communication, and Supervision

In this chapter, you will learn:

1 How project teams are formed and the dynamics at play in the group formation process.
2 How your effort and team commitment during your first year of study impacts your options in later group formation processes.
3 How a group contract supports commitment, effort, presence, and communication quality within your team.
4 The right content of a group collaboration contract.
5 How to prevent conflicts through active and continuous use of your group collaboration contract.
6 How to ensure effective group meetings.
7 How psychological safety and trust are key to great teamwork.
8 How to handle conflicts in your team.
9 How to make the best use of your supervisor.

When you start a project-based course, you immediately face two challenges: understanding the learning objectives and content of the project, and becoming part of the right project team. The energy is usually focused on the latter.

The first semester of a degree course is special in several respects:

- project teams are often formed by your lecturers
- you do not really know your classmates that well
- you have the lowest level of project skills during your whole degree.

Leading and participating constructively in project work are skills you learn just as you would learn thermodynamics and algebra. Project skills include the ability to plan and manage a project, as well as preventing and handling conflicts during your project.

You get your first experiences with project work during your first semester. Because your project skills are not yet matured, project work often feels frustrating and cumbersome in this period. To avoid frustration, students make a considerable effort to get into the right project group. During your second and third semesters, when you often form project teams yourselves as a class, the group formation process in the first week is often considered the most important activity for the whole semester.

Group formation dynamics

Every class differs with respect to the social, cultural, and skills-related characteristics of the students. Some of your classmates are determined, goal-oriented, and have high expectations for their own effort and grades for all the courses they do. A second group of classmates focus less on results and more on learning a skill set for their future work life. Finally, a third group of classmates do not stress too much and focus on wellbeing and having a good time while studying.

Some of your classmates have gotten into their dream course, others have just "settled" for the course, and others might even be thinking about quitting and starting over with a new course. Some students have lots of family commitments or demanding jobs on the side. Some are international students, others already have experience from other courses, and some are mature students.

These personal, cultural, experience-related, and age differences make the group formation process complicated. The most common driver for a group formation process is that people who are alike seek each other out. The familiar feels safest. During your first semester, you do not know your classmates well. If your lecturers do not form project teams, then you are thrown into an (often stressful) group formation process, where you choose each other based on what you can decode by looking and listening to each other (e.g. age, haircut, loud or soft voice, tattoos, accents, etc.). When you reach your second semester, you know your classmates much better and other attributes replace age, hairstyle, and so on. The new traits are effort, physical presence, commitment, grades from the first semester, humor, and whether you are a nice person in general.

It is important to recognize that your individual effort, presence, seriousness, and social skills as a team member will have a substantial impact on your options in future group formation processes. Do your classmates perceive you as diligent or lazy? Through your participation in your university's project-based courses, you acquire project skills. You get to know yourself as a project participant, you get to know your personal strengths and weaknesses, and you learn to thrive and be cool at the (often chaotic and cumbersome) beginning of projects. Equally important, you learn how to handle the personal, cultural, and skills-related differences that naturally exist in a project team. These differences, by the way, do not go away when you graduate. You will need your project skills in your work life.

When the group is formed

Once project groups are formed, your project process begins. Your job as a team is to ensure a complete understanding of the project's purpose and methods as well as an effective mode of collaboration within your team.

To support the process of developing effective collaboration in your team, consider conducting one or two personality and role preference tests. Such tests provide an overview of the personality traits and preferences in your team. The tests can help prevent conflicts in instances where two or more of your teammates do not understand each other's prioritizations, task perceptions, preferred methods, and so on. Role preference tests can explain your teammates' behavior. Having explicit explanations of team member behavior available minimizes the level of conflict in your team.

Explained: personality and role preference tests

Personality tests

A personality test usually consists of a set of questions and a set of personality archetypes. When you answer the questions, the test will reveal which of the archetypes your personality matches best. The test always has a description of each archetype so you can read about the characteristics of the archetype your personality matches best and become wiser about your behavioral patterns (e.g. why you react to things as you do and why you like some things and dislike others).

If you and your teammates all do the same personality test, you will gain a valuable overview of which personality types you have in your group. The knowledge you and your teammates gain from taking the test helps you understand the behavior of your teammates. If you happen to think that two of your teammates act "really weirdly," the test might provide you with an explanation. The test can help you understand that teammates act as they do because of their personality and not necessarily because they are disingenuous or uncommitted to the project.

The process of conducting the test can, of itself, provide you with important information about one another. Consider this conversation about a personality test between two teammates:

Person A: "What was your answer for question 12?"
Person B: "I answered B."
Person A: "What!?! Seriously! You're kidding, right?"
Person B: explains the reasoning behind answering B.
Person A: "Oh, I see. That makes sense."

Role preference tests

A slightly different type of test is a role preference test. A project has a number of archetypical roles (e.g. initiator, idea generator, producer, planner, chairperson, finisher, etc.). You might not be aware which role you prefer. A role preference test will show you. Knowing the preferred roles of all your teammates not only helps you organize your project work better, but also helps you understand, explain, and forecast teammate behavior. One additional insight: you identify which roles your team has in surplus and which roles your team lacks (e.g. the critical finisher role). Lacking one or two roles indicates that you as a team have a common responsibility of helping each other in filling these roles.

You can find numerous personality and role preference tests online. Search for "personality test" or "preference test." Two popular tests are the Myers-Briggs personality test and the Belbin team role preference test.

Group collaboration contracts

Using a group collaboration contract supports engagement, presence, and effective communication within your team. Writing group collaboration contracts at the beginning of project-based courses is common practice in many disciplines. The process of writing such a contract supports a better working environment in your team as well as reflections about what you and your teammates consider professional and laudable behavior.

A group collaboration contract contains the rules that describe the behavior you and your team considers professional. In addition, the collaboration contract should be clear about the penalties for violating the rules. The following list suggests a number of rules that you can consider including in a group collaboration contract:

1 How often and where you gather for group meetings.
2 Whether you allow the use of social media during group meetings.
3 Whether group members are expected to participate in lectures conducted as part of the project.
4 How and when a person must communicate a missed deadline or a potentially missed deadline to the rest of the team.
5 How and when a person must communicate a no-show to the rest of the team.
6 How you expect each other to address dissatisfaction with other team members or the general state of the project.
7 Your expected weekly work effort and hours.
8 Your means of communication and communication behavior (including electronic communication).
9 Whether and how you document decisions and other important issues.
10 The use of meeting agendas and summaries.
11 Whether working at home is allowed.
12 How to handle the fact that some team members have jobs on the side and others do not.
13 How to handle difficulties in finding common time slots for weekly meetings.
14 The consequences and penalties for not complying with the group contract, including the circumstances for involving your supervisor in conflicts.
15 How you organize yourself (e.g. whether you designate one team member as manager or planner).
16 How you assure the quality of each other's work (a quality assurance procedure).
17 How you ensure coherence in your final project report.

Write your group collaboration contract with the mindset that you *will* have to enforce it – more than once. A project often goes through a series of stages. A classic theory within project management (Tuckman 1965) describes how a project has four phases: forming, storming, norming, and performing:

● During the *forming phase*, the group is formed.
● *Storming* means that individual group members or factions of members battle for the right behavior, the real objectives for the project, and which elements of the project are worth prioritizing. During the storming phase, the group collaboration contract is often a weapon of the ambitious project group faction ("No, the contract clearly states that we meet *every* week!"). When the battle of the storming phase ends, the group has reached the norming phase.
● In the *norming phase*, the "winners" are found and the group now follows the norms of behavior, objectives, and so on of the winning faction.

- Once the dust has settled completely, the group begins working better and enters the *performing phase.*

If (and this is a big "if") you are aware that you have indeed gone through a storming phase, then update your group collaboration contract. For example, clarify your project goals, the new ideal for professional behavior, and so on.

Project group meetings

During your first and second semesters, group meetings are essential for coordination and ensuring progress. Semester projects usually require around 25–30% of your time during the semester. You therefore have around 70–75% of your time for other activities that require your attention and thought processing capability. In addition, some of your group members may have part-time jobs, others may have a child to pick up from daycare, and others may participate in university organizations (e.g. student groups and committees). In short, finding a time when everyone is available for group meetings is often not that easy, but you should aim for, at minimum, once a week and, at best, twice a week.

It is a mistake to replace group meetings with emails or texts. Communication functions far better when you are able to see and hear each other. If you can see and hear another person, you are much better equipped to decode the full extent of their message. One of the higher purposes of using project work as a pedagogical method is to facilitate discussion. These discussions might be noisy and annoying at times; for example, a debate about whether it makes sense to include a certain theory in your project. Discussions work terribly when conducted in writing. You can easily misinterpret a message or read all kinds of meanings into your discussion partner's written words. Feedback, in particular, is a high-risk activity when conducted in writing.

During final projects, the best circumstances for a two–three person group is sitting in the same office on a daily basis. Ideally, this office is located at your industrial partner's location. For final projects, make an effort to get your own room in your industrial partner's building. Your daily presence allows for daily informal face-to-face talks between you and the relevant employees of your industrial partner. Such communication is much more effective than sending emails that your industrial partner can misinterpret, forget, "save for later," or delete. You also avoid the long periods of waiting for replies.

If you sit together in the same room on a daily basis, then having formal group meetings is not necessary. Instead, simply discuss issues across the table.

Preventing conflict through your group collaboration contract

Most people perceive conflict and dissatisfaction as unpleasant. As a consequence, conflicts are often allowed to smolder and grow before you address them. Once you get around to addressing a smoldering conflict, it may have grown to such a size that you need help handling it and therefore involve your supervisor.

Before addressing how to avoid this situation, you should know that conflicts during your educational projects are not all bad. The biggest individual jump in your project skills is often related to your first large conflict while studying. The frustrations from this first big conflict are often huge and you now know precisely what you want to avoid at all costs in future projects. You take the learning experience from this first conflict with you for the rest of your career.

To avoid resolving conflicts way too late, make sure to address potential conflicts when they are mere ripples on the surface. These ripples can develop into full-blown conflicts if not addressed early. So, make sure to discuss ripples while they are just ripples. Write an explicit rule in your group contract requiring you to address potential conflicts. The rule can describe that you *must* discuss at least one potential conflict at each meeting. You might consider this unnecessary ("Good morning, professor, we are not seven years old!"). However, the method is effective for avoiding large conflicts. Sometimes, you might even have to provoke discussions of ripple-size conflicts by insisting that each group member mentions one thing they find slightly annoying or see as a potential conflict.

The risk of conflict is especially high during the first month, where you (explicitly or implicitly) establish your ways of working, and during the last few weeks before the deadline.

Using online platforms for communication and file sharing

Establish an online communications platform for your group, such as a Facebook group with Messenger communication. This platform can come in handy when you need to communicate in real time as a whole group or with just two or three other group members.

Do remember, however, that written messages are often misinterpreted or overinterpreted. Examples are, sentences such as "But I thought that you …" or "We agreed about this on Monday last week." It is easy to imagine conflict-prone replies such as "Well, you thought wrong!" or "No, *you* agreed on Monday last week, I didn't!" Only use Messenger for practical or smaller issues. If you have several issues to discuss, then wait for your next group meeting or use the phone, so you can hear each other's voices.

For file sharing, consider Dropbox or Google Drive. File sharing is not as prone to conflict as communications.

Trust and psychological safety are key to great collaboration and communication

Working well in a project setting is an acquired skill just as much as math and mechanics. You learn to collaborate. Conducting project work in your course is the best way of learning project skills. During your first year at university, you have yet to learn these skills and you are therefore on a steep learning curve.

The keys to great collaboration are *trust* and *psychological safety*. If a team member is missing from a group meeting, then your common trust towards this member decreases. You naturally ask yourself whether you can trust this team member and count on them when your project's pivotal tasks approach their deadlines.

Psychological safety means that you feel safe when taking interpersonal risk (Edmonson 1999). An example of such a risk is telling your teammates that you need their help because you are unable to conduct a task that you promised you would do. If you trust each other and feel psychologically safe, then the chance of conflict decreases, frustrations over other team member behavior is low, and the chances of great performance and results are high.

Trust and psychological safety are the basis for knowledge-enhancing team discussions

Great projects have plenty of discussions and debate. There is tremendous learning potential in these discussions. You must allow for these discussions in your team.

Different people have different thresholds for when discussions feel unpleasant. Often, one or two of your team members think that you are engaged in a fruitful, vibrant debate about a given topic, while other team members think the discussion is way too personal and they feel uncomfortable. If you experience such a situation (e.g. early in your project), then address the problem explicitly at the next group meeting. Addressing the problem means that your loud team members who enjoy the discussion understand that they should consider moderating their language to a more neutral tone, while the uncomfortable students understand that their teammates do not consider their arguments as personal attacks. Simply having the conversation about the nature of your group discussions leads to a better working atmosphere in your team. Consider instigating a signal when discussion becomes too vibrant, for example the Vulcan "Live long and prosper" hand gesture.

Another classic problem in team discussions is that one team member hijacks the conversation by talking non-stop and not letting others join the discussion. In the long run, this is a problem for the talkative team member that will extend into their career. For your group's sake and for the sake of your talkative team member, address the problem at your next group meeting. Again, think about a hand gesture that signals "take a break" to your team member. In addition, appoint one (other) team member as discussion moderator.

In general, explicitly discuss when necessary (and this is often the case) how you address one another. This is particularly important when giving feedback on an assignment or a written text. The teammate receiving feedback should act professionally and be capable of receiving the feedback without letting their emotions get in the way.

Good team collaboration is characterized by:

- trust between group members
- team members feeling safe from rude comments
- lots of requests for help between group members
- lots of help between group members
- members listening to one another's ideas and challenges
- a common wish for a pleasant and safe working climate.

Inability to finish a task on time

All members in your group must trust each other to make a real effort and spend time on your project. If you or a teammate cannot finish an agreed task on time, then it is of paramount importance to tell your group well ahead of the deadline. If the reason is lack of time due to personal problems (e.g. a sick aunt), then other group members might be able to help and your team as a whole can still finish the task on time. Make sure to minimize these personal hindrances and remember to factor them in when making promises to your group. You want your team to trust that you will deliver what you promise.

If the reason for a delay is a task that proved more difficult than anticipated, then tell your group as quickly as possible. If you have made a real effort to complete the task, then you are not responsible for the delay as an individual. Instead, your entire team is responsible and must step in to help.

Remember, you conduct projects to learn. You do not know how to solve all tasks prior to the project. Therefore, you will often experience having trouble completing tasks on time. Completing tough tasks is the responsibility of your group at large. As a group, make sure to nurture a working climate where you can disclose your shortcomings without fear of retribution (e.g. a snarky comment or a suggestion that you are not very bright).

Handling conflicts in your team

The best advice about handling conflicts is to deal with them as soon as possible. An effective method is discussing potential conflicts before they become actual conflicts. For example, discuss the issues that this chapter mentions. Talk them through and make sure they do not happen in your team.

The most common problem that supervisors are drawn into is situations where a project group thinks that one member is not behaving properly, that is, their behavior does not meet the standard that the remaining group considers the right behavior. The group's collaboration contract might even clearly show how the one student's behavior violates the contract. If one team member does not contribute enough to your project, you might have a resource problem. This is, however, only the case if you need an all-person effort to complete your project within the timeframe. Instructors often try to match the workload of a project with the number of people in the project teams, so you might have a serious resource problem if one team member does not make a real effort. Typical consequences of lacking resources are spelling mistakes, missing references to appendices, and other tasks that are usually conducted in the final week prior to the deadline.

However, often a project is doable with fewer people than in your team. A project might even be doable with three students working effectively rather than five students making an average effort. If this is the case, then the problematic team member constitutes a problem for reasons other than lacking resources. Two potential reasons are a sense of injustice for the teammates and a lack of learning for the problematic student. The remaining group might not consider the second reason as *their* problem. Instead, they consider injustice as the real problem. The team finds it unfair that one team member completes the project course and gets credits while only making half the effort.

If you involve your supervisor early in the project, then your supervisor will first ask you as a team to try to fix the problem at your next group meeting by discussing the problem outright and giving the problematic student two or three weeks to change their behavior. If the behavior of the one student does not change, then the supervisor might have a meeting with the student or your whole team. This meeting often leads to yet another chance for a behavior change. Finally, the situation has two potential endings:

1 Your supervisor divides your group into two new groups, where the problematic student constitutes their own group. Both new groups own all the material you have completed and worked on prior to the date of separation, so make sure that both new groups have copies of all this material.

2 In less common cases, your supervisor might consider that the behavior you require from all members in your team is above and beyond the formal number of work hours required in the project course. In these cases, your supervisor might act as a mediator to find a reasonable balance between the two different perceptions of the right behavior in your group.

If you involve your supervisor late in the project process, the result is usually that you must stick together for the remainder of the project course. A supervisor almost never separates groups two or three weeks prior to the hand-in deadline. The only exceptions are violence, threats of violence, and other extreme cases that may involve people above your supervisor's pay grade in the university's hierarchy.

It is worth noting that an oral project exam often results in differing grades between group members. It may be that your report only serves as the foundation for the exam, and that your oral performance at the exam is what really counts for your grade. Ask your supervisor how different student performances during the exam impact individual team member grades. Project reports that explicitly state which students wrote which individual sections are a rarity in engineering because the art of writing is less important than technical skills.

The following sections detail a number of teamwork pitfalls and provide advice for handling them.

Differences in team member effort and commitment

Discuss the problem of differences in team member effort and commitment and what you expect from one another. Describe as explicitly as possible the minimum amount of work effort that is required to leave ambitious team members satisfied and enable your group to function without frustration.

If one team member consistently makes less of an effort than the rest of the group, involve your supervisor, who will talk to all parties. If your supervisor finds the team member's effort has been above the minimal expectation for passing the course, then the supervisor might tell you to solve the problem within your team. One option is to organize yourself differently. For example, have the team member making a lesser but still acceptable effort conduct a set of limited and specified tasks with short deadlines (one by one).

If your supervisor finds the team member's effort below the minimal expectation for passing the course, then your supervisor will require more effort and give the student a chance to follow through. The student often makes many promises, and if these promises are kept, the problem is solved. If not, then the supervisor is likely to separate the student from the rest the group.

Differences in the perception of the project's objectives and direction

The problem of differences in the perception of the project's objectives and direction is usually a matter of discussion. If you cannot come to an agreement, then involve your supervisor. Your supervisor often gladly participates in these discussions. Usually, the problem is solved then and there because your supervisor has an opinion (and probably has had the discussion several times in the past).

A risk is that individual group members interpret your supervisor's statements as arguments for *their* view on the matter. For example, person A has perception X and person B has perception Y. Person A listens to the supervisor's statements and remembers word for word those statements supporting perception X. Person B also listens to the supervisor's statements and remembers word for word those statements supporting perception Y. This situation might require another meeting or perhaps a quick visit by A and B to the supervisor's office. If your supervisor is the kind of person who really values the discussion rather than the outcome, you might get the (really annoying) answer: "That is a great question. By all means, keep the discussion going and please let me know what you ended up deciding."

In more extreme cases, a person or a faction of your group may not accept a compromise or a majority ruling. This may result in supervisor involvement and separation of your group into two new groups with two separate objectives. Although this means more work for your supervisor, the learning outcome of such a split might be better than keeping your group together. Two small but determined groups might lead to better learning outcomes than one group stuck in everlasting discussion.

Difference in team member skill sets

In principle, differences in team member skill sets should not be a problem. One of the higher purposes of project work is having the smarter students help the less smart. This way, all students learn.

If you still perceive skills-related differences as a problem, then organize your way out of the problem. Make the less smart student act as a "supplier" to a smarter student. Then, the smarter student can check the quality of the contributions and make revisions if necessary.

A supervisor only rarely allows skill-related differences to cause a division in the group. Instead, the supervisor might encourage you to help the weaker students to complete the project course. Remember, explaining a complex subject to a teammate aids your own understanding of the subject and trains your ability to discuss the subject at your own exam. Some courses have project teams write smaller reports about their process. Handling the problem of differences in skill sets might well give you points for a better grade.

Differences in skill sets between group members is, as with so many other differences, a condition for your group. Do not consider it a problem, but a challenge from which you will learn. Be happy about these opportunities for personal development.

Major conflicts

Major conflicts that push project teams back to the beginning are luckily a rare occurrence. Imagine a situation where no members can work together, members insult each other, and the rare group meetings lead nowhere. That such a group sticks together past the current project course is highly doubtful, but the group still needs to pass the current course. The good news is that even these seemingly hopeless cases can be saved. Saving the group requires building up trust and psychological safety from scratch.

An effective method is having two-person conversations. Bob speaks with Bill, Jenny speaks with Jill, and James speaks with Phil. Such conversations often lead to mutual understanding rather than mud-throwing. The first conversations might revolve around slandering; however, they often develop into more constructive talks. Individual group members begin to understand one another, including the motivations behind group member actions. With a bit of luck, these two-person conversations lead to a set of requirements for continuing the group project. After half an hour, change the combinations and repeat the half-hour conversation in a new two-person pairing. After the second and perhaps a third round of conversations, the group gathers as the full team. From here, you might be able to see the light at the end of the tunnel and begin working towards completing your project report.

The supervisor is often involved in the process, but the key to building trust and psychological safety begins with the two-person conversations.

International students in project groups

Universities usually offer exchange programs, which provide you with great opportunities for gaining international experience. You may find yourself as the one international student in a project team or have an international student in your team.

Having cultural differences play into your group dynamics in addition to personal differences can complicate things and you should read this chapter even more carefully.

TOP TIPS

- Recognize that misunderstandings often arise due to cultural differences and differences in project work practices, and be prepared to address potential issues openly with your team.
- In some countries, students are expected to be the main drivers and leaders of their own work. In other countries, students rely on supervisors and instructors for weekly tasks.
- Discussions around a group contract and a project plan can be very fruitful for bringing problems caused by cultural differences to the surface.
- If you are an international student in a project group, then utilize your team members' knowledge about local project work practices.

Supervision

The first step in supervision is choosing a supervisor. You might not always have the opportunity to choose, but late in your engineering education (certainly for your final project), you are usually able to submit a request for a specific professor. The right supervisor usually teaches the class that covers the subject you want to work with. If you have several professors to choose from, then think about the professor's practical availability and whether you communicate well. If you have a professor with the right skills but little time, then consider a different supervisor. However, do book a meeting with the original professor to pick their brain for your project. With most fields, the whole faculty is at your disposal for short meetings.

Supervision is important early in your project period, when you set the direction. Your supervisor can help you decode the situation of your industrial partner and help you develop a problem statement that fills the academic requirements and satisfies your industrial partner. See Chapter 3 for guidance about problem statements.

At your first supervisor meeting, your supervisor will try mentally to "map the landscape" to identify a proper problem for your project to address. The landscape consists of:

- the type of industrial partner you will work with
- the broader theme of your project
- any specific wishes that your industrial partner has for your project.

A typical situation is that your industrial partner has a wish for either a specific solution or a wish for you to optimize something without specifying exactly what they want improved. For example, a firm might want a new type of component designed or have you optimize a material or product flow.

Your supervisor will ask questions about the purpose of any optimization. If you want to optimize a product flow, the goal might be reduced costs, higher capacity, quicker delivery, or a fourth distinct goal. If you want to redesign a component, the goal might be to reduce production costs, improve durability, increase strength, or improve another component function. These questions need (preferably quick) answers and they are prime candidates for the agenda of your first supervision meeting.

During your project, supervision often occurs through supervision meetings or written feedback on text pieces. How large a text piece a supervisor will comment on varies among courses. For texts of any length, accompany the text with a set of specific questions. Without these questions, your supervisor may not touch upon the issues you need feedback about. Avoid broad questions such as: "Can you check if we have missed something?" or "Does this make sense?" Friendly or inexperienced supervisors might answer such questions, but whether the text makes sense depends completely on your remaining project. So, make sure to guide your supervisor's feedback with specific questions.

Inside information: your supervisor only sees the texts you send, and therefore provides feedback based on what they *think* your overall project concerns. For this reason, the feedback you receive might appear random to you as authors.

Good subjects for supervisor discussions

Topics commonly discussed at supervision meetings are problem analysis, problem statement, selection of literature and methods, data collection and analysis, and solution design. These subjects must be coherent. If your problem statement and analysis are incoherent, you might hear your supervisor talking about "apples and oranges." The goal is having just apples or just oranges. Typical questions for supervisor meetings are as follows:

- What is the problem that the project will address?
- How do we argue for the choice of problem?
- How do we use literature or theory in our project and where do we find this literature?
- How do we argue for our choice of methods?
- How do we ensure a necessary amount of data? What do we do if we lack data?
- Which tools can we use to analyze data?
- When do we know that our analysis and solution fit together?
- How do we know whether our solution will solve the problem?
- How can we assess the financial feasibility of the solution?
- What do you expect from an implementation plan?

These questions are or should be supervision meeting classics. In addition to these questions, supervisors help to answer practical questions concerning the exam, page numbers, how and to whom to hand in the report, and whether to hand in one large report or separate the main report from appendices.

Critical reflection about supervisor ideas and suggestions

A common misunderstanding is that a supervisor can approve sections of your project, such as the problem statement. Your supervisor cannot and should not formally approve any sections of your project during the project. A formal approval would mean that your supervisor cannot hold you accountable for the approved sections, question those sections at the exam, and include them when grading your project.

You might have experienced a supervisor nodding at your problem statement saying: "Yeah, that works fine." This statement is not a formal approval. Keep in mind your supervisor's limited knowledge of your project. Once you hand in your report, a problem statement that made sense in itself two months ago might not fit at all with the finished report (a classic reason is that a project has taken a turn here and there without problem statement updates). Formal student complaints often read: "Our supervisor criticized a section at our exam that they had approved earlier" and "We had important sections criticized. But our supervisor could have just told us about the shortcomings during supervision." It is important to understand that the report (all sections included) is the responsibility of the student team. Your supervisor has neither responsibility nor *co*-responsibility.

A good supervisor can make suggestions during supervision sessions and criticize the very same suggestions at the exam because a supervisor does not have intimate knowledge about your whole project. Think back and you might recall how your supervisor always asked the same question 5–10 minutes into *every* meeting: "Remind me again, what was your problem statement?" Note that you will experience these seemingly sudden memory lapses from your future bosses as well. Make a rule of giving your supervisor "the big picture" every time you tell your boss about the latest developments in your work.

Your supervisor only meets your project sporadically during the project period and "shoots from the hip" when giving advice. Because your supervisor has ample experience, these remarks usually hit the target, but that is not a given. During and after meetings, your job is to reflect critically on your supervisor's ideas and suggestions. Make sure to assess any idea's relevance and quality with respect to your project.

When your supervisor morphs into an examiner

Once you have handed in your project, your supervisor first turns into a random lecturer. A few weeks later your supervisor turns into your examiner. In other words, when you have handed in your report, your supervisor is not your supervisor anymore. This does not prohibit you from asking questions about your exam, but keep your questions general and ideally only about practicalities. For example: "How long should our group presentation be?"

Reviewing this chapter's objectives

Tick those objectives you feel you have achieved, and review those you haven't yet accomplished. In this chapter, you have learned how to:

❏ Deal with the dynamics in group formation processes, including how your first year effort and commitment impact your options in later group formation processes.

❏ Develop a group collaboration contract that supports commitment, effort, presence, and communication quality within your team.

❏ Prevent conflicts through active use of your group collaboration contract and ensure effective group meetings.

❏ Increase psychological safety and trust among the members of your team.

❏ Make the best use of your supervisor.

Cooperating with Industrial Partners

In this chapter, you will learn:

1 How to identify an industrial partner that fits your project.
2 How to "sell" your project to a potential industrial partner.
3 The nature of the first phase of your cooperation including reaching a problem statement.
4 Identifying and setting up meetings with all the relevant actors within or outside your industrial partner organization.
5 The nature of continuous cooperation throughout the project process, including how to collect data in a timely fashion and ensure the availability of all the relevant actors you want to involve in your project.
6 How being physically present and having continuous talks with industrial partner staff contributes to great cooperation.
7 About the pitfalls of industrial partner cooperation, including the perils of an overly engaged department head, a seemingly sudden loss of industrial partner interest in your project, and how your industrial partner may want to include more and more subjects into your project even though you have agreed about your problem statement months ago.

It is important to ensure the best possible basis for cooperation with your industrial partner. Great cooperation is a cornerstone for developing a solution that both you and your industrial partner are happy about. The first task is to identify the right industrial partner for your project. In the later stages of your degree, you and all your classmates have a personal network to draw upon when searching for an industrial partner. Often, an industrial partner is a firm where you or a classmate have been interns.

However, earlier in your degree, you might have to identify a potential industrial partner and make the first contact. Finding a potential industrial partner is easy in principle: you just do an internet search for relevant firms. More difficult is identifying those actors within a potential industrial partner organization who can decide whether to engage with you in your project and thereafter act as your contact. You can meet these individuals directly, meet their colleagues who can refer you to them, meet them at trade fairs or exhibitions, union meetings and seminars, at alumni events, professional network meetings, and at seminars arranged by industry organizations.

How to "sell" your project to an industrial partner

You need to find an industrial partner that is willing to commit at least some resources to your project. The firm needs to see the benefits of engaging in your project. Ideally, when contacting potential industrial partners, you need to know which topic the firm will be interested in. This is difficult without having either insider knowledge or reading something about the firm in the media (e.g. an industry magazine). The two steps in selling your project are:

1 Increase your knowledge about a number of potential industrial partners.
2 Using this knowledge, draft suggestions for potential project topics.

Increase your knowledge through internet searches including industry media outlets, by attending trade fairs, exhibitions, and union meetings, and then draft some suggestions. A classic problem when drafting suggestions is finding the right balance of specificity. Industrial partners usually like student teams that know what they want. Then the industrial partner can easily assess whether they want to engage in the project. So, do not aim too widely in your suggestions: "We are interested in anything within mechanical engineering as long as you want to cooperate with us." On the other hand, by being too specific, you risk missing a topic that the firm might be interested in. So, avoid very specific suggestions such as: "We want to work with 3D printing of items made of the EN AW 2007 alloy."

An effective strategy is suggesting two or three topics and including the three words – "or related topics." This way you are really suggesting many potential topics and aid the thought process of your recipient. Ideally, your recipient will think: "Hmm … well … Oh, Susan is working on (topic). The students might be able to help her with that."

The introductory phase of your industrial partner cooperation

This section deals with your first industrial partner meetings and describes how you can ensure the best possible foundation for your cooperation throughout the project period. The very first meeting, when you sit across the table from your industrial partner contact, usually concerns your project topic and limiting your project scope within that topic. Prior to the meeting, you have probably had an email dialogue. The purpose of this first meeting is to discuss your project's scope and map the problem landscape for your problem analysis. In addition, the meeting often concerns the practicalities of your cooperation (e.g. will you have an office in your industrial partner's building, a computer, and access to relevant employees and perhaps suppliers or customers?).

In addition to these tangible issues, the meeting has a few implicit goals. You get to meet each other for the first time, establish trust, and test the "chemistry" between you. It is important that your industrial partner contact understands how your project contributes to the firm because this very contribution is your contact's argument for committing their own and their colleagues' time to your project.

Following your first industrial partner meeting, you check in with your supervisor. Your supervisor will immediately seek to understand your problem landscape and might even suggest possible problems to address. Supervisors usually meet highly motivated students who are happy with their industrial partner involvement and ready to throw themselves at a problem. This level of motivation is a fantastic driver for getting things done. In this phase, be careful about setting the right direction for your project.

At this early point, your problem statement is naturally vague and unclear. An early draft of a problem statement might be "to optimize a material flow" or "to improve the quality of a product." Your supervisor will challenge you on specificity and focus. Your supervisor might ask which specific variable you want to improve when optimizing a material flow (do you want to reduce costs, increase speed, or reduce inventory levels?).

Between meetings, you work on your problem analysis and specifying your problem statement. At the following meeting with your industrial partner, one agenda point is getting your industrial partner to approve the specified problem statement. You should expect your industrial partner to want to influence your problem statement. They often want you to include new issues ("could you also include X and Y?"). Including new issues usually counters the notion of a focused problem statement, so think critically about whether you should indeed broaden your problem statement. One solution is to find an overarching problem that covers the issues you want to address *and* the issues your industrial partner wants addressed.

The good news is that these first meetings with your industrial partner often end with big smiles and lots of expectations for a great solution ("This project is going be great!"). This great atmosphere goes on for a few weeks. It is the "honeymoon" period of your industrial partner cooperation. After these first few weeks, you may find their interest dwindling. For this reason, act early. Lock down employees for meetings weeks and months in advance. Make sure to gain direct bilateral access to all relevant actors within the first few weeks. Make an effort to unfold the circle of relevant people as soon as possible and ask for contact details for all potentially relevant contacts (see Figure 10.1). Your contact should have the opportunity to forewarn their colleagues, but other than that, ensure (explicitly) that you are allowed to make direct contact with others without your contact acting as "middleman" for all communication.

EXAMPLE: UNFOLDING THE CIRCLE OF RELEVANT PEOPLE

Two mechanical engineering students have had an email dialogue with a manufacturer of mixer taps for bathrooms and kitchens. The mixer taps are surface treated with a zinc coating to resist corrosion. However, too many mixer taps have uneven, spotted surfaces when returning from the surface treatment supplier (who is the best in the business). The two students will address this problem.

During their first meeting, the students discuss the problem with the firm's chief product designer, who is the students' contact. They juggle different ideas for solving the problem. During the second meeting, the two students unfold the circle of relevant actors by asking repeatedly about potentially relevant people, departments, and other organizations that might have a stake or an interest in the project.

Together with the chief product designer, the two students develop a list of relevant actors within and outside the industrial partner's organization. They include the firm's production manager, the team leader in the mixer tap production department, the firm's quality manager, and staff from marketing and sales, who are familiar with customer preferences and taste. Among the external entities are bathroom installation consultants, the surface treatment supplier, the mixer tap material supplier, and the public organization that regulates safety in piping installations.

During this meeting, the students receive the contact details of all these people, departments, and organizations. The chief product designer promises to contact those on the list they know.

Earlier chapters described the interactions between a project group and an industrial partner as a meeting between *two* parties. The example above shows that that the circle of relevant persons, departments, and external organizations consists of many entities both within and outside the industrial partner organization (see Figure 10.1). The students involve other departments, suppliers, and public authorities.

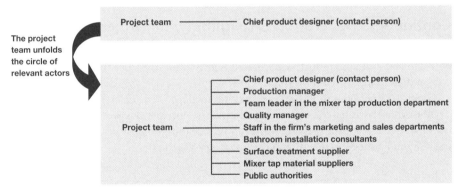

Figure 10.1   Unfolding the circle of relevant actors

Unfolding the circle of actors is often easiest during the first meetings, where your industrial partner's interest in your project is at its highest (the honeymoon period).

Problem statement agreement

After two or three meetings, all parties (you, your industrial partner, and your supervisor) have an interest in agreeing on a problem statement. During the period when these first few meetings occur, you are fully engaged in your problem analysis (see Chapter 2 for specific problem analysis tools and advice).

Chapter 3 describes how a project can improve an existing entity or design a new entity. If your project improves an existing entity, then your discussions with your industrial partner as well as your supervisor should revolve around identifying that one variable that your project will improve (e.g. durability, speed, cost price, performance on a function, etc.). These two questions can help you focus your industrial partner discussions:

1 Which one variable is the problem?
2 Under which limits should the project improve the performance on the variable?

These questions sound simple and straightforward, but identifying that one variable can be quite a complex task.

For projects that design a new entity, the task differs. For these projects, the aim is a detailed and precise description of the *solution need*. The solution that fills this need could be a machine, a building, a software program, a procedure, or chemical process. In your industrial partner discussions, the important questions to ask are:

1 What is the basic need that the solution will fill?
2 Who has the need and who will be the future users of the solution?
3 How and for what purpose will the solution be used?
4 Which known requirements do users and other parties have for the solution?

Often, it is not possible at this early stage of the project to answer these questions fully. Dealing with these questions is the objective of your later analysis. However, the dialogue about these questions does help focus your industrial partner discussions.

Continuous cooperation throughout your project period

The agreement on your problem statement is one of the important interactions between you and your industrial partner. It is important to ensure the most effective cooperation going forward from this agreement.

Figure 10.2 shows a series of important interactions for a project – the "red letter days" of your industrial partner cooperation. Seven interactions are shown, starting with two or three industrial partner meetings, including the first meet and greet meeting and a meeting for settling on a problem statement.

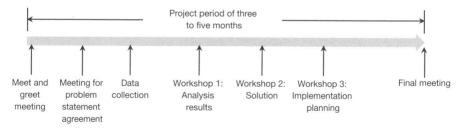

Figure 10.2   The most important industrial partner interactions

A project usually lasts one semester, that is, three–five months from the first day to the submission deadline. After the first four–six weeks, you will have scoped your project, formulated a problem statement, read the relevant literature, and worked on your methodology for data collection and analysis. At this point, your data collection begins, followed by analysis, solution design, and planning the solution's implementation.

Data collection and the three workshops are described below. Workshops are meetings of one–two hours with two or more industrial partner employees. The key purpose of workshops is the continuous involvement of industrial partner employees. Continuous involvement results in "reality checks" of your work and industrial partner ownership of your solution. The goal of successful projects is that solutions are actually implemented and industrial partner ownership will increase implementation chances.

Data collection

Around four–six weeks into the project, your project has advanced to the data collection stage. This usually begins with one large round of data collection followed by a series of rounds collecting smaller but more targeted datasets. The first round of data collection is the first time you will need a real effort from your industrial partner employees. See a later section for advice on how to ensure employees' availability and help.

Workshop 1: analysis results

Once you have collected the first round of data, your analysis begins and you will generate analysis results. Once the analysis results are clear, you should involve industrial partner employees to ensure the validity of these results. In addition to involving industrial partner employees to increase ownership, ensuring the validity of the analysis result is the purpose of workshop 1. For example, a group of civil engineering students have found two distinct causes of cracks in a building wall. The team involves industrial partner employees through a workshop to ensure that the two causes of wall cracks are in fact the real causes. If all workshop participants agree, then you are ready to continue to solution design.

Workshop 2: solution(s)

When you have developed a rough-cut solution or perhaps two or three alternative solutions, involve industrial partner employees once again. This time the purpose is to reach an agreement that the solution will in fact solve the problem. If you have developed several alternative solutions (as in the either/or solution) or a series of potential solutions elements (as in the multiple elements solution), this workshop is a great opportunity for making decisions about which solution or solution element to select.

Workshop 3: implementation planning

When you have reached agreement about your solution(s) and then appropriately specified the selected solutions, the next step is planning the implementation of your solution. Planning the implementation is the next possibility for involving your industrial partner. Prior to the workshop, develop a rough-cut suggestion for an implementation plan as a basis for your workshop discussions. See Chapter 7 for implementation plan details.

The final interaction with your industrial partner is a meeting where you (ideally) discuss how to execute the implementation of your solution. A later section describes this meeting.

Ensuring timely data collection and industrial partner employee availability

Data collection is often the activity that requires most time from your industrial partner employees. All too often, project teams wait days and weeks for data. Occasionally, these data collection wait times impact the grade of a project because the time for analysis gets squeezed.

Industrial partner employees continuously prioritize how to spend their time. This includes which emails to answer immediately and which to save to a later date. Emails from students are often of low importance. This is particularly the case if the employee is not involved in your project.

The most effective guard against long data wait times is *presence* in the minds of your industrial partner employees. Ideally, be physically present daily in your industrial partner's site (depending on your engineering discipline, a "site" could be your industrial partner's office buildings, laboratories, production floor, construction site, etc.). Make yourselves known to your data sources. Have lunch with your data sources or stop by their offices from time to time to ask quick questions.

This ideal situation of being physically present on a daily basis might only be realistic in your final project. Without daily presence, plan for your data collection well in advance. If industrial partner employees know well in advance that you will request reports, ask for a tour of the plant, or conduct a workshop or milestone meeting, your chances of success are greater. Once you have developed the first draft of your project plan (e.g. a Gantt chart containing all activities), book the relevant employees in their calendars through electronic calendar appointments. A tip is to book employees immediately following your project's introductory meetings, when you are still in the cooperation honeymoon period. Three weeks after this, the relevant employees, who are busy people, may only reluctantly prioritize their time for your project.

Obviously, much is unclear at the beginning of your project and you might consider booking people in their calendar as premature. However, an important principle is that cancelling a meeting is much easier than booking a meeting at short notice. At your first or second meeting, lay out your data collection wish list for your contact. They can then evaluate what is possible. For example, explain that you would like to book:

- five or six interviews within three or four weeks
- a set of data dumps within four or five weeks
- two or three employees for three workshops for analysis, solution, and implementation
- two or three managers for a midterm meeting following the analysis workshop.

If you successfully book all these meetings, your chances of long data wait times and unavailable employees are greatly diminished. In addition, these booked meetings function well as milestones in your own project plan. The booked meetings are your incentives to complete your activities on time.

Your most important calendar bookings are the workshops where you need more than one employee. To book two employees plus a department head is often not possible one week in advance. Often, students are uncomfortable booking industrial partner employees without knowing exactly what the meeting will concern. These are laudable thoughts that show respect for the time of your industrial partner's employees. However, if you are not ready for a meeting, then just cancel or postpone. Cancelling or postponing a meeting is a completely natural and unproblematic practice, which industrial partner employees are used to. In fact, having a meeting cancelled means having an hour of two of extra time. Most employees would see this an unexpected gift. Cancelling meetings is only a problem if it becomes a trend, and your project is not there long enough for that to happen.

When you book industrial partner employees in their calendars, use a meeting headline such as "Workshop" or "Milestone meeting" and write that a specific agenda will follow. Such bookings are common practice if they occur a month in advance. Remember to book those employees who need time to collect data on your behalf, even if it is only half an hour to extract a data dump from the firm's IT system. Write to the employee that you are taking the liberty to book half an hour to ensure time to discuss the data you need. If, when the time comes, you are able to describe your data specifically, then the industrial partner employee has half an hour to extract the data.

For semester projects, where you work at the university's site, Figure 10.2 provides a framework for planning your interactions with your industrial partner. Even for final projects where you are present daily at your industrial partner's site, it might be necessary to book meetings with two or more people well in advance. Remember that even with the best intentions of your industrial partner, your project is an activity for which the firm has not prioritized its own employees, but instead uses students. This gives an indication of the firm's prioritization of your project.

Ensuring workshop success and preventing problems

The workshops and milestone meetings where you present your work to your industrial partner usually create extra work for you. The industrial partner employees naturally have greater insights into the workings of their own processes, products, technologies, and so on. For this reason, you should include time in your project plan for conducting the extra work following each workshop.

You can do quite a bit to prevent a large amount of extra work by hitting the target the first time around. The most effective method is continuously sharing information with the workshop participants prior to the workshop. For example, "randomly" run into relevant people in the elevator or at lunch, and give them a status update of your work. Fully informed industrial partner employees will quickly accept your work and perhaps be a bit bored at the workshop.

Ending your industrial partner cooperation

You report to your university by writing a report. Supervisors are often asked by students how to report project recommendations to the industrial partner. Asking about how to report to an industrial partner indicates a bit of a misunderstanding. Remember, great projects do not simply summarize solutions; they make sure their industrial partner implements the solution and (in time) reaps the benefits.

As the Introduction of this book describes, engineering projects do not conduct research that investigates unanswered questions. Engineering projects design solutions to problems. The objective for these solutions is actual implementation. You should work actively with implementation planning. Ideally, your final meeting with your industrial partner concerns discussions about implementation execution.

A (newly formed) project organization within the firm will execute the implementation and your final meeting is where you officially hand the baton to the newly appointed project manager. The meeting represents the culmination of your work. Perhaps the most telling indicator for whether your project is a success is whether the industrial partner employees and managers who you have booked for the final meeting accept your meeting invitation.

The possible pitfalls in industrial partner cooperation

There are a number of possible pitfalls in industrial partner cooperation. These pitfalls are described below, as well as advice on how to avoid them or how to handle them if they have already happened.

Your industrial partner loses interest

A common problem is a quick loss of interest from your industrial partner. The first sign of this problem is long waits for email answers. The most effective method for avoiding the problem is keeping the interest level high from the first days of your cooperation. Keep the dialogue with your industrial partner running. Avoid long breaks where you do not communicate. In periods without meetings, write at least one email per week. If you do not need anything, then give your industrial partner updates on your work. Remind your industrial partner of the benefits of your cooperation and how soon they will materialize.

For projects where you are physically present in your industrial partner's building, make sure the relevant people know you. If those who are relevant for your project know you well, then they will likely keep helping you, if not for the project then for you personally.

Contact denies you access to the rest of their firm

Having direct, bilateral access to your contact's colleagues and perhaps suppliers, customers, and regulating authorities is key to conducting a good project.

If your contact has initiated the project, it may come as a surprise that you want to interview several of their colleagues across several departments. Such a situation might be uncomfortable for a contact because they suddenly need to justify spending their own time and their colleagues' time on your project. Suddenly, your contact needs to "sell" your project. You risk your contact wanting to avoid that situation. You will find out when your contact:

- insists on collecting all the data without involving colleagues
- will not allow you to interview colleagues and insists that they know everything you need to know
- insists that there is "no need at all" to involve suppliers, customers, or other external organizations.

If you find yourself in this situation, you have three options:

1 Accept the conditions, use the information you do get, and work with a set of assumptions that replace information you cannot access.
2 Convince your contact and later your contact's boss that your project is worth spending time on.
3 Jump ship and find a different project.

Remember to consult with your supervisor. A version of option 1 is often the result and replacing inaccessible data with reasonable assumptions is a viable path, albeit not ideal. A practical method for operating within option 1 is writing up a list with all your information needs and asking your contact how to access the data. You might be lucky that your contact allows for one or two interviews with their close colleagues. If your contact keeps insisting, "I can answer all those questions" or "That idea won't work in our organization, I just *know*," then discuss these specific issues with your supervisor. Your supervisor can participate in discussions about reasonable assumptions that can replace data.

Although your supervisor's help increases the quality of your assumptions and thereby your project as a whole, the situation is not ideal. Heavy supervisor involvement will likely increase your grade. However, whether the base is a B or an F depends entirely on the overall quality of your project.

In your final report, remember to describe your original plan for your industrial partner cooperation, and why you could not execute this plan. Blame your industrial partner if your industrial partner is to blame. Do not protect your contact and remember that your examiners are the target audience of your report, not your industrial partner.

Avoid the pitfall altogether by explicitly discussing the conditions for the project with your *potential* contact. Make sure that your potential contact understands the conditions under which you expect to work. If in doubt about whether the lines are clear, look directly at your potential contact and ask: "Will you allow us to interview your boss for the project?" Asking this question should clarify the situation.

Overly engaged department heads

With respect to your industrial partner, your project is usually anchored in one particular department. This department is often your contact's department. Your contact has a boss, who may have signed off on engaging in your project.

Bosses are usually smart, skilled and successful. That is often why they have been promoted and are the boss. Bosses are used to contributing to all the activities around them with ideas, feedback, help, and decisions. Bosses are used to acting with vigor and expect their influence to matter. These are great assets for the firm that employs them and for you as a project team it is fantastic to have bosses who are willing to help you.

However, a pitfall in industrial partner cooperation is having a department head who wants to turn your project's focus in a new direction mid-project. The new focus may be more relevant for the department, but less fortunate for your team because making big changes mid-project means wasting a lot of work and the new direction may decrease your project's academic qualities.

It might be difficult to resist making changes and given that the boss is your contact's boss, your contact may be of little help. This pitfall is particularly deep if the department head is inexperienced with university projects, and therefore unfamiliar with the requirements of academic projects.

Prevent this problem by making a big deal out of the meeting where you lock in the problem statement, mention this particular meeting from time to time and refer to the meeting, as "the meeting were we locked down the problem statement." In addition, channel the boss's contribution wish into a direction that is useful for you. Remember, a student project is not a boss's first priority. If your project were pivotal to the future of the department, then the boss would have given the task to his best employees or a team of expensive consultants.

An overly engaged boss usually just wants to help you and considers their help as a positive contribution that will help you get a better grade. This may be the case even though the "help" is making trouble for your project. Think ahead about how you channel the boss's contribution to your benefit. One way is using the boss as a source of knowledge. Simply, ask lots of questions.

If you are in real trouble, then invoke your supervisor as "the bad cop," and therefore your common enemy. Discuss the matter with the overly engaged boss and argue as follows: "Our supervisor will only accept a project with one focus" or "Our supervisor tells us that the idea falls outside the scope of our project."

The industrial partner wants breadth and the university wants focus

A classic schism in engineering projects is breadth versus focus. In industry, a project may be a collection of vaguely related tasks. Therefore, a new task that relates to a project's other tasks will be the project manager's headache ("Give that task to Brian, he heads the quality project"). An education project has one focus and does not add new random subjects to the project.

At the beginning of a semester, your goal is to find an industrial partner who is willing to commit their resources to your project. Naturally, you are inclined to nod and say "Absolutely" when the firm details its wishes for the project. Later, your supervisor enters with the academic requirements and you face the task of reconciling an industrial partner's wish list with a set of academic requirements.

EXAMPLE: DIALOGUE BETWEEN PROJECT TEAM, INDUSTRIAL PARTNER, AND SUPERVISOR

Imagine a project about the redesign of a handheld temperature and moisture measuring instrument. The project team's contact is the sales manager for Belgium, the Netherlands, and Luxembourg.

The team's contact wants to improve the ergonomics of the instrument to increase the time before a user feels uncomfortable using the instrument. The problem statement therefore concerns the "use length prior to feeling uncomfortable (measured in minutes, e.g. 126 minutes)."

The following describes a dialogue between the project team, the head of the sales department (your contact's boss), a few colleagues, and the team's supervisor.

The project team tell the department head about their project, redesigning the handheld temperature and moisture measuring instrument.

The department head replies:

> OK, interesting. Could you also have a look the instrument's weight? A weight reduction might mean saved material costs. Also, I'd like you to discuss the instrument with Robert and Sara from marketing. They have a great plan for entering the German market with this instrument. ROBEEERT … [Robert comes running down the hallway.] Hi Robert, can you tell these students about your plans for Germany? [the department head leaves the room]

Robert replies: "Err, yeah … what were you working with?"

The project team tells Robert about their project.

Robert replies:

> Great project! … What I think the core issue with this problem is that the Germans want strength and corrosion protection so the instrument can be used for lengthy periods on ships and oil drilling platforms. Can you include these issues in your project? I really think you can make a difference with this project. I must run …

The project team reply: "OK, so we'll look at the weight, the material cost, the strength, and the corrosion issue … Right?"

Three days later, the team tells their story to their supervisor. Their supervisor responds:

> It's perfect that you have access and a genuine interest from all persons and departments. However, didn't you say last week that the problem was the use time before users get uncomfortable? Remember, when you improve an existing entity, your problem should be one variable. Is the variable going be use length, material costs, weight, strength, or the ability to withstand corrosion?

The students don't really know what to say.

Chapter 3 details problem statements in engineering projects.

The situation in the example above is not easy to deal with. One solution is focusing on one problem (e.g. use length) in the project, but report back to the firm with your knowledge about the other issues. Tip: wait until you hand in your report, so you are not stuck with an annoyed department head at a time when you are still depending on the firm for data and employee availability. Alternatively, consider your project not as improving an existing entity, but as designing a new instrument from scratch. Assemble all the wishes the firm has for the instrument and write a design requirement specification. See Chapter 5 for the specific steps in projects that design a new entity.

To examiners, a project that wants to improve an entity on several variables simultaneously will confuse and appear incoherent. So, avoid making everyone at your industrial partner happy at the expense of the focus in your project.

Figure 10.3 illustrates the general rule for an industrial partner's influence over a project. The X-axis is time and the Y-axis shows influence. Figure 10.3 shows how the industrial partner's influence is high to begin with when the project is scoped, but the influence decreases sharply thereafter. During the later parts of your project, the industrial partner's influence is close to nonexistent. Do not allow large changes mid-project. Think of your project as a building. Once the foundation is done, it is too late to make further changes.

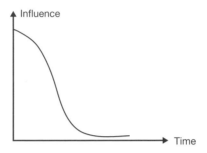

Figure 10.3   Industrial partner influence on a project

Informants with a natural and convincing credibility, passion, or high rank

Some employees and managers have a natural credibility that may make you take their statements as fact without viewing them through your critical mindset's lenses. They could be high-ranking managers, employees with lots of passion for their work, or older, more experienced employees. These informants have a certain vibe, a charisma, that makes you believe their statements instantly. Such informants simply *know*, period.

Generally, having credible informants is tremendous. Your challenge is that these informants might say things you instantly believe without asking for reasons. At your exam, your examiners might ask for reasons and all you can answer is: "But Edwin told us, and he really knows," "Lisa knows this subject well and she is really skilled," or "the sales director supports the suggestion." These answers will not suffice. Remember, engineering projects make decisions based on facts and logic. The personal credibility of informants counts only to a lesser degree.

The industrial partner requires a very restrictive confidentiality agreement

You can experience that an industrial partner (at the last minute) wants you to delete bits and pieces in your report, citing the confidentiality agreement you have signed. If you have signed a restrictive confidentiality agreement, the firm can formally stop you from handing in a report with the bits and pieces they want deleted, and this may turn into a real problem. To prevent this situation, remember two pieces of advice:

1 If you sign a confidentiality agreement (sometimes called a non-disclosure agreement), make sure that the statement includes a passage that explicitly allows you to share information with your supervisor and external examiner. If the firm has a standard form they want you to sign, then write up a piece of paper stating

that your supervisor and external examiner are exempted from the agreement, and have your contact sign it (remember the date). With such an amended agreement, it is more difficult for the firm to stop you from handing in your report (provided that you hand in your report directly to your supervisor). Remember to write "CONFIDENTIAL" on the front page of your report.

2 In many countries, public employees (which includes your supervisor if your university is public) are bound by law not to disclose private companies' secrets. External examiners are often subject to a non-disclosure obligation by virtue of their appointment as external examiners. If both supervisor and external examiner are under public confidentiality agreements, then the firm has covered all bases.

Reviewing this chapter's objectives

Tick those objectives you feel you have achieved, and review those you haven't yet accomplished. In this chapter, you have learned how to:

❐ Identify a potential industrial partner that fits your project.

❐ "Sell" your project to an industrial partner and settle on a problem statement.

❐ Identify and organize meetings with all relevant actors within or outside your industrial partner organization.

❐ Ensure continuous cooperation efforts from your industrial partner throughout the project process.

❐ Avoid the possible pitfalls inherent in industrial partner cooperation.

Managing Stakeholders

In this chapter, you will learn:

1 Who the stakeholders are for engineering projects.

2 How you can analyze stakeholder interests in your project and keep a continuous overview of your project's stakeholder landscape including sources of resistance to your solutions.

3 How to spot stakeholder-related barriers and pockets of resistance against your solutions.

4 How to manage stakeholder interests throughout your project.

5 That a project has different sets of stakeholders in the project period, the implementation period, and when operating solutions.

6 How to handle milestone meetings where your project is subject to direct stakeholder evaluations.

This chapter deals with managing your stakeholders and their interests in your project. It describes how to conduct a stakeholder analysis that provides you with an overview of stakeholders, their power, their relations to other stakeholders, and their interests in your project.

Your key stakeholders

Figure 11.1 shows the classic stakeholder categories for engineering projects. A stakeholder can be a person or a department within your industrial partner's organization, or an organization outside the boundaries of your industrial partner (e.g. a labor union). The most important and often most complex stakeholder is your industrial partner.

Figure 11.1 shows that engineering projects have a whole array of very different stakeholders. The reason that your industrial partner often is your most important stakeholder is due to your dependence on access to data, employee work hours, and in some projects materials and equipment. The number of people you need time with varies from project to project, but you will often need access to several departments. Later sections deal extensively with your industrial partner as a stakeholder.

Figure 11.1 shows several stakeholders outside the boundaries of your industrial partner. Competitors and labor unions are often unaware of your project prior to implementation. Public organizations and authorities have a stake in your project because their job is ensuring solutions that meet public safety requirements,

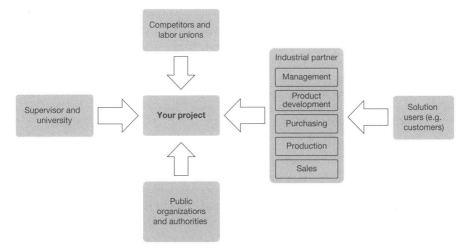

Figure 11.1   The classic stakeholder groups for an engineering project

regulations for the built environment, and so on. Your supervisor and university have the objectives that the project leads to a great learning experience and a passed exam for you and maintaining relationships with industry.

Solution users are key stakeholders in your project

A key stakeholder that you should involve in your project is the group of future solution users. Often future users are employees and managers within your industrial partner organization; for example, a project that improves a production facility's performance. For projects that improve products or design brand new products, users are often your industrial partner's customers. Examples are projects that develop software applications, mechanical components, or buildings.

Understanding user needs and requirements is of paramount importance for developing great solutions. External examiners focus much of their evaluation energy on the relationship between the solution and user needs (regardless of whether a project report states these needs explicitly or not). Perhaps the most universal critique of engineering solutions is that engineers develop products, processes, and systems with exciting and technically challenging functions that no one needs. The critique is a sore point for the engineering field in general, and therefore the inclusion and understanding of user needs is a theme that is often discussed at project exams.

Your supervisor and university as a stakeholder

The general rule is that your supervisor's and university's interest in your project is limited to ensuring *your* learning experience and a passed exam. There are a few exceptions to this rule. These exceptions most often apply to those projects that are component parts in larger research projects conducted by your university. For other projects earlier in your education, your supervisor and university may have objectives related to the satisfaction of external partners that the university has an interest in keeping as partners.

Most universities have a set of "regulars." These are firms that have internships every semester and hire graduates every year. Your instructors have an interest in keeping their regulars. In addition, your university might wish to extend its set of regulars. If a firm establishes an internship or enters into project cooperation for the first time, your instructors might be interested in making sure the firm is happy to commit resources to the internship or project.

Your industrial partner as a stakeholder

While your university can be a source of annoyance during a project, your industrial partner can be a whole minefield of pitfalls. The minefield metaphor is particularly real for projects that result in tangible consequences with your industrial partners, for individuals, groups, or whole departments. Be aware that your project might be a pawn in a power struggle or political "game" within the organization. You might find it improbable that an engineering project is a pawn in such struggles, but this is frequently the case.

Your contact may well have an agenda that is unfamiliar to you. For example, a group of civil engineering students cooperate with a large contractor, who sells and builds predesigned houses. The group's contact is dissatisfied with the firm's window supplier and asks you to alter their house designs with windows from a different supplier (without telling you the real motivation for the project).

It happens that an informant, mid-interview, realizes that they are able to use your project as leverage in their own agenda if your conclusion happens to match their own objectives. All of a sudden, your informant has "fresh" ideas for your project.

EXAMPLE: BEING A PAWN IN A POWER STRUGGLE

A team of students work with a manufacturer supplying industrial spray dryers to customers in Europe. The team's contact is a sales manager who wants to show upper management how skilled he is by selling products to US customers. The firm's production manager does not want to expand because the firm's production capacity is already stretched thin for the European deliveries. If the firm were to sell additional products to US customers, the production manager would have to establish a high-cost night shift, which would increase average unit costs and therefore decrease the production manager's bonus.

To gain the attention of upper management, the sales manager has engaged two manufacturing engineers in one project and two business engineers in another project. The manufacturing engineers will design a logistics system for US deliveries, while the business engineers will analyze the market size and purchasing power of potential customers in California, Texas, and Florida. These two projects are high risk because if the production manager gets wind of them, he might have enough power to simply shut the two projects down immediately.

The stakeholder analysis

For some projects, it is worthwhile for your team to spend time conducting a stakeholder analysis that provides you with insights into which stakeholders are "friends" of your project and which stakeholders constitute potential barriers for either data collection, employee access, or the later implementation of solutions. Table 11.1 describes how to conduct a stakeholder analysis using a spreadsheet.

Table 11.1   How to conduct a stakeholder analysis

	Step	Description
1	Develop a list of all potential stakeholders for your project (input the list into a spreadsheet column)	Think through the whole project period including the time for implementation and the time for solution operation. Consider both employees and managers, whole departments, and external organizations (suppliers, customers, labor unions, etc.). Include in your list both friendly stakeholders and antagonists (current as well as potential)
2	In the column to the right, briefly describe the stakeholder's interest in your project	Answer the question: What interest does each stakeholder have in your project? Some stakeholders may be unaware of your project, but they still have a potential interest if they learn of your project. Remember, a stakeholder's interest may relate only to the consequences of operating the solution
3	In the next column to the right, assess the stakeholder's power	Assess the stakeholder's power in the organization on a 1–10 scale, where 10 indicates much power and 1 indicates no power whatsoever. If a stakeholder has enough power to singlehandedly boot you out of the firm within minutes, then give the stakeholder an 11 (the numbers become relevant in a later step in the analysis). Power can be based on not only the formal place in the organizational chart, but also on the control of information or top management's agenda, personal knowledge and substitutability, and informal relationships to other powerful persons
4	In the next column to the right, assess the size and direction of the stakeholder's interest	Assess the stakeholder's interest in.your project on a scale from –10 to +10, +10 indicating that the interest is huge and positive (a big "friend" of your project) and –10 indicating that the stakeholder thinks your project is the worst initiative ever taken in the history of the firm
5	In the next column to the right, note any network, alliances, or strong personal relations the stakeholder has	Power and influence increases exponentially when powerful people get together. If three people want to influence a position, their combined power is larger than their individual powers. Therefore, note (if possible) which alliances the stakeholder has, including strong personal relationships
6	In the last column, describe the strategy (if any) you want to use to manage the stakeholder	Do you involve the stakeholder from the first day, do you keep a low profile, and do you keep the person informed? These are potential strategies. Think about whether you should act to ensure a clear path forward for your project. This may be important particularly with powerful stakeholders. A later section provides details of potential strategies

Include in your analysis the period when you conduct your project, the time for implementation execution, and the time for operating solutions. The head of the department where you conduct your project might have complete indifference towards your solutions, but may be very attentive to whether you are using their employees' work hours during your project. Other stakeholders might be indifferent about your work hour usage, but care very much about your solution's consequences for work environment, bonus schemes, and task division. This could be a human resources department, a quality department, or a department for regulatory compliance. Figure 11.2 illustrates the three phases in a project that each have their own sets of stakeholders.

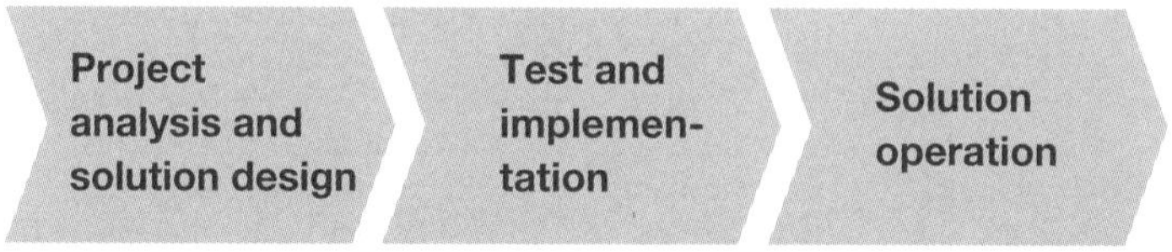

Project analysis and solution design ⟩ Test and implementation ⟩ Solution operation

Figure 11.2 **The three phases of a project that each have their own set of stakeholders**

You can summarize your stakeholder analysis using a diagram illustrated in Figure 11.3. Specifically, you can insert your results from Table 11.1's first five steps (the method is adapted slightly from DeLuca (1984).

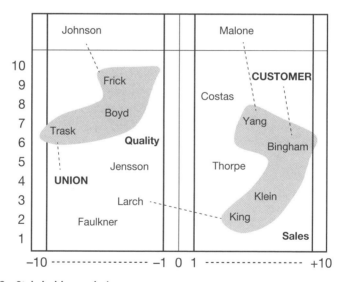

Figure 11.3 **Stakeholder analysis summary**
Source: Adapted from DeLuca, J. (1984) "Managing the sociopolitical context in planned change efforts", in A. Kakabadse and C. Parker (eds) *Power, Politics, and Organizations: A Behavioral Science View*, Chichester: Wiley. Used with permission

Figure 11.3 displays a set of people (e.g. Johnson and Frick), a set of departments (Quality and Sales), and a set of other organizations (CUSTOMER and UNION). These organizations reach into the power structures of your industrial partner. All these people, departments, and organizations are stakeholders in the project. Horizontally, the figure is divided into a left and a right side. The right side displays project friends (e.g. Yang, Thorpe, and Sales) and the left side shows the antagonists (e.g. Trask, Jensson, and

UNION). The analysis places a stakeholder on the horizontal axis following the principle of "the bigger the friend, the further to the right, and the bigger the antagonist, the further to the left." Vertically, Figure 11.3 is divided into a small field at the top and a larger field below. The larger field has a 1–10 scale on the left. The more power a stakeholder has, the higher the stakeholder is placed on the map. If the stakeholder can singlehandedly stop your project, then place the stakeholder in the small upper field. In Figure 11.3, Johnson and Malone are in this smaller field, as they are the stakeholders you gave an 11 in step 3 in Table 11.1.

Figure 11.3 contains two blue areas that include two or more stakeholders (e.g. the field with Yang, Bingham, Klein, and King). These four stakeholders form an alliance of people, who quickly take the same position on any subject. The dotted lines in the figure (e.g. between Johnson and Frick) indicate a strong personal relationship. A stakeholder can exploit such a relationship for their own benefit. Figure 11.3 shows a strong personal relationship between Johnson and Frick, which is of key importance because Frick might be able to use the relationship for his benefit.

The stakeholder analysis, which you can summarize and illustrate with a figure like Figure 11.3, constitutes the foundation for your decisions about whether and how to manage each stakeholder. Whether and how to manage a stakeholder depends on the following factors:

1 Where on the map a stakeholder is located, that is, whether the stakeholder has power and whether the stakeholder is a friend of the project.
2 Whether the stakeholder has strong relationships with powerful actors or is part of an alliance.
3 Which specific interest the stakeholder has in your project.

Managing the risks your stakeholder analysis reveals

A thorough stakeholder analysis enables you to take preventive action when necessary. Consider the early involvement of actors who could become antagonists of your project. If you involve them early, there is a chance they will develop a sense of ownership for your project and become project friends rather than potential show stoppers.

Remember to utilize your own relations with your project's natural friends, so they can help you back up the project and provide the necessary access for you to conduct your activities. Think about how to present information about progress, results, and benefits resulting from your solutions. Often, you will need to "sell" your project to a stakeholder. When you present information, make sure to begin by presenting the advantages of the project to the stakeholder. Do present the whole project, but if you begin with disadvantages pertaining to the stakeholder, they might not really listen for your remaining presentation and instead think and reflect about countering the disadvantages. Prior to the presentation, prepare yourself by getting to know the stakeholder's interest and overall objectives.

A special challenge is dealing with a department head, who might have approved engaging in your project, but fiercely guards the time his employees spend on the project. For this challenge, use the incremental method. Avoid giving the department head a long list of people you want to interview. Just ask for two half-hour interviews; the next week, ask for one more half-hour interview. During your interviews, ask for permission to make telephone calls for follow-up questions. Slowly, but surely, you will get all the information you need. If all else fails, "run in" to people in the hallway or sit with them at lunch.

Particularly critical projects

A stakeholder analysis comes in particularly handy for projects that result in layoffs, changes in work conditions, offshoring positions to other parts of the country or world, ending the sale of particular products, or changing the power balance between two department heads or vice presidents. For such projects, conduct a stakeholder analysis that is as detailed and precise as possible and update the analysis weekly so you keep track of all possible barriers for your project. The weekly updates should include discussions about whether to take preventive actions vis-à-vis one or more stakeholders.

Some projects are, by nature, high risk. These are projects about cost reduction and radical innovation that potentially lead to large and unpredictable change.

Monthly meetings with your contact's boss or (worse) several department heads

The vast majority of student projects create no significant changes in the firm and run their course without any trouble. However, every once in a while, a project is important to a manager and the manager insists on monthly progress meetings. The first piece of advice is to avoid this situation. Working with a project that is of key importance to managers is asking for trouble and extra work. If your industrial partner insists on these monthly meetings, make them as dull as possible by making sure that all participants know everything in advance. A strong success indicator for this strategy is the number of times a manager says: "Could we move things along, please." If you are really successful, the department head will call off the meetings and trust you to conduct a great project without monthly meetings.

Reviewing this chapter's objectives

Tick those objectives you feel you have achieved, and review those you haven't yet accomplished. In this chapter, you have learned how to:

- ❏ Identify the stakeholders for your engineering project.
- ❏ Analyze stakeholder interests in your project and keep a continuous overview of your project's stakeholder landscape.
- ❏ Spot stakeholder-related barriers and pockets of resistance to your solutions.
- ❏ Manage stakeholder interests throughout your project period.
- ❏ Manage milestone meetings where your project is subject to direct stakeholder evaluations.

The Project Report

The Project Report: Structure and Content

> **In this chapter, you will learn:**
>
> 1 Which sections a report typically comprises.
> 2 The content of each of these sections.
> 3 How the ideas and principles from Chapters 2–8 feed into the final project report.
> 4 How to write sections to ensure coherence throughout the report.
> 5 How to ensure clarity and coherence within each section.

This chapter is about your project report and it differs from Parts 1 and 2 by addressing the final result rather than the project *process*. Chapters 2–8 describe the activities of a project and this chapter will refer back to Chapters 2–8 where relevant.

The content of a project report depends on the learning goals and traditions within your engineering discipline. During your early semesters, projects often have predetermined problems, objectives, and methods. These reports follow specified, fixed rules and perhaps forms or templates that you apply directly. The free, independent projects, where you as the project team make decisions about problem and methods, are the focus of this book. This chapter therefore concerns the structure and content of project reports for these projects.

A well-known structure for academic reports is the IMRAD structure, which means Introduction, Methods and materials, Results, And Discussion. This structure works well if the report documents a research study that contributes to your field's body of knowledge by investigating one or more unanswered questions. If you conduct such a research study, see Chapter 16, which describes how to write your report with the IMRAD structure. However, if your project concerns designing a solution to a problem, then stick with this chapter. The IMRAD structure is not sufficient because IMRAD does not contain an S for Solution design, which is the crux of engineering projects. Using the structure outlined in this chapter ensures that you remember all relevant sections in an engineering report that solves a problem.

If your university requires the use of an official standard for project reports, then be sure to adhere to this. An example of a national standard is the British Standard for technical report writing. Your university may have its own standard.

In addition to report headings and structure, these standards describe writing style and how to use tables and figures.

The sections of a project report in engineering

A report in engineering usually consists of sections that follow each other in a logical, natural sequence. These sections vary slightly between engineering disciplines, but usually align well with this list:

1 Front page and project title
2 Abstract or executive summary
3 Introduction
4 Problem statement
5 Delimitations from the problem statement
6 Concept definitions and literature review
7 Methodology
8 Analysis
9 Solution design
10 Solution test
11 Solution implementation
12 Conclusion and recommendations for the industrial partner
13 Perspectives, critical reflections, and discussion of results
14 List of references
15 Appendices and data documentation.

This chapter details each of these sections, beginning with the front page and project title.

Front page and project title

The front page of a report has three general purposes:

1   Align the reader's first impression of the report with the actual report content.
2   Inspire the reader's interest in the report.
3   Communicate practical details about the project (e.g. group number, name of course etc.).

The following sections describe great project titles, front-page illustrations, and how the front page should communicate practical details to make the examiner's job of evaluating the report easier.

Project title

Perhaps the most important words in the entire report are those comprising the report title. The title is your first opportunity to create clarity for the reader about the content of your report. A classic pitfall is having a title that is so broad that the reader only gets a vague impression of the report's content. A tip is to use a title that is a rephrased version of your problem statement.

EXAMPLE: A TITLE THAT EFFECTIVELY COMMUNICATES THE PROJECT CONTENT

A project deals with the reduction of downtime of the injection molding machines that produce plastic items for the (fictitious) firm Worldwide Plastic. Downtime is when machines are not operating due to sudden stops, breakdowns, scheduled maintenance, waiting for material, etc. The title of the project is:

Optimizing plastic component production at Worldwide Plastic

At first sight, this might sound like a fitting title, telling the reader where the project takes place and the theme of optimizing plastic production. However, this title is vague and can mean all kinds of things. Worldwide Plastic's logo is probably on the front page, so naming the firm in the title is redundant. The verb "optimizing" can have many meanings. A title should be much more precise about the specific content of the report. A better title is:

Reduction of downtime of injection molding machines

From this title an experienced reader can immediately deduce the problem statement: "How can Worldwide Plastic reduce the downtime of its injection molding machines?"

Front-page illustrations

In free projects, you usually get to design your front page. Some project teams use generic Word templates as a front page (e.g. a set of lines, squares, or circles). Other project teams use a figure or a photo that directly illustrates something relevant to the project. This book recommends the latter.

Use a figure or photo that illustrates the core of your project. If you design a building, then show the building, and if you design an instrument, then show the instrument (e.g. an illustration or artistic sketch of the instrument). Front-page illustrations serve two of the front page's purposes, aligning the reader's first impressions with project content and inspiring reader interest. Illustrations can be a photo, a diagram, a sketch, and so on. Avoid using your industrial partner's logo as the only front-page illustration: it only tells the reader where you conducted your project, and does not indicate the project content.

Practical information on the front page

Your report's target audience is your supervisor and your external examiner. Your external examiner often evaluates not just your report, but several other reports, perhaps even reports from your whole class. For this reason, make sure to write your group number on your report's front page. If you are handing in a main report, an appendix report, and a set of technical drawings or diagrams, then make sure all documents have the right (and the same) group number.

Imagine an examiner, who has two or three evenings (besides their day job) to evaluate the reports from ten project teams. All teams hand in a main report, an appendix report, and a set of technical drawings. That leaves the examiner with a total of 30 documents. If all documents from the same group have the same group number *and* front-page layout, it is easy for the examiner to make ten piles, each with three documents. If reports have different layouts and the wrong group numbers, then the examiner's first evening is spent matching documents from the same groups, which leaves the examiner with a poor first impression.

Executive Summary or Abstract

The purpose of the abstract or executive summary, which is usually a page in length, is to communicate the key content of your report. Almost all reports require some form of abstract or executive summary. As an engineer, you must be able to communicate the key content of your report to busy managers and colleagues. While the target audience for your whole report is your two examiners, consider the target group for your abstract as:

1   People without the time to read the whole report (e.g. a department head).
2   People who want to assess whether the report is worth reading in its entirety.
3   People who might be interested in your solutions only, and not methods, analysis, and so on.

Academic literature usually begins with an abstract. If the abstract is one page long, then a template for an abstract is as follows:

- *Introduction* and background to the project: 2–4 sentences
- *Problem statement* and perhaps one or two major delimitations: 2–3 sentences
- *Methodology*: 2–4 sentences depending on the field's traditions
- *Analysis findings*: 3–4 sentences
- *Summary* of the solution including a financial feasibility evaluation: 2–4 sentences
- *Conclusions* and recommendations for the industrial partner: 2–4 sentences.

In addition to this abstract, universities often require a half-page abstract for publication. Engineering projects are often confidential because they contain privileged information. So, when you write this half-page abstract, make sure to anonymize your industrial partner. Use the term "manufacturer" or "organization" when referring to your industrial partner. Naming the industry might be too revealing, so you may have to think of a broader term, such as "industrial equipment" instead of industrial dryers or "clean energy" instead of photovoltaics.

Introduction

In this book, "Introduction" refers to all text between the abstract and the problem statement. The introduction contains the project's background information including a profile of your industrial partner.

The purpose of the introduction is to ensure your readers' understanding of your project, particularly your problem statement. To do this, use a *hierarchical* introduction that begins with the big picture and ends with your problem statement.

EXAMPLE: A HIERARCHICAL INTRODUCTION

The project is about reducing the downtime of injection molding machines at Worldwide Plastic. The plastic components produced through injection molding are used in tools, consumer electronics, and even hearing aids. Downtime is the number of hours when machines are not operating because of breakdowns, waiting for materials, and so on. The student team conducts the project at Worldwide Plastic's production site in Liverpool, UK.

Prior to the introduction, the reader is only familiar with the front page, the project title, and the firm's logo and name. The title is "Reduction of downtime of injection molding machines."

The hierarchical introduction is as follows:

1   Description of Worldwide Plastic.

2   Description of the firm's product. This includes photos of products so the reader becomes familiar with molded plastic components.

3   Description and illustrations of Worldwide Plastic's worldwide production sites, including a map of the world with dots for each of the firm's sites.

4   Description of the firm's UK sites, including a map of the UK with dots for each of the firm's UK sites.

5   A local map of the factory buildings at the firm's Liverpool site, where the injection molding production for northern European markets is located (the site where the students conduct their project). Mark the building housing the firm's injection molding machines.

6   Ground plan of the injection molding building showing the molding machines in question.

7   Photos of the molding machines detailing which component types each machine produces.

8   Diagrams showing two selected machine's current downtime vs. total time (e.g. 45%).

9   Descriptions, including diagrams, quantifying the consequences of high downtimes, for example a description of how a 5% downtime reduction can reduce the need for two rented machines, which reduces the firm's cost of rent and maintenance among other things.

Following this introduction, the reader clearly understands the problem statement and why the problem statement is important to address. The problem statement is:

How can Worldwide Plastic reduce the downtime of its injection molding machines?

The example shows the hierarchical build-up of the introduction. The section begins with the big picture – the firm, its products, and global presence. The introduction then moves into the details of the problem, ensuring that the reader always has the necessary knowledge to understand the next point.

Verifying the actual existence and size of the problem

The introduction to the Worldwide Plastic project does not just tell the reader about the downtimes. It also documents the problem and tells readers the size of the problem using diagrams (step 8 in the Worldwide Plastic example). That a project's problem actually exists is the basis for conducting the project. Without a problem, there is no project. Therefore, make sure to document the problem and its size. See Chapter 2 for details.

If the firm has already measured the size of the problem, then use these data in your introduction (as in the Worldwide Plastic example). If there are no data, then collecting and analyzing data is your task. Perhaps generating data and taking your own measurements is necessary. The introduction should make clear to the reader that the problem exists (at a minimum through indications or anecdotal evidence). Measuring the exact size of the problem might be a bigger task and if this is the case, present the result of your measurements in your analysis section.

See the description of how to present these size-measuring data in your report later in this chapter, and see Chapter 6 for methods and advice for the actual measurement activity.

Problem statement

The problem statement follows the introduction. If your introduction is clear, then you simply present your problem statement with little further explanation. Make sure that your report makes clear to your readers which line on the page is the problem statement. Use the page's layout to emphasize the problem statement; for example, bold text and line breaks before and after. Avoid shadows, new colors, or a different font (unprofessional).

The importance of a proper, clear problem statement cannot be emphasized enough. Chapter 3 details what a great problem statement is for engineering projects.

If you use subquestions to the problem statement, place these immediately after the problem statement. If your subquestions are what Chapter 3 calls "acceptable subquestions," then your subquestions are self-explanatory to your reader. The reader will not need any further explanation.

Delimitations from the problem statement and other delimitations later in your report

Chapter 3 explained that delimitations have two functions in a project:

1 To delimit themes from the problem statement that the reader can reasonably expect your project to address.
2 If necessary, to make delimitations locally in particular report sections.

These two delimitation types are now described.

Delimitations from the problem statement

Place a delimitation section immediately after the problem statement. This section has the purpose of shaping your readers' expectations for the remainder of your report. Imagine your reader has just read your introduction and problem statement.

Now, put yourself in your readers' shoes and assess what you can reasonably expect from your report. If these expectations include issues that the report does not cover, then delimit them.

For example, a report deals with the reuse of a manufacturer's used products. It is reasonable to expect such a report to address "green" issues, such as how reuse will affect the firm's image, CO_2 emissions, or the firm's ability to support the UN's Sustainable Development Goals. If the project does not address these issues, then delimiting the issues is an effective way of aligning reader expectations with report content.

Avoid delimiting subjects that are only vaguely related to your problem (or completely unrelated). Such delimitations, which readers would not think of even in their wildest imagination, only confuse. Imagine a reader thinking: "Well, if this issue is delimited, then I may not have understood the project at all so far. I'd better read the introduction again."

TOP TIPS

Have three university-educated friends or classmates read your introduction and problem statement. Then, ask them for their expectations of the rest of your report. Pose the following questions:

1. What do you think the report is about?
2. Which themes will the report cover?
3. What do think the report will analyze?
4. Which expectations do you have for the solution?
5. What do you think the conclusion will say?

The answers to these questions will show whether your introduction and problem statement fit with the remainder of the report. If report content and reader expectations do not align, then either delimit the themes your report does not address or revise your introduction.

Your dialogue about expectations might also reveal any inconsistencies in your report, including between problem statement and analysis, and analysis and solution.

Local delimitations in particular report sections

When you reach the analysis, you may experience new needs for delimitations. For example, you may have identified six causes for why an app's launch speed is too long, but you will only develop a solution that addresses two of these six causes. Delimit the four other causes from your report locally when your reader knows all six causes. Another example where local delimitations are relevant is if you are using only three steps of a four-step method and delimiting the fourth step.

Making delimitations locally in your report is completely acceptable, although you do need to argue for your choices. Keep local delimitations local and do not move them to the delimitations section that follows the problem statement. They would make no sense here to a reader, who is unfamiliar with the context of such delimitations.

Concept definitions and literature review

Engineering projects use the knowledge base in their field. The knowledge base is documented in the field's literature. Chapter 4 describes how engineering projects use literature for a host of different purposes. Three of these purposes are to define the project's central concepts, develop the foundation for the project's analysis, and identify all general requirements for the project's solution. Here, the chapter addresses how and what to describe about your literature in your report.

The "global" theory section

The section that defines your central concepts is usually placed right after the delimitations section. This book will refer to this concept-defining literature section as the "global" theory section. The global theory section may be an integral part of your methodology section. The purpose of the global theory section is to make sure that your reader understands all the key concepts and variables in your project. With a clear understanding of the problem statement and key concepts, your reader is able to evaluate whether your choice of method will, in fact, achieve the right analysis results. The analysis results form the basis for designing your solution. Chapter 4 describes how to use your literature as a basis for conducting your analysis, and how to develop a generic problem tree. In your report's global theory section, describe and illustrate your problem tree.

The global theory section in an engineering report is usually short compared to reports in subjects within the humanities and social science disciplines.

Explained: why theory sections are short compared to other academic fields

Engineering reports rarely contain long discussions about theory, the basic assumptions in a theory, or the circumstances around the theory's origin. For example, an engineering report does not describe who Mr. Ohm was and under which circumstance his theory about electrical resistance came to be. Natural science theory is usually *nomothetic* theory. Nomothetic comes from the Greek *nomos* meaning law. Natural science theories are laws that apply generally to all situations of the same category rather than just for a single phenomenon.

When using theory in the humanities and social science disciplines, discussing the basic assumptions and circumstances around the theory's formulation are often central activities. The reason is that these discussions feed into the argument for why and how a project can apply the theory. Many theories in these disciplines are not nomothetic but *idiosyncratic*, that is, a theory that explains a single phenomenon. For example, a theory explains that a strong middle class with lots of purchasing power is the reason why the USA experienced steep average economic growth between 1960 and 1980. Let us assume that a student team examines the economic growth in Germany during the same period. The question is whether the theory on US growth can explain the economic growth in Germany. The student group must make a considerable (and often lengthy) effort in arguing for their choice of theory.

Local theory sections

In addition to the global theory section, an engineering project contains a series of local sections that describe and use literature with the field's methods and models. For example, methods for constructing the solution or implementing the solution. Keep these local sections local, that is, where you use the methods or models.

EXAMPLE

A project develops a window frame for a new type of energy-efficient windows. The project has identified and specified the design requirements for the window frame and divided the solution design into a set of activities that each concern one important design question:

1   How should the frame keep the glass panes fixed?

2   How will the frame keep the gas between the glass panes?

3   How will rubber strips ensure the necessary tightness between window frames and walls?

For each question, the project applies methods and models. For example, construction codes about the weight of the glass panes impact the mechanical structure of the frame. The project report describes these methods and models in the solution design section where the methods are applied.

The WHY+APPLY principle

Chapter 4 describes the WHY+APPLY questions that tie your chosen methods and models into the overall flow of your project. The two questions are:

1   WHY is a method or model chosen?
2   How do you plan to APPLY the method or model?

Answering these two questions explicitly in your report might not always be necessary. Readers will consider the inclusion of some theories self-evident (e.g. using Bernoulli's principle for dealing with energy conservation in flowing fluids). However, the selection of a method or model might be an actual choice between two or more alternatives. Reflect carefully about whether your reader will consider your selection of a particular theory as self-evident. If not, then answer the WHY+APPLY questions for your choice.

The answers to these questions weave the theory into your project's coherent flow. Comprehensive answers give your readers a complete understanding of the purpose and use of the theory in your project. You avoid the classic pitfall in a report that your reader is thinking: "Why am I reading this?" When answering the WHY question, refer back to your earlier sections, such as the problem statement or methodology. For the APPLY question, refer to forward sections, such as your analysis or solution design. Figure 12.1 illustrates how to use the WHY+APPLY questions to refer back or forward.

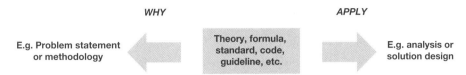

Figure 12.1   The WHY+APPLY questions

The following example shows how the WHY+APPLY questions ensure your reader's understanding of the place in your project's coherent flow of a theory, method, or model.

EXAMPLE

A project deals with increasing the durability of rubber gaskets in hydraulic systems. The gaskets, which sit between steel items, crumble after only a few years, leading to hydraulic oil leaks. The student team examines why the gaskets crumble as fast as they do.

The team applies theory from materials science about gaskets and steel surfaces. A reader might ask: "Why this theory?" or "How does the team plan to use the theory?" To accommodate these questions, the team explains their selections and planned theory application.

The team draws on gasket theory to understand how gasket material and physical gasket design impact durability. Furthermore, the team draws on steel surface theory to examine how the steel type impacts the surface roughness. By explaining the inclusion of these theories, the team ensures that readers do not think: "Why does the team think I need a lecture about gasket and steel surface theory?"

In addition to explaining why the theories are selected, the team explains how they plan to use the theory. The theory about gaskets is used to assess whether the firm has chosen the right gasket type. The theory about steel surfaces is applied to examine whether the firm applies a steel type and surface treatment that leads to minimal surface roughness.

Identification of the general requirements for the solution type

Chapter 6 describes the identification of design requirements relevant for engineering solutions. A solution should meet the specific needs of the user including the right functions and other features. In addition, the solution must meet a set of *general* design requirements that apply to the type of solution. Table 12.1 shows three examples of general design requirements.

Table 12.1 Three examples of general design requirements	
Example	**Engineering discipline**
Public regulations for the construction of a dam	Civil engineering
Technical requirements for electrical power components in a machine	Mechanical engineering
Standards for quality management procedures in food production	Manufacturing engineering

Because these general design requirements are not unique to the solution, you can begin your identification of design requirements early in your project. If the solution is a building, then identify requirements in building regulations and district plans. If your solution is a chemical process, then identify requirements for safety and sustainable waste management. If your solution is equipment for the healthcare sector, then look for requirements about cleaning and maintenance of equipment for hospitals, clinics, and laboratories. Make sure to include these design requirements in your report.

Methodology

The purpose of the methodology section in your report is to describe your method so the reader is convinced that your method will in fact lead to a great solution to your project's problem. Before presenting a practical, easy-to-use and reader-friendly way of writing your methodology section, this section deals with a question that engineering students often find puzzling: Why are methodology sections usually so short when compared to disciplines in the humanities and social sciences?

Explained: why methodology sections are shorter in engineering compared to other academic fields

Many engineering students have had questions from (often flabbergasted) humanities students such as: "Haven't you got a methodology section?!" or "Is your methodology section only TWO pages?!" The reason for these reactions from humanities students is that the methodology section in humanities is very long and embeds a comprehensive thought and discussion process. There are (at least) four reasons for the length of methodology sections in non-technical fields:

1   Projects in the humanities and social sciences rest on important choices within the philosophy of science. Reports must adequately present and argue for these choices. Because the philosophy of science is an abstract discipline, presenting and arguing for choices takes up a lot of space. Engineering reports only rarely use any space for discussions of the philosophy of science (see Chapter 5 for reasons why).

2   Projects in the humanities and social sciences do not revolve around designing solutions to problems, but instead conduct a study that answers one or more currently unanswered questions. Because such projects conduct one study, the report describes the methodology *once* in one large section. An engineering project uses several methods for several purposes and describes these methods in several sections throughout the report rather than one large section early in the report.

3   Engineering projects design solutions and the report demonstrates the authors' solution design skills. Because projects in humanities and social study disciplines conduct a research study, the report must demonstrate students' research skills. The methodology section is *the* section that demonstrates the students' research skills and therefore the section is long and comprehensive.

4 Projects in humanities and social science disciplines often apply "soft" concepts that need space for definition. Examples of soft concepts are happiness, upward mobility, competitiveness, and innovation capability. Engineering projects usually use concepts whose definitions are known by all parties. Examples are energy consumption in kWh, weight in grams, and noise level in decibels.

Practical and reader-friendly methodology description

An intuitive easy-to-understand way of describing a project's methodology is the hierarchical method. With the hierarchical method, you first describe the overall steps in your project structure, and then describe each of the overall steps in detail. Chapter 5 describes which overall steps usually constitute the project structure of an engineering project. When the reader reaches the report's methodology section, they will already have read the introduction, problem statement, and definitions of key terms. Describing the methodology for these sections is therefore not relevant. Only describe the methodology for future sections.

Often, the methodology section focuses on the project's analysis only. Some projects include methods for design, test, and implementation in the methodology section, but leaving these methods until later in the report is equally acceptable. Where the analysis identifies the causes of the project's problem, projects can only vaguely describe solution design methods because the causes for the problem are formally unknown at the time when the methodology choices are made.

Figure 12.2 illustrates how you can describe the method in your report. The top of Figure 12.2 shows the project structure in diagrammatic form and beneath it a short description. Do include an illustration of your project structure in your report. For inspiration, see Chapter 5.

Once your reader is well acquainted with your overall report structure, the section moves on to describe the methods for each of the individual sections in the report structure. Figure 12.2 shows one piece of paper, but use as much space as you need. When you describe these single steps in your methodology, be specific about:

- how you plan to generate data (e.g. through an experiment) or collect readily available data
- how you plan to ensure data validity and reliability
- how you plan to analyze your data and extract the conclusions you seek.

If you have developed a generic problem tree (as described in Chapter 4), then use this tree actively in your methodology section to show the reader which specific analyses you plan to conduct. Show your reader a version of your problem tree that deduces the relevant analyses. See Chapter 4 for an example.

Experiment-heavy projects

In some engineering disciplines, a project's analysis is often an experiment. If an experiment constitutes your analysis, then describe your experiment carefully and in detail. Describe equipment, protocols, materials, the dataset your experiment will produce, how you analyze the dataset, and how you extract conclusions.

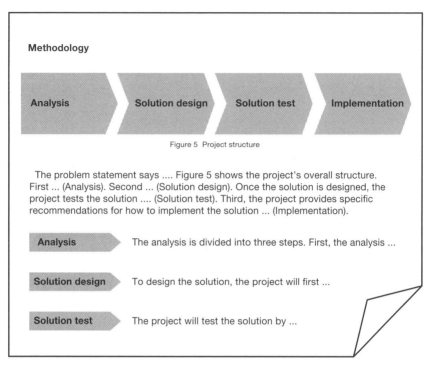

Figure 12.2   The methodology description in engineering projects

Experiment-heavy engineering projects have much in common with research projects. For example, the reader might expect a review of related literature and an explicit discussion of how the result of your experiment adds to this literature. Chapter 16 covers engineering research projects.

Locally placed shorter methodology sections

Describing how you conduct a task locally in the report is common for engineering reports ("As a basis for implementing the solution, the section builds on methods X and Y"). These local method descriptions can be detailed versions of methods briefly described in the methodology. If this is the case, remember to refer back to the main methodology section where you initially tell the reader that the method will be used later in the report. These local descriptions of methods can also be descriptions of methods not previously mentioned. For example, solution design, test, and implementation are sections that often include one or more new methods. These methods are then described in the same sections as they are applied.

When you draw on methods not described or referenced earlier in the report, make sure to argue for their selection if need be. In addition, remember to base your methods in your field's literature. Your literature usually contains rules and guidelines for how to properly design and test a solution; for example, how to design a software application or construct a machine. Your reader should know that your inclusion of methods locally in your report is solidly based in your subject's knowledge base. Such use of literature gives credibility to your solution.

The almost mythical nature of a project's coherent flow

The subject of coherence in project reports is well described in books about writing. One principle often referenced in these books is that in a coherent report, all sections are part of one, large argument for the project's conclusion. This principle makes great sense for engineering reports. When your reader reads your report, they should get a sense of *"of course-ness."* Great reports make your think as follows:

1 *Of course* this is the problem statement when your problem analysis shows what it shows.
2 *Of course* this is the literature and theory that the report applies when the problem statement is what it is.
3 *Of course* this is the methodology when the problem statement and the selected literature are what they are.
4 *Of course* this is the analysis when the methodology is what it is.
5 *Of course* this is the solution when the analysis says what it says.
6 *Of course* this is the implementation plan when the solution and the organization are what they are.

If your reader has these thoughts when reading your report, then your report's coherence is rock solid. To reach this level of coherence and flow from section to section, you must write your report as a *formal, ideal sequence.* See Chapter 5 for details about the typical sequence. Your actual project might feel like a chaotic set of random activities that far from resemble an ideal sequence of tasks. But, in spite of your chaotic, actual process, write your report *as if* it were conducted as the ideal sequence that leads to an effective solution, a set of great recommendations for your industrial partner, and a valid conclusion (solution summary).

Analysis

Chapters 2–8 describe how a project either improves an existing entity or designs a new entity. If your project improves an existing entity, then the purpose of the analysis is to identify the cause (singular or plural) of your project's problem. If your project designs a new entity, then the purpose of the analysis is to identify the entity's design requirements. For these projects, the analysis may also include an analysis of the entity's subsystems and the potential technical solutions for each subsystem. First, the analysis section in projects that improve an existing entity is described and, second, the analysis section in projects that design a new entity is explained.

Analysis section in projects that improve an existing entity

The project's problem statement states the problem. The purpose of the analysis is to find what causes the problem. Your analysis section must describe and preferably also illustrate the causal trajectories between the problem and its cause(s). However, prior to describing the analysis of causes, you may have to describe your analysis of the size of the problem.

Chapter 3 describes how projects that improve an existing entity should focus on one key variable. Examples are product durability, production scrap rate, and the speed of a liquid separation process. The problem in your project is constituted by the gap between the firm's current performance on the variable and the desired performance. The size of the gap is the size of your project's problem. For example, a manufacturer wants to reduce the product scrap rate from a production line (too many products are scrapped). The current scrap rate is 23% and the firm would like a scrap rate resembling the scrap rate on its other production lines, which is 3%. The 20% that is the difference between 23% and 3% constitutes the size of the problem.

Often, your industrial partner knows the current performance on the variable well. The current performance might be the reason for your involvement in the project. In this case, you will have already presented the problem size in your report's introduction and then you can head directly for the analysis of your problem's causes. You might, however, be in a situation where the performance is unknown. In such cases, you must measure the current performance and present your analysis of the problem's size. The measurement might require weeks of data collection and this analysis is therefore a large part of your project's analysis. Remember to describe the method for this problem size analysis in your methodology section.

Analysis of the cause(s) for your project's problem

Once the problem and problem size are clear to your reader, the following analysis of the problem's causes is easier understood. In this section, your task is to show the reader how you analyze your way through the causal trajectories. If you apply a generic problem tree, then use this tree explicitly in the analysis section as an illustration. If your tree cannot fit into a page, then show one large but unreadable version of the tree to begin with and smaller but readable parts of the tree later. Alternatively, show an aggregated version of the tree first and then disaggregated versions of tree branches later.

Figure 12.3 shows a problem tree. The dark line is one causal trajectory through the tree, beginning with the project's problem on the left-hand side and ending with a cause for the problem on the right-hand side. The tree itself is a set of boxes and arrows. See Chapter 2 for an explanation of the tree's format and Chapters 4 and 6 for detailed examples of how to use the tree.

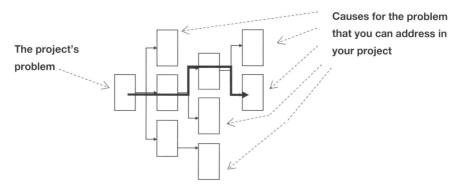

Figure 12.3　Problem tree with causal trajectories

Your earlier report sections show the generic version of the tree. For your readers' understanding, you may want to repeat the generic tree at the beginning of your analysis section. The purpose of your analysis is to replace the generic tree with the actual tree. The actual tree contains the causal trajectories that are actually present in your project. See Chapter 6 for an example of how to conduct such an analysis.

To ensure your reader's understanding of interbox relations, either use quantitative analyses (e.g. a regression analysis) or qualitative analyses (e.g. interviews with two informants who, independently from one another, provide the same explanation of an interbox relation). Irrespective of the data type, your reader must be convinced that one box logically impacts the other and why. Using logic to connect boxes might also be possible.

If you use quantitative analyses, show these analyses in your report using diagrams. Avoid pasting half or whole pages of numbers directly into the report. When writing your report, it is your job (and not your reader's job) to present the important messages with clarity. Use diagrams to show your results, so your reader easily sees your results. Remember to include all your raw and processed data among your report's appendices (electronically if necessary). Chapter 13 details how to include diagrams and numbers in your report.

The relative importance of causes (important and unimportant)

Once you have reached the actual problem tree that often contains two or more causes for the problem, the next natural step is assessing the relative importance of the causes. An important cause is a cause that has large impact on the problem.

EXAMPLE

A project wants to minimize the time that a user of a high-tech rental bike takes from approaching the bike to being ready to ride the bike. The time between these two points is spent registering name and credit card information on the bike's software, unlocking the bike, and getting to grips with the bike's GPS system.

The team has measured the average time between bike approach and being ready to ride as seven minutes. The team has analyzed each step in the process and examined possible technical solutions for speeding up the steps. The team has found three major causes for the lengthy process:

1 Users wait an unnecessarily long time for software start-up. In their analysis, the team has identified several options for improving the start-up process.

2 Users wait an unnecessarily long time for the registration of credit card information. The team has identified several options for speeding up the registration.

3 Users spend a long time unlocking bikes from their stands due to various mechanical theft-proofing devices. The team has found ways of reducing the time spent unlocking bikes.

The question is: "Which of these three causes are important for the total time between bike approach and being ready to ride?" The team measures the average time 50 times and found that the unnecessary time (that can be eliminated when implementing the solution elements that the team has identified in their analysis) is 2.23 minutes for software start-up, 0.84 minutes for registering credit card information, and 0.41 minutes for unlocking bikes. These numbers reveal that cause number 1 is big, and that 2 and 3 are small. In your report, an effective way of communicating the relative importance is through a column chart, as shown below.

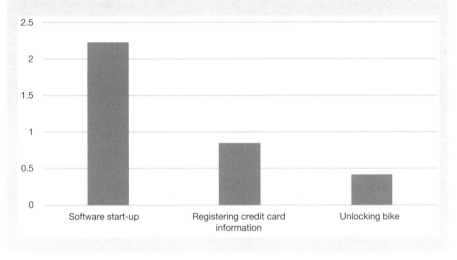

Ideally, use diagrams that quantitatively demonstrate the relative importance of causes. You may not have data for such a representation. Often, a Pareto chart requires data collected over a long period prior to your arrival. If you lack the right data, then use qualitative data. Remember to involve the relevant actors in your industrial partner's organization and perhaps your supervisor to ensure that your conclusions from qualitative datasets are reasonably reliable. Chapter 6, which deals with this problem in more detail, describes the alternative to a Pareto chart of having two boxes: "Important causes" and "Unimportant causes." In your report, make your reasoning for your categorization process and arguments clear to the reader, so the reader is able to assess your reasoning.

Once you have presented the relative importance of causes to your reader, you can argue why you chose to exclude one or more causes in your work. Chapter 6 describes a project at Bing & Co. that investigates a large number of failures in a final product quality test. The analysis identifies five causes, of which the team excludes three because they have very little impact on the failure rate in the product test (the project's problem).

Analysis section in projects that design a new entity

The analysis in projects that design a new entity must identify all design requirements. In addition, in some engineering disciplines, the analysis identifies the entity's subsystems and the potential technical solutions for each subsystem.

Identifying all design requirements

Your solution must adhere to all design requirements. In some projects, the industrial partner has already defined a complete requirement specification, but often identifying the requirements is your job. The basis for identifying design requirements is the *solution need* specified in your problem statement (see Chapter 3).

Some design requirements are general in nature and apply to all solutions of the same type (e.g. a building, bridge, a machine, etc.). An earlier section in this chapter described how you can apply your field's literature to identify the general requirements and provided three examples of general requirements.

Identifying the design requirements that are specific to your solution is the job of your analysis. When your reader reads your analysis, they are familiar with the solution need that your problem statement states. Prior to presenting the total requirement specification (the "spec"), insert a section that describes how you "extract" the specific design requirements from the solution need. The reader needs to follow your reasoning for how you translate the often vaguely defined solution need into a set of distinct and precise design requirements. Then present the total design requirement specification. Describe your requirements one by one. If necessary, group your requirements into logical categories. Consider including a description for how each requirement will impact the solution design, and also mention whether a requirement is an absolute requirement or an "as good as possible" (AGAP) requirement. See Chapter 6 for a detailed distinction.

The identification of design requirements may be a recurring step in an iterative solution design process. Although your design process is iterative (or agile), the report is most often described as one, linear process that identifies and describes design requirements once in one design requirement specification.

Requirements should be operational for your use in the solution design

An operational requirement does not need additional interpretation or specification. A non-operational requirement might be "the solution must adhere to existing quality standards." You might ask: "What *are* these with respect to your solution?" Be precise when formulating design requirements. Rather than "the item must operate for long hours in both warm and cold temperatures," write "the item must operate 24/7 within a −30 to +70°C interval." You can use the latter requirement directly in your solution design when selecting materials for wear parts, when designing the item's outer isolating shell, and when determining the right maintenance frequency for the user manual. Use numbers in your design requirement specification and remember to use clear units of measurement.

If your requirement specifies the use of specific components (e.g. "the machine must employ a 4.5-liter V-8 Duramax diesel engine"), then state the requirement in your spec and include a white paper of the particular component among your appendices.

Subsystems and their technical solutions

In addition to the identification of the design requirements, the analysis in projects that design new entities may include an analysis of the entity's subsystems and the potential technical solutions for each subsystem (a subsystem is also referred to as a *function*). Following your analysis, the solution design will select a technical solution for each subsystem and ensure that all the selected technical solutions are consistent.

In your report, describe and perhaps illustrate each subsystem. To support your reader's understanding as well as your decisions in your solution design, consider applying and showing a "subsystem solution" matrix, as shown in Figure 6.8.

Solution design

Your report must describe the specific nature of your solution and how your solution solves your project's problem, using text, drawings, illustrations, calculations, and so on. An engineering project may test the solution. If so, the test results will show (or at least indicate) whether the solution will in fact solve the problem. Many engineering projects do not reach the test phase or require an expensive real-life test. Without a test, the credibility of your solution is embedded directly in the coherence of your report's sections. Section by section, your reader must be convinced that a section's results are correct and that following sections build on these results. For projects that improve an existing entity, the reader must be convinced that the analysis has identified the real causes of the project's problem and that the solutions eliminate these real causes or reduce their effect on the problem.

Chapter 7 describes three solution archetypes – a single solution, an either/or solution, or a multiple elements solution. A single solution is an app that a team develops so the app meets all the design requirements in its requirement specification. An either/or solution is two or three solutions from which the industrial partner or industrial partner client will choose one; an example is two bridges and a tunnel as three alternative traffic connections between two islands. A multiple elements solution is a set of solution elements that each address one cause in a causal analysis; together, the set of solutions elements comprise the full solution.

Your chosen archetype solution greatly impacts your solution section. For either/or and multiple elements solutions, the section must not only describe and illustrate one solution, but also rough-cut sketch solutions and the process that leads to the selection of the final solution. For example, the section should describe how a project selects one of the alternatives in an either/or solution. The sections below describe a project's solution section for each of the three solution archetypes.

The single solution

In your report, describe the solution so your reader clearly understands the solution, its functions, and, if necessary, the interaction between the solution and its environment. Often, a team does not develop the solution "in the flesh," but draws technical drawings, makes the necessary calculations, and perhaps develops a prototype.

The single solution is often the result of projects that develop a new entity more or less from scratch. In such projects, the analysis has identified and specified a set of design requirements. For the coherence of your report, readers must understand how the solution meets the design requirements. The solution design process sheds light on requirements that are difficult to meet in combination; for example, a relationship between weight and tensile strength or between functionality and speed in software.

The process for developing the single solution varies. One method is the traditional method where you identify and specify all design requirements once, and then develop the solution. Other methods are iterative in nature and work through a number of cycles that each develop a prototype or component parts of a prototype. The team then tests the prototype, and determines whether design requirements need adjustments and how the prototype needs changes for the following cycle. In iterative development methods, cycles often result in new requirements or new functions that users want. In your methodology section, make sure to detail your specific method and argue for why your method will lead to the best possible solution. Ideally, back up your arguments with your field's literature, stating how your carefully selected method is genius for the particular type of development your project happens to conduct.

Make sure to describe and illustrate your solution. Engineers are visual by nature and expect graphical communications of all sorts – drawings, sketches, diagrams, graphs, charts, photos, and so on. Some forms of graphical communication are standardized within the industry that your particular field targets. For example, technical drawings express tolerances with Geometrical Product Specification, software developers follow UML (Unified Modeling Language) deployment diagrams, and optimization projects that follow lean manufacturing principles use the rules in value stream mapping.

If your project improves an existing entity, make sure to present the effect of the solution on your project's problem. In addition, for projects that improve an existing entity and projects that design a new entity, present the financial performance of the solution. See how to calculate financial performance in Chapter 7.

The either/or solution

The guidelines for the single solution apply to the either/or solution as well; for example, that a solution must meet design requirements and that a solution section should present the solution's financial performance. However, the description of the either/or solution requires a few additional subsections.

A solution section for either/or solutions often uses a three-step structure, as shown in Figure 12.4.

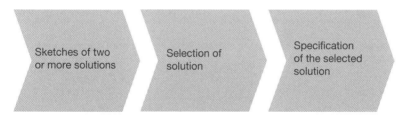

Figure 12.4   Three-step structure in either/or solutions

The first step presents two or more solutions as sketches or rough-cut versions of solutions. Each of these solutions meets the design requirements presented in the project's analysis section. Often, an engineering discipline has standards for rough versions of solutions. In civil engineering, architects or engineers develop a sketch version of a project for the construction client. The sketch project shows the client how the building will look when finished, but does not include foundation drawings, material specifications, location of lamps and power outlets, and so on. In manufacturing engineering, a team can sketch three different production systems with varying degrees of automation and robot technology. These sketch versions of solutions include rough assessments of financial performance and ease of implementation.

Once a project team has developed the set of alternatives in the either/or solution, the project reaches a critical decision: the choice of the one final solution. When you describe this choice, consider detailing the decision-making process and the actors who participate in making the decision. Think about how you as a project team facilitate the decision-making process; for example, which information the decision makers should have. The decision makers should have thorough information about the following:

1 The project's problem (in an either/or solution, the problem is often a defined solution need; see Chapter 3).
2 The design requirement that you have identified and your analyses of how each solution meets the requirements.
3 The solution alternatives in their rough version.

Remember points 1 and 2 because they constitute the foundation for assessing the solution alternatives. If you have analyzed how well each solution meets the design requirements, then remember to include your analysis as information in the decision-making process. See Chapter 7 for an example of such an analysis. Describe the decision-making process in your solution section so readers (examiners) can clearly see your professional application of the decision-making process.

The last part of the solution section details and specifies the selected solution following the academic requirements in your discipline. This specification of your solution concludes the solution section for either/or solutions.

The multiple elements solution

The guidelines for single solutions apply to multiple elements solutions as well. However, as is the case for the either/or solution, the description of the multiple elements solution requires a few additional subsections. A solution section often has a three-step structure, as shown in Figure 12.5.

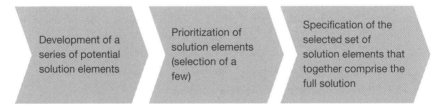

Figure 12.5   Three-step structure in the multiple elements solution

The multiple elements solution fits well with projects that improve an existing entity (e.g. the durability of a product or the delivery speed of a logistics system). The analysis in your project has identified the cause(s) of your project's problem (why the durability or delivery speed is low). Finally, the analysis has evaluated which causes have the highest relative impact on your problem. For each high-impact cause, your solution develops one or more solution elements.

A project team wants to increase the speed of a measurement instrument. The team wants to reduce the time from when a measurement begins and a result is presented. The team has found three causes for the long measurement speed:

1   To reach a precise result, the instrument conducts 25 single measurements and combines the result. The team finds that the precision the firm requires is reachable with only four measurements.

2   Transferring signals from the instrument's sensors to the algorithm that calculates the result is slower than necessary. Newer generation sensors transfer signals quicker.

3   The instrument validates test results by communicating with a cloud-based test procedure. Validating through a procedure placed in the instrument is quicker.

The team develops a total of eight solution elements, including quicker sensors and local result validation. All elements reduce the instrument's measurement speed. The next step is prioritizing which elements to include in the full solution.

In your report, your job is to describe each solution element to a level of detail that enables an assessment of each element's effect on the problem and ease of implementation. The section presents solution elements in a rough version similar to the detail level of the either/or solution's alternatives. Chapter 7 shows a method for prioritizing among solution elements. The method provides a complete overview of all solution elements' individual effects and ease of implementation.

Include in your description of the prioritization process a description of how you involve your industrial partner in the prioritization decisions. End the solution section by describing the selected solution elements in greater detail.

Describing the solution's effect and ease of implementation

As part of your solution section, communicate to your reader the effect of your solution on the project's problem, as precisely as your data allow. If your solution is a single solution or the selected solution from among two or three alternatives, then describe the effect and ease of implementation of your one solution. If your solution is a multiple elements solution, then describe the effect of your total set of selected solution elements.

You may not able to assess the solution's effect precisely; for example: "The solution will increase durability by 9.46%." In these cases, consider one of two options; either write the effect as a round number with few significant figures, such as "roughly 10%," or present the effect as an interval, such as "between 5% and 15%." The difference between 5% and 15% is substantial, but you do tell your reader that the effect is not 1% or 50%. In your report, remember to argue for your choice of interval boundaries. A relevant exam question might be: "Why do you think the solution will have a minimum effect of 5%, why not 3%?"

Once you have described your solution's effect, the next step is presenting your assessment of the effect's value. Remember to provide a unit of measurement of the value – "€ per employee," "€ per year," "€ per item," "€/hour/product." Once you have presented the value, move on to the necessary investment, operating costs, and finally the solution's financial feasibility. See Chapter 7 for methods to calculate a solution's financial feasibility.

When describing your solution's investment and operating costs, think 360 degrees around the solution. Your solution may not have many cost parameters (e.g. no investment in machines, software, or buildings), but remember the smaller costs. Examples include, one or more of these cost parameters:

- employee hours spent in development and implementation participation
- project management for the implementation
- time spent by expensive external consultants
- time spent by employees from the firm's IT department if software needs development
- costs for training employees in new procedures
- costs of developing proposals and tenders
- time spent by industrial partner employees controlling the solution's continuous operation
- time spent developing and receiving information and communications
- time spent by the firm's legal department in updating customer or supplier contracts.

A last rule of thumb for assessing a solution's financial performance is to make sure that cost savings are realizable. A solution might reduce time consumption in production by 15 seconds here and 10 seconds there. However, if these seconds do not amount to 40 hours per week of a specific role in the production line, the cost savings will likely not materialize.

Solution test

If practically possible, test the effect of your solution. In your report, describe the test methodology and test result. Your test description can be an integrated part of the solution section or (if the test requires a lot of time and effort) as an independent section immediately following the solution section.

A test's place in the coherent flow of the report

Tests have a natural place in a project's flow. In projects that improve an existing entity, the project's problem has one or more causes that your analysis has identified. The solution or solution elements that you have designed eliminate these causes or reduce their effect on the problem.

Figure 12.6 shows a problem tree, in which a solution is symbolized by the blue box on the right-hand side. The test can show two results:

1 Whether the solution does, in fact, reduce the cause it addresses.
2 Whether the elimination of the cause does, in fact, reduce or perhaps completely eliminate the problem.

In projects that develop a new entity, the project's problem is often a defined solution need (something someone wants that currently does not exist). In such projects, the analysis specifies all design requirements and assembles them in a

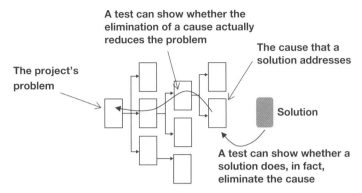

Figure 12.6   The two functions of a test

design requirement specification. Once you have designed the solution, you may be able to test whether the solution actually meets the design requirements. Perhaps you are unable to test the complete solution, but are able to test the functionality of one or two major solution components.

Engineering disciplines have varying traditions for including a test in a project

Individual engineering disciplines each have their own traditions for including solution tests. Those disciplines that use tests often have their own test methods. In fields where a team of engineers draw and specify but do not construct the solution, tests often happen in test and simulation software. In software engineering, the team continuously tests solution components, and later the whole solution. In this field, testing a solution is an integral part of the solution design. Tests may examine functionality, speed, and so on. In mechanical engineering, a team might test one or two single components of the solution in simulation or if necessary live action; for example, the tensile strength or stiffness of a cast iron item.

Solution implementation

A great project not only designs a solution, but also includes planning the solution's implementation. In your report, describe an effective implementation plan. The term "implementation" has different meanings across engineering disciplines. Implementation can mean building the house, embedding new code in a program, developing a product for mass production, and changing a machine's maintenance process. The latter involves changing human behavior (of users and maintenance engineers). This section is most relevant for solutions that require changes in human behavior (e.g. from industrial partner employees or customers).

Chapter 8 describes how an implementation plan consists of three components: a project plan, a chart of a project organization, and an assessment of sources of resistance to change, including actions to prevent and handle the resistance.

Chapter 5 describes how to plan a project using Gantt charts. A Gantt chart shows an implementation's activities, the actors responsible for each activity, and how activities are logically sequenced.

Table 12.2 An example of a Gantt chart for developing and constructing a building

Months

Activity	Person	1	2	3	4	5	6	7	8	9	10	11	12	13	14	15	16	17	18	19	20
Write tender offer	Architect	▓	▓																		
Communicate with potential contractors	Engineers			▓	▓	▓															
Receive offers	Engineers						▓														
Negotiate final contracts	Engineers							▓	▓												
First construction meeting	Architect										▓										
Lay foundation	Bricklayer												▓	▓							
Construct wall and roof elements	Carpenter														▓	▓					
Mount wall and roof elements	Carpenter															▓					
Electrical installations	Electrician											▓	▓					▓			
Indoor carpentry	Carpenter																	▓			
Kitchens and bathroom furniture and plumbing	Carpenter																	▓	▓		
Painting the whole interior	Painter																			▓	

Implementation in "close-to-reality" projects

Some projects are close to reality, but not conducted in cooperation with industrial partners. Such a project could be the design of a building based on real, publicly available tender offer documents. In the implementation section for such projects, great subjects include how to avoid the typical challenges and pitfalls of a construction project; for example, the practical, political, financial, and technical pitfalls, and the risks the project faces.

Conclusions and recommendations for the industrial partner

Write your conclusion as accurately as possible. Students often look a bit baffled when supervisors emphasize the importance of answering the problem statement in the conclusion. Yet, a classic pitfall in project report writing is conclusions that really just summarize the project activities without concrete problem statement answers ("First, the project selected X, then analyzed Y, and then validated Z"). The reader immediately thinks: "Yes, but what do you conclude?"

Advice for writing a conclusion that answers your problem statement

First, follow this procedure:

1 Open a new word processing document
2 Copy your problem statement into the document
3 Answer the problem statement as accurately as possible
4 Replace the problem statement that you copied with the word "Conclusion."

Have a look at the very first word of your problem statement (the interrogative). The interrogative decides the nature of your conclusion text. The relationship between your problem statement and your conclusion is:

- How can ... $\Rightarrow$ Summary of your solution
- Which elements ... $\Rightarrow$ List of elements
- Why ... $\Rightarrow$ An explanation

If the interrogative is "How", then your reader expects a summary of your solution, because your solution is the answer to the how question. Some projects might search for elements and begin their problem statement with "Which." The answer is a list of elements. Finally, some projects ask "Why," which means the project is looking for an explanation for something. Your conclusion is the explanation, perhaps in a shorter version that the full explanation given in the body of your project. It is an absolute no-go to cross over and answer a how question with a list of elements, or a why question with a solution. Stick with the congruence in the list above.

If your problem statement is a solution need (see Chapter 3), then carefully describe how your solution fills the need. You might consider including a sketch drawing and a description of how the solution meets two or three important design requirements.

The validity of the conclusion

A great subsection in the conclusion is a section describing your reflections about the validity of the solution. A valid conclusion is a *true* answer to the problem statement.

Because an engineering project's conclusion is often a summary of the solution, the validity of the conclusion is in effect the mirror image of the solution's effect on the problem. Reflect on questions such as:

- Will the solution actually solve the problem?
- How sure are you, really? And why?
- Which limitations impact the solution's effect?

Reflecting on your conclusion and solution's effect demonstrates skill and an ability to critically evaluate your own work.

Prefer sure intervals to uncertain single numbers

The implementation of a solution will result in gains of some sort (lower costs, prolonged durability, higher efficiency, etc.). Your conclusion summarizes these gains, which you have calculated in earlier sections. Your calculations are based on a string of input numbers that are more or less certain. The size of your gain is at minimum as uncertain as the uncertainty of all input numbers combined, that is, often very uncertain. If you want to build higher certainty into your conclusions, then avoid writing single numbers (e.g. "the durability will increase by 35%"). Rather, write intervals that take input number uncertainty into account (e.g. "the durability will increase by 20–40%").

Perspectives, critical reflections, and discussion of results

Often, examiners expect you to write a section that reflects on the broader themes of your projects – "We like it when our students lift their heads, gaze at the world, and look at their work from a broader perspective."

This section is often a bit of a puzzle to engineering students. In a classic research study, a discussion section has a fixed, standard function. In this section, the researcher places their findings on "the shelf of all science." More specifically, the researcher tells the reader which previous studies and theories the findings support, which theories the study contradicts, and which theories the findings extend. In the discussion, the researcher puts their own findings in perspective vis-à-vis the world of science at large.

Although this type of discussion is often not fitting for an engineering report that solves a problem for a particular industrial partner, a discussion of other issues is still relevant. For example, reflect on whether your solution is useful in other contexts, perhaps other industrial partner departments or other firms within or outside your industrial partner's industry. A new procedure might be useful in other industrial partner factories; a new public building might be useful in other municipalities, countries, or continents; and a chemical process might be useful in other types of process than the process you deal with in your project. In general, reflect on how your solution might contribute to making the world a bit better.

List of references

Write your reference list as one, alphabetically ordered sequence following the last name of the publication's first author. For textbooks and papers, remember to use one referencing style consistently throughout your list. Examples of styles are APA, Harvard, and ISO 690. Using Google Scholar, you are able to copy book or paper references in three or more different styles.

If your source is an organization, use the name of the organization. If your source is a webpage, write the name of the organization that runs the webpage, the URL, and the time and date for when you accessed the page.

EXAMPLE LIST OF REFERENCES

Directive 2012/19/EU of the European Parliament and of the Council of 4 July 2012 on waste electrical and electronic equipment (WEEE), https://eur-lex.europa.eu/legal-content/EN/TXT/?uri=celex%3A32012L0019. Accessed April 2018.

Engineering Today (2018) Experts are unsure of the future of bioethanol, January 2. Accessed January 2018.

Kalpakjian, S., Schmid, S.R. & Vijai Sekar, K.S. (2014) *Manufacturing engineering and technology* (7th edn). Singapore: Pearson.

Kreyszig, E. (2010) *Advanced engineering mathematics* (10th edn). Hoboken, NJ: John Wiley & Sons.

Larsen, S.B. & Jacobsen, P. (2016) Revenue in reverse? An examination of reverse supply chain enabled revenue streams. *International Journal of Physical Distribution & Logistics Management*, 46(8): 783–804.

The textbooks and papers in the list are referenced using the APA referencing style.

Appendices and data documentation

Your discipline's traditions decide which texts, figures, tables, and other material belong in the main report and which belong in the appendices. However, there are a few basic rules. The main report should contain explanations, argumentation for choices, method descriptions, conclusions from analyses, and solution descriptions. Raw data and documentation (e.g. technical drawings and spreadsheet files) belong in the appendices.

Large data quantities

If your data is massive (e.g. a spreadsheet file with 45,000 rows), then hand in these data electronically. If your university has an upload option, then use this option, and otherwise add a USB key to your report. You want to make life easy for your reader, so if you have a spreadsheet file with 45,000 rows, then add the top of the list (that includes column names) to your printed appendices and refer the reader to the large electronic file from the printed appendix.

Page numbers for appendices

Remember page numbers for your appendices as well. Adding one ongoing sequence of page numbers for all appendices might constitute a practical challenge because your appendices come in so many different software packages (SolidWorks, Excel, Maple, etc.). A trick is to open a new Word document, insert 150 page breaks, and add page numbers. Then, print the 150 pages and reinsert them in the printer paper cabinet. Then, print your appendices one by one in the right sequence.

At your exam, your examiners often ask you to flip to a certain page number among your appendices. Without page numbers, you might spend valuable time looking for the appendix. Your examiner is waiting for you to find the appendix, while you become more and more stressed and nervous about whether you perhaps forgot the appendix in your report copy. In addition, the time is subtracted from your time to shine.

Reviewing this chapter's objectives

Tick those objectives you feel you have achieved, and review those you haven't yet accomplished. In this chapter, you have learned how to:

❒ Describe the analysis well in the project.

❒ Describe the solution designed in the project well in the project.

❒ Write sections that ensure coherence between sections throughout the report.

❒ Ensure clarity and coherence within each section.

Communicating Clearly and Professionally

In this chapter, you will learn:

1 That the writing style in engineering project texts is neutral, impersonal, correct, specific, concise, and (above all else) clear.
2 How to ensure correct spelling, grammar, and punctuation.
3 How to increase the clarity of your texts.
4 To increase readers' understanding of your report's coherent flow through meta-texts.
5 How to effectively communicate results from quantitative analyses.
6 To communicate through figures, illustrations, tables, and other graphical means.

The content of a written engineering report includes regular text as well as tables, diagrams, figures and other types of graphical communication. Communicating effectively in reports requires that both language and all graphical communication are clear to the target audience. Chapter 5 describes how engineering education builds on a positivistic, "natural science" worldview. This worldview is embedded in readers' minds and influences their perception of what professional and clear communication is. The worldview considers professional and clear communication as *neutral, impersonal, concrete, specific, correct,* and *concise*. These characteristics of communication are the foundation for the advice in this chapter.

Correct and clear language in engineering reports

As it is one of the most important life skills, a great deal is written on how to write and communicate effectively. This chapter deals with those issues that pertain to engineering reports in particular. The next two sections give advice about how to ensure a report free of spelling, grammar, and punctuation mistakes, and then how you achieve clarity in your report through the use of meta-texts.

Correct spelling, grammar, and punctuation

To spell correctly, construct correct sentences, and use correct punctuation are all important issues for engineering reports; perhaps more important than one might think.

If your examiners become annoyed with spelling or punctuation mistakes, you risk getting an assessment that is worse than your project really deserves (perhaps even much worse). External examiners base most of their assessment of a project on the written report. If the report is full of mistakes, then they may have a difficult time seeing beyond the mistakes and appreciating the report's technical qualities. So, make sure to proofread. See the top tips box for how to clear away all language mistakes.

TOP TIPS FOR AVOIDING LANGUAGE MISTAKES

1. If time permits, leave your report alone for a couple of days and then proofread it from start to finish.
2. Persuade a friend to proofread the report. Think carefully and identify in your social circle someone who once in a while corrects your *spoken* language. This person is perfect for proofreading.
3. Read your own report, but read it backwards – sentence by sentence – beginning from the last sentence in your conclusion and ending with the first sentence of your introduction. When reading backwards, you naturally avoid focusing on the flow of text and are therefore more keenly focused on language mistakes.

Meta-texts

Good reports contain massive amounts of meta-texts (or meta-communication). Meta-texts are those paragraphs that "lead the reader through the forest." Consider meta-texts as spoken by the report's storyteller, who continuously weaves together all the important threads of the report. The meta-texts are those pieces of text that ensure readers' understanding of the report's coherent flow.

Make sure to insert meta-texts at the beginning and end of all sections, regardless of whether sections are whole chapters or short subsections within chapters. The two lists below provide examples of meta-text. The first list presents meta-text examples of section introductions:

1 "The purpose of this chapter is to plan the implementation of the solution."
2 "Because the problem statement is about product weight reduction, this chapter will examine alternative, lighter materials for the product."
3 "As detailed in the methodology section, the analysis will first collect material prices and then examine how these materials impact cutting tools abrasion."
4 "This section will present the project's solution."
5 "The section will first summarize the results of the analysis, and then describe the solution design's three steps."
6 "First, the section provides an overview of all strategies that are theoretically possible, and then the section describes how workshop participants have selected their favorite solution."

The next list of meta-text examples are for section endings. The examples show how section ending meta-texts should tie section results together with future sections in your project:

1 "The section selected low carbon steel for the outer casing. The following section will test the bending ability of steel plates."
2 "The section's results are used when calculating the laminar flow speed through the back end of the system."
3 "The workshop prioritized four of six solution elements. The following section specifies each element."

Make sure that all sections (whole chapters as well as small subsections) begin with at least one sentence of meta-text about the content of the section; for example: "This section details/presents/demonstrates/examines/shows/links/summarizes/ compares …"

Large sections or chapters often have subsections. The chapter's introductory meta-text is the right place to tell readers which subsections the chapter includes and why.

EXAMPLE OF USING META-TEXTS

"The chapter first defines the concept of inventory and delineates a method for calculating inventory costs. Then, the chapter details the theoretical reasons for carrying inventory and methods for reducing inventory costs.

Definition of the concept of inventory
Inventory is …

Method for calculating inventory costs
Inventory costs consist of rent, salaries, risk costs, lost opportunity costs

The theoretical reasons for carrying inventory
The theory about production and logistics contains a number of reasons why firms hold inventory …

Methods for reducing inventory costs
A manufacturer can reduce inventory costs through several means. First …"

Notice the following two characteristics of the description in the example above, which improve the section's clarity:

1 The introductory meta-text lists four terms that each constitute one subsection in the chapter.
2 The terms mentioned in the introductory meta-text (e.g. "concept of inventory" or "theoretical reasons") are then used as the headings of the subsections.

A great rule of thumb is never have a heading immediately followed by a subsection's heading, as shown overleaf.

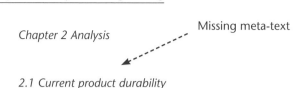

Chapter 2 Analysis

Missing meta-text

2.1 Current product durability

At a minimum, write some meta-text that tells the reader which subsections the section consists of (as in the boxed example).

Sentence construction

You might have heard a lecturer or a classmate utter a firm opinion about whether the active or passive voice is best (e.g. "Passive voice is more objective!" or "Active voice is clearer!").

In a sentence in the active voice, the actor who conducts the action expressed by the sentence's verb is the grammatical subject; for example: "The quality engineer continuously measures product weight." The subject is "The quality engineer" and the verb is "measures." The passive voice version of the same sentence is: "Product weight is measured continuously by the quality engineer." Although the quality engineer is still the actor who performs the action in the sentence, the grammatical subject is now the item that the action is done to – "Product weight."

Engineering reports should communicate with the maximum amount of clarity. Reports achieve clarity more effectively with sentences using the active voice. An editor of a major international journal once said:

Avoid the use of passive voice as much as you avoid death! (Reid 2010)

While this particular statement is overly dramatic, active voice sentences *are* clearer to the reader for the simple reason that the subject is the actor. Passive voice sentences do not include the actor in the sentence's central subject + verb structure. The actor must be added to the sentence using the preposition "by." The sentence about product weight includes the actor by adding "by the quality engineer." Because the addition of the actor is voluntary, passive voice sentences often leave out the actor. In such sentences, it is the reader's job to identify the actor from the sentence's context. If the context is a bit too ambiguous, readers might get confused. Table 13.1 provides examples of sentences in both the active and the passive voice.

Table 13.1 Examples of passive and active voice sentences	
Passive voice	**Active voice**
The windows were delivered without the necessary certificates	The manufacturer delivered the windows without the necessary certificates
The robots have their processing speed tested 12 times per year	The production engineering department tests the robots' processing speed 12 times per year
The product control test equipment is calibrated daily	The operators calibrate the equipment for product control tests daily

The argument that the passive voice is more objective than the active voice is still debated. One explanation for the perception might be that sentences in the passive voice avoid the use of the personal pronouns – "I" and "we." Engineering reports should be impersonal and therefore avoid using personal pronouns. Because the use of the passive voice easily enables the omission of the pronoun, some lecturers consider the passive voice to be more objective. In this author's opinion, the objectivity has to do with the *personal–impersonal* distinction rather than the active–passive voice distinction. Constructing sentences that are both active and impersonal is possible. See the examples in the next section.

If your supervisor is of the opinion that the passive voice is more objective, then do indulge them. Convincing your supervisor that the active voice is equally objective (as well as clearer) is not among your project's objectives, and although your report becomes clearer, you might end up annoying your supervisor, who will be your future examiner as well.

There is one important exception to the "active voice is clearer" rule. When you introduce new and hard-to-grasp terms, a sentence using the passive voice often achieves more clarity (Booth et al. 2008). For increased reader understanding, place the new term as the last part of a sentence. This is often only achievable with a sentence using the passive voice. For example:

> The manufacturer Nelson Lotions Inc. has three production lines for skin creams. The three production lines are labelled P1, P2, and P3. During production, the product flows through a set of pipes. Production line P3 was stopped by increased liquid viscosity.

The last sentence is passive. The actor "increased liquid viscosity" stops the production line. Increased liquid viscosity is not the subject, but is added to the sentence with the preposition *by*. Although this should make the sentence less clear, the reader gets a better understanding of the term, because when the reader gets to the term, they already know that the term is the cause for the production line stoppage.

Generally, readers are better equipped to understand a difficult term if the term's context is clear prior to the introduction of the term itself.

Impersonal language

The credibility of an engineering project builds on solid arguments, calculations, and reasoning, and not the personal qualities and credibility of the report's authors. Therefore, write the report as impersonally as possible. Avoid using personal pronouns such as "I" and "we" and possessives such as "my" and "our." Avoiding personal pronouns as actors might be difficult if you want to write sentences using the active voice. In these cases, replace personal pronouns with impersonal, neutral terms. The following list provides several examples:

1 The analysis shows ...
2 The calculations demonstrate ...
3 The section delineates …
4 The chapter details …
5 The dataset indicates …
6 The cause impacts ...

7 The problem statement focuses …
8 Figure 4 exemplifies …
9 Table 3 summarizes …
10 Appendix 5 contains …

A neat trick is using synonyms for *study* as a noun or a verb. For example:

- the study examines …
- the examination studies …
- the investigation analyzes …
- the examination investigates …
- the analysis examines …

In addition to this trick and the ten suggestions in the prior list, you can use impersonal pronouns, such as: "*This* shows …" or "*which* shows … ." Avoid using "it," which is often unclear.

Figure 13.1 shows four ways of describing the same idea, depending on the use of active/passive voice and personal/impersonal actor. Where possible, use formulations as in the top-right box in Figure 13.1.

	Personal	Impersonal
Active voice	"We have analyzed that …"	"The analysis shows …"
Passive voice	"… was analyzed by us."	"… is shown by the analysis"

Figure 13.1   Active/passive and personal/impersonal

Use short prepositions

Students often use long prepositions, such as "in relation to," "with respect to," "in connection with." Long prepositions are unclear. Consider this example: "The analysis verifies the results in relation to product performance." Readers will wonder how the numbers and product performance relate to one another. Do the results represent product performance or do we compare results with product performance, or do we verify the results on the day of receiving numbers for product performance? The reader is not informed about this relation. Instead, use the short prepositions – of, for, by, with. The example would be much clearer using the preposition "for" – "The analysis verifies the results for product performance."

Footnotes and references

Some lecturers have firm opinions about footnotes, while others have no opinion. The advice of this book is simply to avoid footnotes because they break up the reading flow. For every footnote, your reader stops their reading flow and looks to the bottom of the page.

To avoid the use of footnotes, insert appendix references directly into your text. For example: "the investment results in a surplus of £1.3 million over a five-year period. See Appendix 23 for details." Supervisors often want literature references as footnotes, and if so use footnotes. Otherwise, consider using either the traditional Harvard (or APA) academic in-text citation – "According to Johnson and Beamon (2014) the Earth is round" – where the reference is then found in the alphabetical list of references, or a more anonymous notation – "the Earth is round [18]," – where [18] means reference 18 in your report's list of references.

If your university has an explicitly stated referencing system (e.g. APA or Harvard), then make sure to apply that system.

Numbers in engineering reports

Numbers constitute a large portion of an engineering report's communication. A report should present numbers so that readers clearly understand every "number including" point the report makes. Three classic pitfalls that do not help understanding are forgetting to add units of measurement, presenting varying decimals, and using too many significant digits. The following sections detail and give advice for each pitfall.

Units of measurement on all numbers

Insert units of measurement on all numbers in the report including appendices and when numbers are components in formulas in the main report.

In tables, insert units of measurement in column headings; for example, in square parenthesis following the heading name – "Weight [kg]," "Pressure [hPa]," and "Temperature [°C]." Alternatively, insert an extra row below the heading names and insert units of measurement, as shown in Table 13.2.

Table 13.2 Showing units of measurement in a table				
Demand	Price	Weight	Max temperature	Density
pieces/year	$	kg	°C	kg/dm³
10.000	345.70	2.34	1.670	4.69
2.000	576.80	1.25	1.980	4.87
5.000	456.12	5.79	1.670	4.13

Variation in decimals in numbers of the same kind

Table 13.2 also shows that all numbers in the same column have the same number of significant digits. The *full points/commas* are placed in line with each other vertically down the columns. Make sure to align all numbers in a column as soon as you can, as this improves your own ability to draw conclusions from the table. Aligning numbers is quickly done using the Align button in the Excel task bar. As a minimum, remember to "clean" your tables of decimal variance prior to handing in the report.

Use a reasonable number of significant digits

A classic critique of a project is that students present calculation results with too many significant digits. A report might tell the reader that implementing the solution will result in a surplus of £3,483,657.89 over a five-year period. This number is much too precise (the more significant digits, the higher the precision). The number is highly uncertain, as the five-year timescale alone means considerable uncertainty. A more appropriate number presentation would be "approximately £3.5 million."

Any calculation has input numbers and each of these input numbers comes with its own level of precision. A rule of thumb is to include in your calculated result only as many significant digits as the input number with the lowest amount of significant digits. For example, a calculation says 34.82 liters per hour x 6.56 hours = 228.4192 liter. Because 6.56 hours only has three significant digits, the report cannot present the result with more than three significant digits, that is, 228 liters.

Many significant digits indicate high precision and engineers should know that unnecessarily high precision often results in unnecessarily high costs for producing an item. So, only include as many significant digits as necessary.

Tables, figures, charts, and other graphical displays in engineering reports

Tables, figures, and charts are very common in engineering reports. These graphical displays often represent the essence of both analysis and solutions. A report often presents analysis results with diagrams and charts (e.g. column or bar charts, or scatter diagrams). The solution is often explained using illustrations, such as "box-and-arrow" diagrams, construction sketches, and 3D technical drawings.

At best, a graphical display is self-explanatory. This is, however, often not the case and you might need to help your reader understand the display. A general rule for presenting any type of graphical display is to, first, present the display's *form*, and second the *content*. Table 13.3 gives examples of explaining the form of visuals.

Table 13.3 Examples of explaining the form of visuals	
Type	Explanation
Coordinate system	Explain the units of the X and Y axes
Column chart	Explain the unit of the chart's Y-axis and the meaning of a tall column
Box-and-arrow diagram	Using a legend, explain which types of boxes the diagram contains and how the diagram displays the box types (e.g. using different colors or box shapes)
Table	Explain each column in the table (e.g. product number, order numbers, or material) and (if necessary) how information flows from one column to another column

Then, when you are positive that your reader understands the form of the display, explain the content. The content is the message you want the reader to take from looking at the display. The following example shows how a report first explains a display's form and then the content that the readers should understand.

EXAMPLE: FIRST *FORM* AND THEN *CONTENT*

A project report deals with errors in the production of two types of pressure testing instruments used in offshore oil drilling (Product A and Product B). The text below shows how the report first explains the form and then the content of a columns chart.

First form ...

"Figure 12 shows how the instrument's errors are distributed across error causes. Blue columns represent Product A and orange columns Product B. The height of a column indicates the percentage of all errors that are attributed to the cause that the column represents."

and then content

"For Product A, the figure shows that 82% of all errors are caused by cracks of the outer casing or imprecise test measurements. The remaining causes only result in 18% of errors. The results for Product B are similar. The project will therefore address the production of casings and examine why test measurements are imprecise."

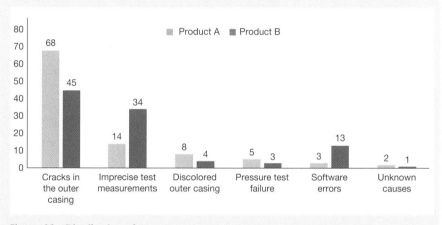

Figure 12   **Distribution of errors across error causes**

The chapter has so far focused attention on displays presenting quantitative analyses. Reports often need to present results from a qualitative analysis (e.g. interview data). Tables are an effective way to show qualitative analyses. For example, a study addresses five issues in three interviews, each with one informant. Use a table with one column for each informant and one row for each issue. Then, summarize each informant's statements on each issue in the table. For a qualitative analysis, this table constitutes an analysis result, just as a bar chart does for a quantitative analysis. So, when using a table to present a qualitative analysis, explain first *form* (what are the rows and columns) and then *content* (for example, patterns in informant statements about a particular issue).

Insert references to all graphical displays in your written text

A report's analysis often consists of many diagrams and tables, and the solution section often contains many illustrations. Remember that your written text must contain references to all displays. When you are close to your hand-in deadline, go through your report and check for these references. Formally, the text is the reader's guide, so if the text does not refer to the displayed material, the reader will (formally) not see it.

Reviewing this chapter's objectives

Tick those objectives you feel you have achieved, and review those you haven't yet accomplished. In this chapter, you have learned how to:

❐ Write using language that is neutral, impersonal, correct, specific, concise, and (above all else) clear.

❐ Ensure correct spelling, grammar, and punctuation.

❐ Increase the clarity of your texts and your report's coherent flow using meta-texts.

❐ Effectively communicate results from quantitative analyses.

❐ Communicate using figures, illustrations, tables, and other graphical means.

The Project Exam

Examination of Engineering Projects

In this chapter, you will learn:

1 How you (as a project team) can present your project effectively at your exam.
2 Some guidelines for designing professional presentation slides that effectively communicate your presentation's messages.
3 How to structure a coherent presentation with a flow that is clear and easy to follow.
4 How you can "own the stage" and use your body language, eye contact, hand gestures, and voice to support your presentation.
5 How you (as an individual student) can perform well during oral Q&A examinations.
6 The nature of an oral examination that is run by your examiners.
7 How to handle nervousness.
8 How to deal with dissatisfaction with your grade, receive feedback in a professional manner, and considerations about filing a formal complaint.
9 How to quickly clarify your own situation if you happen to fail an exam (e.g. second attempts).

Although evaluations and grading in project-based courses differ among universities and courses, a common method for evaluating the overall performance of a student project is evaluating the sum total of (a) the written report, (b) an oral group presentation of the report, and (c) student's individual performance in an examiner-led, Q&A-style discussion. Because examiners have already evaluated the written report prior to the day of exam, the examination consists of the group presentation and the individual examination.

Chapters 12 and 13 focus on the characteristics of a great written report. This chapter deals with group presentations and individual Q&A-style examinations. In addition, it provides advice for tackling grade dissatisfaction, the decision about whether to file a formal complaint, and (if you did not pass an exam) looking ahead towards the resit.

Group presentations at your exam

In group projects, you often present your project together with your teammates. Usually, you and your teammates stand in front of a whiteboard or projector screen and present a set of PowerPoint slides. Your examiners sit across from you behind a desk. At other times, you and your group might present a poster instead of a PowerPoint presentation.

The next two sections give advice on the design and content of PowerPoint slides, and how to ensure a coherent thread in your presentation. See a later section in this chapter for advise about designing great posters for poster-based exams.

Professional slides in your presentation

There are many opinions about the nature of good PowerPoint slides. Table 14.1 summarizes the guidelines for designing professional PowerPoint slides.

Table 14.1 Designing professional PowerPoint presentations	
Bullet points	Some slide templates encourage the use of bullet points, but bullets do not support an effective presentation well. Great presentations are visual, which a list of bullet points is not. Take a bold decision in your group not to use bullet points. Instead, use a great visual for each point that would have been a bullet point on its own slide. Then, use speech to convey the message
Text on slides	Avoid long chunks of text on a slide. Illustrate your point on the slide and convey your messages to your audience verbally instead
Figures, charts, diagrams, etc.	Your presentation should be stuffed with illustrations and visual displays of all sorts; for example, charts, photos, maps, box-and-arrow figures, 2x2 matrices, thought bubbles, stick figures, flow charts, all kinds of diagrams (see Figure 14.3)
Slide headings	Place the heading in the top-left corner of all slides in your presentation. Make sure that the first letter of all headings begins on the same pixel, so your headings do not jump from left to right, when moving between slides. Font size 28 is appropriate for slide headings. Your presentation heading of the first slide is an exception (see Figure 14.2)
Shadows and colors	Avoid using shadows on figures and text, and use colors conservatively. Pick a set of three coordinating colors and use these as your color theme. One of these colors could be the color of your industrial partner's logo. If you cooperate with an industrial partner that has a firm-specific PowerPoint template, then use the template
Placing figures on slides	If a figure is small, then place the figure in the center of the slide. If a figure is large, then align the left-hand side of the figure with the left-hand side of the first letter of your slide heading. The distance between both sides of the figure and the slide edges should be the same. In more creative presentations, a neat method for keeping your audience's attention is using edge-to-edge illustrations, e.g. a photo. Do consider your audience though. What works well in the advertising business might be considered unprofessional in banking or shipping (see Figure 14.3)
Font style and size	Use the same font throughout your presentation. Some people (including the author of this book) would say that Arial is the only professional font in a PowerPoint slide, but what's most important is consistency. As much as possible, use the same font size throughout any one slide. Exceptions are the slide heading, footnotes, and source

Sources	Explicitly stating the source of a slide's content is often considered professional; for example: "Source: Bureau of Labor Statistics, August 2018." When your own project is the source, consider inserting either "Source: Project report, page 34" or "Source: Project analysis." Write sources in the bottom left-hand corner of the slide so the S in Source aligns with the first letter of the slide's heading. An appropriate font size is 14 for a source (see Figure 14.1)
Footnotes	Mark footnotes with an asterisk (*) on the slide where appropriate. If you have several footnotes, use *, **, ***, etc. or numbers. Place the written footnotes above or below the source at the bottom of the slide, so asterisks align with the S in Source (see Figure 14.1)
Table of contents	Insert a "Table of contents" slide following the presentation's front page. Insert the same Table of contents slide every time you go from one agenda point to the next in the presentation. Mark on each version of the Table of contents slide which particular agenda point you have reached; for example with a light-blue box behind the next agenda point (see Figure 14.2). If your presentation has 12 agenda points, then repeat the Table of contents slide 12 times. A Table of contents slide can be a figure (e.g. a flow chart, a solution sketch, etc.). Every time you shift agenda point, mark on the figure which agenda point you will now turn to
Excel tables in slides	Avoid copying Excel tables directly in your slides. Instead, use diagrams that illustrate the key points in your material
Slide messages	All slides should have a message. Sometimes the message is a bit vague (e.g. a slide that provides an overview of an area or the build-up of a product). Most slides (e.g. slides with diagrams) have a specific point. Write these points either in the slide's heading or following a "giant arrow" (see Figure 14.1)
Presentations that "speak for themselves"	Some presentations should be designed so they "speak for themselves." These are presentations that you will not present orally, but instead send via email to a recipient without accompanying words. In such presentations, text pieces are necessary
Slide numbers	Remember to number your slides so your listeners can follow your presentation better. Consider using number notation such as "23/50" or "23 of 50"

The following three figures present three examples of slides that follow the guidelines given in Table 14.1 for professional PowerPoint presentations.

The slide in Figure 14.1 provides an overview of which activities a firm conducts in-house. The giant arrow connects the slide's main content with the main message. The heading is placed on the left-hand side. The first heading letter aligns with the left side of the figure, the S in Source, and the footnote asterisk.

The slide in Figure 14.2 is a "Table of contents" slide. The presentation has eight agenda points. The blue tint panel indicates to the reader that the next agenda point is "Introduction to the project."

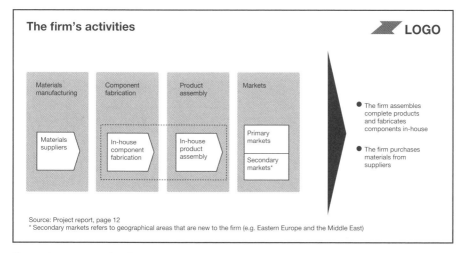

Figure 14.1   Example of a slide that provides an overview of a firm's activities

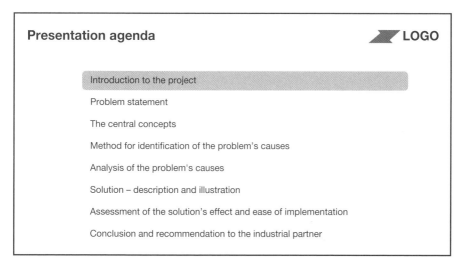

Figure 14.2   Example of a "Table of contents" slide

The last example of a professional slide, Figure 14.3 overleaf, shows an illustration of a project's solution using a "box-and-arrow" chart. The solution could be a flow of water, power, information, or goods. Notice that the slide's heading contains the slide's main message that the solution consists of nine component parts.

Building the presentation's coherent flow

Most presentations use the flow from the report (the "Table of contents" slide is an example). This is the safe way of conducting a presentation. Your audience receives what they expect and you are well equipped to design a presentation with a

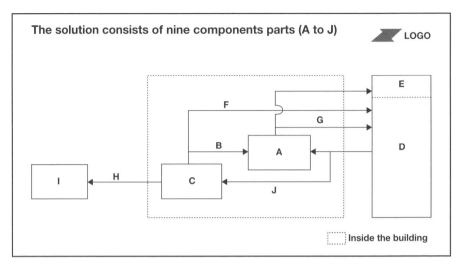

Figure 14.3   Example of a slide that expresses the main message in the slide's heading

coherent flow that is easy for your audience (your examiners) to understand. Add to your presentation any other points you want to make in addition to your report. See a later section about adding new content to your presentation.

"Owning the stage": body language, eye contact, hand gestures, and voice

In your exam, use your body language and voice to more effectively convey your messages. See the top tips box below.

TOP TIPS FOR GIVING A PRESENTATION

- Plant your feet solidly on the floor and stand up straight.
- Speak loudly and clearly.
- Look at your examiners and avoid staring at your slides.
- Stand still and use your arms as living conductor batons.
- If you present as a team, when it is your turn, assume ownership of the stage by moving closer to either your audience or your slides.

Your examiners alternate their view between looking at your slides and looking at you as the presenting student. Avoid looking at your own slides. Instead, keep your eyes on your audience. Instead of looking at your slides for your talking points, write them down on small cards or place your computer in front of you, so you are able to follow your slides without looking at the projector screen behind you.

Some students speak very quietly, which may get examiners thinking that such students are uncertain and perhaps less skilled. If you struggle with this quite common problem, a great idea is to train your ability to speak loudly and clearly. Check YouTube for videos about vocal training or vocal exercises. Here is a short intro:

1 Walk into an empty room.
2 Fill your lungs with air, stand up straight, and pull your shoulders and chin back.
3 Begin making a deep OOOOH sound where you let the air stream evenly from the bottom of your lungs. You control the stream with your stomach muscles. Imagine making your throat as broad as possible.
4 Continue with LOH-LOH-LOH-LOOOOOOH.
5 Continue by reciting sentences using the same technique.

Consider improving your general presentation skills. If your course does not include presentation training, check with your field's labor union or industry organization. Presenting with poise, ease, and elegance requires training. Although some people are great at hiding their nervousness and feel comfortable when presenting, no one is born to present. Everyone becomes better with training.

Presentation content

A great presentation begins with a concise and accurate presentation of the project's main theme. In addition, effective presentations add perspective to their project. When you present your project's main theme, remember to present the problem statement and conclusion so your examiners clearly understand how your project answers the problem statement. The additions to the presentation that add perspective vary among faculties and their traditions. However, typical themes include:

- The current state of solution implementation
- Challenges in the implementation
- The solution's broader relevance, perhaps for other firms in your industrial partner's industry
- Your solution's relevance for society at large and perhaps an environmental impact
- Your own learning process throughout the project
- Reflections on your teamwork – conflict management, planning, and organization
- New projects that naturally follow your project.

Errors in the report you discovered between report hand-in and the exam

Usually, you will hand in your report between two to four weeks prior to the exam. During this period, you often find errors and mistakes of varying importance. Lecturers are often asked whether and how to deal with these errors in the exam presentation. The short answer is that this depends on the nature and gravity of the errors. Table 14.2 presents some more concrete answers.

Table 14.2 How to deal with errors and mistakes in the exam presentation	
Nature and gravity of error	**Recommended action**
Serious errors that alter your conclusions considerably	Include these errors in the first part of your presentation, tell your audience what you should have done correctly in your work, and show the correct version. Use the correct version in the remainder of the presentation so your conclusions rest on the right calculations and presumptions
Medium-sized errors with little conclusion impact	Briefly mention these errors towards the end of your presentation. If you mention these errors prior to your individual examination, you can disarm your examiner a bit. Do expect questions about the errors regardless of whether you mentioned them
Errors that are inconsequential for your conclusion	Do not mention these errors in your presentation. Instead, know what you should have done and hope that your examiners will address the errors during your individual examination

Irrespective of the size of the error, what's most important is knowing that an error is, in fact, an error, and the correct way to put it right.

Poster session exams

A poster is a common tool for presentations and some project courses use a "poster session" as part of the course examination. Your exam is presenting your poster for your examiners and perhaps classmates and industrial partner employees.

A poster should clearly present the main theme of your project. However, because a poster has the natural limitation of being only one (large) piece of paper, think about which parts of your main theme should be on the poster and which parts you provide orally when you present your poster.

The two most important parts of your project are the problem and the solution. If your project improves an existing entity, then be clear about what needs improvement. If your project designs a new entity from scratch, then be clear about the need and the person, organization, or group having the need. If possible, illustrate the problem.

While your problem might be difficult to illustrate, your solution is likely to be more naturally illustrative. Make user-friendly drawings of machines or buildings, box-and-arrow diagrams for software, and flowcharts from processes. If your solution is an idea or a partly developed concept, then consider a conceptual sketch. The list below presents some more advice:

1 Feel free to use emojis, stick men, thought bubbles, arrows, and the like to make your points.
2 Write any technical details that you feel are necessary to convey at the bottom of the poster, so they do not confuse the big picture.

3 If you want to divide your poster into sections, make clear lines and consider whether your readers can follow your flow between sections or whether you should use arrows to guide your readers.

Individual examination

Examiners often test students' individual performance in an examiner-led, Q&A-style discussion that follows the presentation. Such an examination can be conducted as one, long discussion with the full group participating. These lengthy whole-group discussions may include individual student examinations with everyone present. Most of the advice in this section centers on one-student examinations.

Although departments and examiners differ in their success criteria, the most effective method for improving your prospects for a better grade is answering examiner questions correctly. Good answers during the examination usually impact the grade much more than a great group presentation.

The discussion at the exam table

Your examiners read your project report with a critical mindset. A general rule for grading applied by many universities is that a report starts at an A and the frequency and seriousness of the report's errors and inadequacies then reduce the grade. Because of this general rule, examiners spend much of their evaluation effort looking for errors and inadequacies. At the exam, examiners bring with them a set of questions that address these errors and inadequacies. You as students are expected to answer these questions, often by explaining how to carry out an erroneous calculation, assessment, or other activity correctly.

With very good reports, examiners have a hard time findings errors and inadequacies. There are always some errors and inadequacies, but great projects may not contain enough errors and inadequacies to fill the whole discussion time. In these situations, examiners often add questions that address correctly conducted activities. Such questions work well for assessing the knowledge and skills of the particular student in the exam room. Although a whole project team has written the report, project exams often concern the individual students in the group. Examiners use these questions about correct elements in the report to probe the level of the particular student in the room.

When an examiner asks you a questions, assess as quickly as possible whether the question concerns a flaw or a correct element. If the questions concern a flaw, then follow this two-step procedure:

1 Acknowledge that the flaw is indeed a flaw.
2 Explain the correct way of conducting the calculation or activity.

When explaining the correct way, be convincing. For example: "I see that we forgot to multiply with Pi" or "We should have divided by the number of observations before taking the square root." The two examples indicate quite clearly that your skill level supersedes the level of the report.

Even better, but also harder, is if you can spot that your examiner has overlooked something (a premise or special circumstance), meaning that *what your examiner thinks is an error is, in fact, correct.* Your reply could be: "I gather that your question implies (premise). However, in our project (explanation of special circumstance meaning that your use of, say, a method is correct)." If you convince your examiner, you will get lots of credit.

Most importantly, if your examiner addresses a real error (most often the case), avoid fighting to the bitter end. Fighting to the bitter end gives your examiner the impression that you do not understand why your error is an error. Better just say "Good question, I am not sure" and hope for better luck with the next question.

If you do not understand a question, you can still make a few points by beginning your answer with explaining the generalities about the theme the question addresses. For example, let us assume that an examiner poses a question about calculating the center of gravity for a mechanical component. Begin your answer by telling your examiner about the purpose of including the calculation and follow up with what you know about conducting the calculation. Even though you only get a few points for a vague answer to a specific question, you do get points for knowing the purpose of and method for the center of gravity calculation. Although you get points for using this tactic, keep in mind that you spend valuable time that you could have spent giving precise and impressive answers to other questions, which result in many more points.

During your discussion, you might be tempted to disown parts of the report. Examiners do not react well to this tactic. Unless your faculty specifies differently, you all own the whole project. Avoid formulations such as: "well, I did not work with this part of the project," "what they (your teammates) might have meant … ," or "I think they assumed … ." These formulations indicate that you are unfamiliar with these parts of the project.

Managing nervousness

A nervous student taking an exam with a poor report is an unfortunate cocktail. With a poor report, the examiners enter the room with a long list of errors and inadequacies. The examiners will most often ask about these errors from the very first question. The nervous student might quickly think that there is no chance of passing. This is unfortunate because the nervousness may give examiners the impression that a student's skills are even lower than the level of the report.

The trick is to remember that examiners ask about errors and inadequacies even with the best of projects. Keep your cool and use the two steps in the previous section about how to respond to a question about an error: acknowledge that the error is indeed an error, and explain what you should have done to avoid the error. In addition, remember that projects with lots of serious mistakes still pass an exam, only with lower grades.

Dissatisfaction and filing complaints

Students who are unhappy about their grade are quite common. Most often, students are dissatisfied or disappointed with their own performance, but it happens that students are dissatisfied or even angry with their examiners. They consider their grade unfair. Sometimes, emotions fly so high that students leave the room in anger or counter-argue loudly during feedback. Occasionally, examiners may give up providing feedback or arguments for the grade.

It is important to understand that once the grade is given, the only possibility for changing the grade is by filing a formal complaint. Counter-arguing during feedback is pointless. Instead, take thorough notes for a possible complaint.

If you are deciding whether to file a complaint, check whether you risk getting an even lower grade if your report is reassessed by an appeals committee. Even though there might be a risk of getting a lower grade, you may have real cause for filing a complaint. Consider discussing your grade after a few days with your (former) supervisor or study director to assess the viability of a complaint. In addition, consider these guidelines:

1 A classic complaint is: "But you could have told us during supervision." The answer is of course "Yes," but only if your supervisor knew of the error. You need to make the case that you got cheated by a supervisor who "saved an error for the exam" or that your supervisor should have spontaneously opened a discussion about the error without it being an agenda point (or any other prompting from you). Making this case plausibly is difficult.
2 At some universities, students can complain about the supervision *or* the grade. Make sure to complain about the grade even though your argument may be poor supervision. Otherwise, your grade might stay the same regardless of whether the appeals committee agrees with your complaint.
3 Complain about the process rather than the assessment. The process is unrelated to your examiner's professional skills and such a complaint might get a more favorable reception. See if you have a common enemy (e.g. ambiguous grading rules). Argue, for example, that a grade should be "Passed" rather than a C– that impacts your grade point average.

"But I answered all the questions"

From time to time, a student feels that a grade is unfair, because even though the student answered all the questions, the grade is not an A. There are two (and perhaps more) explanations for this paradox:

1 Students "warm up" for every question. A typical oral exam lasts 15–20 minutes per student. This allows for asking around 7–10 questions. If a student spends several minutes getting help to understand each question, there will only be time for 4–5 questions. Even if the student ends up answering each of the 4–5 questions correctly, the overall performance is mid-level because of the level of help needed to understand the questions.
2 Some lecturers cannot help themselves and feel an urge to give students the right answers to questions even though the students could not provide a correct answer. The student hears all the correct answers as part of the discussion and therefore feels that they did an excellent job. The grade is still low because your examiners take notes of who provided the correct answers.

What if I fail?

Around 5–10% of students fail a course and some courses have fail rates of above 30%. In other words, failing a course is not unusual. If fact, failing is quite common.

Consider your failed exam as the dry run, as your final rehearsal, and then consider your resit as the "real exam." If you have once tried and failed an exam, you are much wiser about the exam situation and the specific success criteria of your examiners. After the failed exam, you can begin preparing for your resit knowing more specifically what to study.

For a project exam, you might have to rework or supplement your report. Ask your supervisor what to rework. During your preparation for the resit:

- make the necessary edits to your work
- develop a stronger understanding of the errors and inadequacies in your report
- study the theory that serves as the foundation for your project.

Reviewing this chapter's objectives

Tick those objectives you feel you have achieved, and review those you haven't yet accomplished. In this chapter, you have learned how to:

- ❏ Present your project effectively in your exam.
- ❏ Design professional presentation slides that effectively communicate your messages.
- ❏ Structure a coherent presentation with a flow that is clear and easy to follow.
- ❏ Take the stage using your body language, eye contact, hand gestures, and voice.
- ❏ Perform well during oral Q&A examinations and handle your nervousness.
- ❏ Quickly clarify your own situation if you happen to fail an exam.

Getting Top Marks from External Examiners

This chapter deals with the success criteria of external examiners. The chapter describes what external examiners look for in both the written report and the oral project presentation at the exam. In addition, the chapter describes elements that cause confusion for external examiners. The chapter draws on conversations with external examiners for engineering projects. These were industry specialists and academics. Their comments are included in quotation marks throughout this chapter.

External examiners' expectations of the basics in a project

Although the traditions for the content elements in a great engineering project differ across engineering fields, the following four elements constitute the basics of an engineering project:

1 A problem of reasonable complexity.
2 A sufficient base of knowledge and methods from the engineering discipline.
3 An analysis (e.g. of problem causes, user needs, or technical possibilities for solutions).
4 A solution that will credibly solve the problem.

These four content elements are included in projects across almost all engineering disciplines. The four elements are particularly important in your final two or three semesters when you select your own problem and methods. During earlier semesters, problems and methods are often defined and specified by your instructors. In addition to these four content elements, another four elements are "must haves" for a large proportion of engineering disciplines:

5 An analysis of the problem landscape prior to formulating the problem statement.
6 A detailed description of methods, materials, equipment, and knowledge base for the analysis.
7 A financial assessment of the solution (beyond an assessment of the solution's effect).
8 A plan for implementing the solution.

External examiners' official focus when reading the report

In many countries, the external examiner's official focus when reading the report is errors and inadequacies. A report with none or only a few flaws gets the top mark and reports with a higher number of flaws or more serious flaws get lower marks. Because the official focus is errors and inadequacies, external examiners consider their job as being a detective in search of errors and inadequacies.

The nature of errors and inadequacies differs widely. Some mistakes are simple (e.g. a missing name on a chart's axis) and others are complex (e.g. an incorrect assessment of the solution's impact). Some errors are clear to all parties and others are a matter of discussion. Table 15.1 contains examples of common report errors and inadequacies.

Table 15.1   Common errors and inadequacies in reports
Simple errors and inadequacies*
Using the wrong formula
Using a variable with the wrong sign (plus or minus)
An error in the use of a program (e.g. an MS Excel formula only includes half the data)
Lacking units of measurement or a result with too many significant digits
Mistaken understanding or use of a concept, a method, or measurement instrument
Report mistakes (e.g. wrong figure numbers or missing references to appendices)
Errors and inadequacies in assessments
Selection of the wrong problem (the problem analysis points to a different problem)
Using a method that logically cannot result in a useful solution (regardless of correct use)
Using a test method that cannot provide a useful result (even if the method is used correctly)
Selection of a material that is not durable under the relevant circumstances
Two or more incompatible choices for a project's solution
Wrongful assessment of the effect of a cause on the project's problem

* A simple error can have huge consequences, even if the mistake itself is simple ("You should have typed a minus rather than a plus")

Errors and inadequacies are not of equal size. The next section provides insights into the relative importance of errors and inadequacies in the minds of external examiners.

The relative importance of success criteria for external examiners

Figure 15.1 shows a house with three floors (ground floor, first floor, and attic). The house shows how the importance among quality criteria varies. Generally, the better your project, the higher up in the house is the conversation at your exam. For the ground and first floor, the point to the right of the house indicates what a report must have to get to the next level in the house.

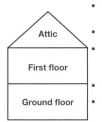

- Comfortable conversation about subjects such as the broad applicability of the solution, the firm's plans for the future, industrial partner developments

- Coversations about your project process and industrial parter cooperation

- The project's use of theory, methods, models from the project's engineering discipline including how and under which circumstances and limitations methods and models are used

- Whether and how the solution as well as critical assumptions match reality

- The coherent, logical flow of the project's step-by-step reasoning from problem and analysis to solution and implementation

- Conducting project activities with a critical mindset (particularly important with data collection and all other industrial partner intractions)

Figure 15.1   House illustrating external examiners' quality criteria

Figure 15.1 shows that having a coherent, logical flow is an important quality criterion of all in an engineering project. When an examiner reads a given section of a report, the examiner should not be thinking: "What is this report really about?" The following elements must be clear to your examiner at all times:

1 Your project has one problem (and not two or more, or perhaps no problem at all).
2 Your project's analysis must deal with this problem (and not any other problems).
3 Your solution should solve this one problem (and not other problems or no problem at all).

With a clear coherent flow, your project reaches the first floor. To make sure you reach the first floor, structure your project as described in detail in Chapter 12. The coherent logic that Chapter 12 describes is very different from writing your project as a "historical account" detailing your actual work process.

In your project, demonstrate how you have used a critical mindset when collecting data (regardless of data type); for example, how you saw through an obvious bias in an interview with a department head. Examiners expect you to assess whether a data source is reliable and how you take action to ensure data reliability if necessary (e.g. interview two or three people about the same issue if you suspect your first informant might have an agenda other than just helping you with information). Notice that the issues in Figure 15.1's ground floor are more important than using the methods and models from your engineering discipline.

A project with a clear, coherent flow that uses reliable data and results in a realistic solution can reach the attic in Figure 15.1 by using the discipline's methods and models correctly. In addition to using your methods and models correctly, examiners expect you to check whether your assumptions, calculation results, and proposed solutions are realistically implementable or whether they are "pie in the sky."

If you demonstrate excellence in both ground and first floor, your project is great and your grade is most likely an A. The conversation around the exam table feels easy, comfortable, and almost fun. Examiners ask you for information out of real interest and not just to assess your skills. Your examiners have assessed the quality of your report prior to the exam and found the report excellent. Your conversation will therefore be largely about explaining correct issues rather than errors and inadequacies. When your examiners (often quite quickly) determine that they are satisfied with this portion of the conversation, the remaining conversation turns to your industrial partner's situation, new opportunities, industry issues, and other issues outside the scope of your project.

Examiner assessment of your report's communicative level

There are two important principles to bear in mind with regard to examiner assessment of your report's level of communication:

1 Write so that your external examiner, who meets your project for the first time when reading the report, understands the project from the first page and section.
2 Write so that your examiners can understand the project without any prior knowledge other than the general engineering disciplines (be pedagogical and explain the basics when introducing the project).

It is not unusual, unfortunately, that an external examiner first understands what a project is about on page 35 of a report. Such reports are written with absolute clarity for the project group members who know the project well, but are close to unreadable for outsiders. This is because the report:

● uses terms that are not introduced until later on in the report or not at all
● forgets the necessary explanations and meta-texts
● discusses subjects that require prior familiarity from the reader.

TOP TIPS

Learning how to write a report for an audience completely unfamiliar with the project is not easy, but there are a few tricks to it:

1. Let a friend or relative read your project's introduction section. This way you receive feedback and a first-hand impression from a person who (just like your examiner) meets your project for the first time.
2. Write a draft of your introduction early and then revisit the introduction a week or two later. Reading any written piece a week later allows you to read the piece with fresh eyes and you are better equipped to find terms in need of introduction, and sections in need of reader-friendly meta-texts.

See Chapter 12 for advice about writing your introduction using a hierarchical structure.

Your examiners are your primary target audience and because your supervisor is already familiar with your report, the external examiner is the core target audience. You might think that the report needs to cater for the needs of your industrial partner contact, their department head, and perhaps the project manager selected for implementing your project. This is a misunderstanding. Your industrial partner is not the target audience and not even a part of the target audience.

External examiners value reports that "say it like it is" even if a conclusion fits terribly with the wishes of your industrial partner. For example, a report finds that the drop in productivity is caused by poorly motivated production equipment operators and that the drop in motivation is caused by the poor management skills of a new group leader (who may be your contact person). Warning: by reading between the lines in your report, seasoned external examiners can detect such situations like bloodhounds. So, even if you please your industrial partner by writing diplomatically, be prepared to discuss the situation.

Mistakes in spelling and grammar, missing figure numbers and titles, and poor quality of appendices (e.g. drawings and photos) often count more than you might expect. External examiners often criticize the lack of proper proofreading that would detect these mistakes. Spelling mistakes, grammatical errors, and so on indicate to your examiners that your quality awareness is low and since examiners are humans, these thoughts can permeate their perception of your project's technical subjects.

The "don't do" list

The following list describes a set of project characteristics that have negative effects on external examiners' assessments:

1 Blaming errors and inadequacies on a lack of time ("If we had more time, we would have …").
2 Having far from complete datasets. If your industrial partner does not have the data you need, then conduct measurements yourselves. If necessary, take sets of representative measurements and extrapolate or use realistic assumptions that you have checked with your industrial partner and supervisor.
3 Inventing your own terms for subjects that already have widely recognized names. Use your discipline's recognized terms if possible and particularly if your examiners can reasonably expect you to know these terms from your classes.
4 Including a problem statement that has two or more issues.
5 Writing imprecise text that is only understandable with prior insights, leaving your examiners to make a series of guesses.
6 Inserting figures and illustrations without references in the text (your examiner is led to think: "What was the point of this figure?").
7 Writing conclusions that are artificially friendly to the project's industrial partner. Make sure to write the conclusion that your well-reasoned arguments point towards, and avoid "pleasing" your industrial partner. In rare cases, it might be necessary to hand your industrial partner a redacted version of the report.
8 Trying to impress your examiners by writing how closely you have worked with a company's managing director or various vice presidents (insight and knowledge matter, not titles).

Reviewing this chapter's objectives

Tick those objectives you feel you have achieved, and review those you haven't yet accomplished. In this chapter, you have learned:

❐ The expectations and quality criteria of external examiners about the content of great projects.

❐ That external examiners' focus is often officially the errors and inadequacies in a report.

❐ Which quality criteria are most important to external examiners and which are less important.

❐ The "don't do" list of project characteristics that have negative effects on external examiners' assessments.

Technical Research: the Master of Science (M.Sc.) Project

The Special Requirements of M.Sc. Projects in Engineering

In this chapter, you will learn:

1 The differences between projects that design solutions to specific problems, and M.Sc. projects that conduct academic research that contributes to general knowledge.
2 How you as the student can manage *two* primary stakeholders: an industrial partner and your university.
3 That problem statements in M.Sc. projects often are research questions and that answering these questions will contribute to the general base of knowledge within your discipline.
4 The typical structure of an M.Sc. project, which follows the structure of academic papers.
5 How M.Sc. projects systematically localize and use theory, conduct methodology choices, and how the project's results contribute to knowledge.
6 How M.Sc. projects describe the methodology, analysis, discussions, and conclusion in the project report.

Universities and engineering fields differ in their traditions. One of these differences is whether they expect their students to design a solution for a specific problem or conduct an academic research project that contributes to the general base of knowledge (and can perhaps be published as a paper in an academic journal or conference proceedings).

There are a great many differences between problem-solving projects and academic research projects. Academic research projects are most prevalent in graduate schools and the most common project conducted as a research project is the M.Sc. project. Universities and even departments within the same university differ in their expectations and traditions for M.Sc. projects. At some universities, M.Sc. projects are traditional problem-solving projects, while at other universities, they are problem-solving projects but with extra academic requirements (often the inclusion of a literature review and a discussion about how results relate to the literature), and at yet other universities, M.Sc. projects are research projects that follow the traditional guidelines for academic research.

Table 16.1 shows these three project types: a problem-solving project, a problem-solving project with added academic requirements, and a pure academic research project. While Chapters 1–15 are relevant for problem-solving projects, the content of this chapter is relevant for M.Sc. projects if they are academic research projects as described at the bottom of Table 16.1. For problem-solving projects that have added academic requirements (e.g. a review of related literature), you can find guidance in all chapters.

Table 16.1 Three types of project	
Project type	**Description**
The problem-solving project	No difference between an M.Sc. project and a traditional problem-solving project. If your university's expectation for your M.Sc. project is a traditional problem-solving project, then skip this chapter and read Chapters 1–15
The problem-solving project with extra academic requirements	Projects of this kind differ from traditional problem-solving projects by including a thorough review of the literature closely related to the project's problem. For example, if the subject of a project is precision in measurements of living cells in milk, then examiners expect you to demonstrate insight into the literature that specifically concerns milk cell measurement and not general literature about liquid measurements, which or may not be part of your subject's curriculum
The academic research project	The academic research project is a fundamentally different activity from a problem-solving project and the resulting report is almost a different literary genre. The purpose of an academic research project is contributing to our common pool of knowledge. An academic research project can be conducted in cooperation with an industrial partner, but only if the cooperation contributes to answering the project's generally relevant research questions. The academic research project is this chapter's focus

If you conduct your M.Sc. project or any other project as an academic research project, use the advice in this chapter. If you conduct a problem-solving project with extra academic requirements, use Chapters 1–15 as well as the section in this chapter about an academic research project's literature review. If you're conducting a traditional problem-solving project, then skip this chapter and read Chapters 1–15.

The nature of academic research projects

The purpose of an academic research project in engineering is to contribute to knowledge within an engineering discipline. In other words, an academic research project does not contribute to the knowledge of an industrial partner *only*.

Academic research projects can constitute their own independent project or be part of larger research project conducted in the university department. An academic research project *can* be conducted in cooperation with an industrial partner and result in the design of a solution. However, designing a solution is only a secondary goal. The primary goal is answering the project's research question in order to contribute to knowledge.

Managing both the industrial partner and the university as stakeholders

Although the higher purpose of an academic research project is knowledge contribution, research projects are often conducted with an industrial partner. Early in the project period, your job as a researcher is to match the interest of both of your primary stakeholders, the university and the industrial partner. Compared to the problem-solving projects described in Chapters 1–15, matching these interests can be a bigger challenge because your supervisor may have a personal/professional stake in your project beyond helping a student learn something and pass an exam. Although matching these interests is standard operating practice at universities, the task is not always easy.

EXAMPLE: MATCHING INDUSTRIAL PARTNER AND UNIVERSITY INTERESTS

Two students plan a project with a firm that carries out galvanization of metal items. The galvanization process enables items to withstand corrosion over time. The industrial partner wants the team to examine the corrosion of a particular metal item that the firm galvanizes for one of its largest customers. When galvanized, the metal item is used for a 20-year period under aggressive levels of environmental acidity. The firm would like the team to assess the impact of the aggressive levels of environmental acidity on the corrosion of the item.

The students' supervisor, a professor of metallurgy, has an interest in the project. The professor wants the students to contribute to the science of metallurgy and conduct a study publishable in the journal *Corrosion Science*.

The students formulate a problem statement in collaboration with their industrial partner and supervisor. The project will examine the effect of the aggressive levels of environmental acidity on the item's corrosion. Specifically, the study will examine the corrosion attack points on the metal item and the annual corrosion rate on the attack points' galvanized surface.

In this project, the students match both stakeholders' interests. This problem statement deals with a particular firm's current challenge, but contributes to the general metallurgical knowledge about corrosion.

Project structure of academic research projects

The project structure of academic research projects follows the traditional structure of academic papers. This structure is often abbreviated as IMRAD for Introduction, Methods and materials, Results, And Discussion. Briefly, the introduction contains the project's purpose, research questions, and a literature review, while the section on methods and materials includes descriptions of methods, datasets, and techniques for ensuring reliability and validity. The results section presents the results, while the discussion section discusses possible explanations for the results and how the results matter. In addition, the discussion section includes conclusions, contributions to the body of knowledge, the study's limitations, and suggestions for future research.

Figure 16.1 illustrates the IMRAD structure and the following sections will describe the academic research project's sections one by one following the sequence in the figure.

Figure 16.1   The typical structure of academic research projects

Introduction

While the introduction of a problem-solving project usually begins with describing the industrial partner, the academic research project takes its starting point in literature. The introduction includes a purpose statement and perhaps explicit research questions. The introduction describes how the project contributes to the body of knowledge in its field by fulfilling the purpose and answering the research questions.

The beginning of the introduction section works well using a hierarchical structure. As Chapter 12 describes, a problem-solving project often begins broadly by introducing the industrial partner to readers and ends with a problem statement and delimitations. The academic research project also begins broadly by introducing the literature field. The inclusion of literature in the introduction serves two purposes:

1 The literature can help to ensure that readers understand the relevance of conducting the study.
2 The literature may point specifically to the gap your project will address.

EXAMPLE

In cooperation with an industrial partner, a student conducts a project about reducing the number of necessary service visits to electrical converters in offshore wind turbines operating in high salinity environments. The firm's technicians are convinced that the salty air impacts the converters' durability. The project's research question is: "How does environmental salinity affect the number of service visits needed by the electrical converters?"

A problem-solving project would have begun the introduction with a description of the industrial partner and ended with describing the problem. Because this is an academic research project with the purpose of answering the research question to contribute to knowledge, the introduction begins by describing the general nature of environmental salinity and the literature on how such an environment affects electrical components. The introduction feeds into the research question and argues (using literature) why the question is worth answering.

If the project in the previous example about service visits to offshore wind turbines had been a problem-solving project, the problem statement might have been: "How can [name of industrial partner] reduce the number of service visits needed by the electrical converters in the firm's offshore wind turbines?" Instead, an academic research project should focus on a question that has general relevance. Answering the question must contribute to the body of knowledge in the field.

Often, conducting academic research means examining relationships between entities. Scientific fields may have their own name for *entity*, such as construct or variable. In the engineering sciences, *variable* is popular. Variables are usually measurable using numbers. Contributing to knowledge means adding to the understanding of how variables relate to one another, that is, how one variable impacts another variable. The variable that does the impacting is the *independent variable*, and the variable that receives the impact is the *dependent variable*.

Table 16.2 presents some research questions about the relationship between two variables.

Table 16.2   Examples of variables across fields

The independent variable	The dependent variable	The science that examines the relationship
The thickness of a carrying beam made from a new composite material	The beam's tensile strength	Material science
The formula for a new type of pesticide	The amount of weeds in a cornfield	Agronomy
The amount of preservative in a finished food product	The food product's durability	Food science
The arrival rate to a queue	The average queuing time	Management science
Martin Luther's perception of the God–man relationship	Martin Luther's preferred form of government	Religious studies or theology
The average amount of vitamin D in a person's blood	Life span	Medicine or pharmacology
The time spent on social media	The feeling of loneliness	Psychology or sociology

Table 16.2 shows that studying relationships among variables cuts across scientific fields. Because academic research projects, both within and outside engineering, often study the relationships among variables, three research questions are quite common. Table 16.3 describes these three research questions.

No.	Research question	Details
1	"Does A impact B?"	The answer to this question might be a resounding "Yes." A great academic research project will qualify this answer, discuss limitations, and reflect on the robustness of the "Yes," and the circumstances under which the "Yes" applies
2	"How does A impact B?"	This research question is relevant in cases where the answer to research question no. 1 is established as a "Yes," but without an understanding of the nature of the A–B relationship. An answer to the research question could be: "If A increases, B decreases." For example, in construction science, an answer could be: "If the density of the material of the wall between two rooms increases, the noise transference between the two rooms decreases"
3	"Why does A impact B as it does?"	This research question is often the most complex. The question is relevant when the nature of a relationship is known, but not explained. In the noise transference example above, the project would seek an explanation for why material density impacts noise transference as it does

Table 16.3 Three common research questions across fields

Variants of the three research questions in Table 16.3 are the most prevalent questions in many scientific disciplines. There are, of course, other questions. For example:

- "Which factors affect …?" The answer: a set of factors.
- "How can X be conducted?" The answer: a method.
- "How can the speed of X method be increased?" The answer: a set of method *changes.*
- "What are the key variables (within a new area)?" The answer: a set of key variables.

Once the research question is formulated, the next step is to review the literature that is closely related to the research question, so the project builds on and utilizes the earlier published theories, methods, and models.

The literature review

The section of a research report that reviews the relevant literature, defines concepts, and (if needed) operationalizes concepts and variables is often called *the literature review.*

In problem-solving projects, students often use the subject literature that is part of the course's curriculum. Academic research projects, on the other hand, are expected to locate and use the literature that is related to the project's research question. It is possible that your engineering faculty happens to include the most relevant literature for your project; however, it is highly unlikely.

Imagine a project working to reduce the delivery time of orders from a fish filleting factory to fish retailers (convenience stores and supermarkets). If this project were a problem-solving project, the student team would most likely use theory about delivery time reduction found in their subject's literature. An academic research project would instead search for theory about delivery time reduction for fish filleting processes. If such theory is nonexistent (or exists but is not useful), then the project would look for theory about delivery time reduction for food manufacturers in general and not limited to fish filleting. Only if this theory is nonexistent or not useful, would the project apply the general theory about delivery time reduction (for any type of product).

Academic research projects are expected to document their search for literature and (if necessary) argue for their choice of theory. Even if you apply the general theory, examiners expect you to document your search and argue why other specific theories were deselected. For the fish filleting example, the project must argue for deselecting any theory about fish filleting or the broader food production theory; for example, a great argument is that a specific theory about fish filleting does exist but only covers preserving filleted fish and other issues unrelated to reducing delivery times.

Documenting the literature review's search and selection process

An academic research project documents its search and selection of literature by describing the search and selection process. The first step in this process is generating the right search string for use in your university library's database.

EXAMPLE

Documenting your process for searching and selecting literature shows your reader which steps you have taken to locate the theory that is most relevant for your project among all literature.

This process consists of a number of steps that begin with the use of search strings in your library's database. A search string contains the relevant keywords that limit your search to the literature that is relevant for your project. The database searches in the titles, abstracts, and keywords of books and papers.

Consider this example that deals with yet another offshore wind turbine component affected by the salty air. In this example, the item is the turbine's hydraulic system. This project looks for the relevant literature using the following search string:

"surface treatment" AND hydraulic*

The search string contains a number of elements that limit the search. The word AND is a so-called "Boolean operator," which tells the search engine only to include books and papers that contain *both* "surface treatment" *and* hydraulic* in the search result. The quotation marks around "surface treatment" indicate that the search engine should only include books and papers where surface and treatment are right next to each other as if they were one word. The search engine considers all words between the quotation marks as one word. The asterisk (*) indicates that words that begin with hydraulic are included, regardless of their ending (e.g. hydraulics or hydraulically).

The search string results in a list of around 1,000 books and papers. Among these is an article in the journal *Materials Research Innovations* titled *"Analysis of antiwear for hydraulic relief valve under different surface treatment processes."* This article examines how surface treatment of a valve impacts the valve's wear. The search is on the right track. If too many books and papers are thrown up by the search, then refine the search string. For example:

"surface treatment" AND hydraulic* AND ("high salinity" OR "high saltiness")

OR is a Boolean operator that broadens your search results. The search engine includes books and papers that contain *either* the term on the left of the operator *or* the term on the right.

Once you have a list of books and papers, begin screening them for relevance. The list will probably only contain a few books and many papers. First, read the titles and abstracts of papers to screen for those that are irrelevant. Following the screening, you have a much shorter set of books and papers. Now, read or skim full papers. You will end up with a complete set of papers for your literature review. Document each step and use clear criteria as arguments for why you deselect certain papers.

Content of the literature review section in the report

The literature review has three overall elements:

1 A summary of the literature that examines related questions and subjects.
2 An argumentation for why your project is needed and adds value to the research field's body of knowledge. Use the summary of existing literature to establish that a gap in the literature needs filling and show that your project does exactly that.
3 A definition of your project's key concepts using existing literature. If your concept definitions do not build on extant literature, then define your concepts in the literature review section without referencing sources.

Occasionally, research projects develop a theoretical framework as the foundation for the study. Operationalizing concepts and building theoretical frameworks are usually the final parts of the literature review. Operational concepts and theoretical frameworks feed directly into the following report section, Methods and materials.

Methods and materials

This section describes an academic research project's use of theory, methods, and materials. When you have defined your research question, reviewed the literature, operationalized your key concepts, and perhaps built a theoretical framework as the base for your study, the next step is choosing and describing the project's methodology.

The first choice is selecting the overall method for your analysis. In engineering projects, the overall method is often mathematical modeling, case study research, a survey, an experiment, or a combination of these methods. In addition to the choice of overall method, you make a set of smaller methodological choices. For example, methods for collecting data, methods for displaying and analyzing data, and methods for ensuring data validity and reliability. A method can be either purely quantitative (e.g. a statistical study), purely qualitative (an interview study), or a mixture of the two (e.g. a case study leading to a mathematical model).

Your study should argue why the reader can trust your method to produce a valid and reliable result. Argue for your methodology choices by drawing on your research question ("Because the research question …, the methodology …"). Ideally, having read the methodology section, your reader has the feeling of: "Of course this is the best method. Anything but this method would lead to a less valid conclusion or even complete nonsense." If this is what your reader thinks, your methodology is solid and your methodology section is written perfectly.

There is often a relation between methodology choices and the maturity of your field of study. If your field is newly established, research often concerns uncovering the landscape and identifying relevant variables and research questions. For such research, consider using an exploratory method such as case study research. If your field is well established and has a long tradition, your project could develop mathematical models that bind variables together in precise expressions, or use survey research, which requires a thorough understanding of the subject by both researchers and survey respondents.

Results

The results section follows the methodology section. This section describes the results of your data analysis as they are *without* interpretation or discussion of causes. You can describe results with regular prose or through diagrams, tables, mathematical expressions, drawings, a set of interview quotes, or a combination. The right format depends on the research type and your field's traditions.

The results section portrays results without explanation or discussion of their meaning and implications. These activities are the subject of the following sections – discussion, conclusion, and reflections about study limitations.

Discussion, including conclusions, contributions, limitations, and future research suggestions

After the results section, the final sections in your project must achieve a number of objectives. These sections should:

1 *Discuss results* – see specifics in Table 16.4
2 *Present the conclusions* – answers to your project's research questions
3 *Describe your project's contribution* to your field, including to the industrial practice of your engineering discipline
4 *Describe and discuss your project's limitations* and the validity of your conclusion
5 *Suggest new projects* – perhaps a project that could verify your results.

The discussion section reviews the results, which specifically means answering the two questions posed in Table 16.4.

Table 16.4 Two important questions and their answers	
Question	**How to answer**
Why are the results as they are?	Suggest and discuss possible explanations for your results and present hypotheses arising from your results. The discussion section is a relatively free section, so you are free to suggest explanations
How do your results compare with existing research?	Discuss the existing literature that your results support, which literature your results might contradict, and which literature your results might extend. Include references to papers from your earlier literature review and discuss how your results support, nuance, extend, detail, operationalize, or contradict these papers. A great literature review provides the basis for a great discussion

Finally, summarize your results and perhaps one or two major points from your discussion in your conclusion section. Answer your research questions specifically and do remember that your conclusion is not a summary of what you have done in your project. Then, reflect on your study's limitations, and, from your limitations, make suggestions for future research.

Reviewing this chapter's objectives

Tick those objectives you feel you have achieved, and review those you haven't yet accomplished. In this chapter, you have learned how to:

❐ Distinguish between projects that designs solutions to specific problems and M.Sc. projects that (often) conduct academic research in order to contribute to the general base of knowledge within your discipline.

❐ Manage *two* primary stakeholders: an industrial partner and the university.

❐ Structure an M.Sc. project following the traditional structure of academic papers.

❐ Systematically localize and use theory and conduct methodological choices.

❐ Describe the methodology, analysis, discussions and conclusion in the project report.

References

Booth, W.C., Colomb, G.G. and Williams, J.M. (2008) *The Craft of Research*, 3rd edn, Chicago: The University of Chicago Press.

DeLuca, J. (1984) "Managing the sociopolitical context in planned change efforts", in A. Kakabadse and C. Parker (eds) *Power, Politics, and Organizations: A Behavioral Science View*, Chichester: Wiley.

Edmondson, A. (1999) Psychological safety and learning behavior in work teams, *Administrative Science Quarterly*, 44(2): 350–83, available at http://web.mit.edu/curhan/www/docs/Articles/15341_Readings/Group_Performance/Edmondson%20Psychological%20safety.pdf.

Kotter, J.P. (2007) Leading change: why transformation efforts fail, *Harvard Business Review*, 85(1): 96–103.

Lippman, L.H., Ryberg, R., Carney, R. and Moore, K.A. (2015) *Workforce Connections – Key "Soft Skills" That Foster Youth Workforce Success: Towards a Consensus Across Fields*, cited in R.M. Golinkoff and K. Hirsh-Pasek (2016) *Becoming Brilliant: What Science Tells Us about Raising Successful Children*, Washington, DC: APA.

Reid, N. (2010) *Getting Published in International Journals*, Hauppauge, NY: NOVA.

Sirkin, H.L., Keenan, P. and Jackson, A. (2005) The hard side of change management, *Harvard Business Review*, 83(10): 108–18.

Tuckman, B.W. (1965) Developmental sequence in small groups. *Psychological Bulletin,* 63(6): 384–99.

Index

Abstract, *See Project report, Executive summary*
Analysis, 68, 71–83, 157–62
    Foundation for, 39, 45–8, 209
    Investment analysis; *See Solution, Financial feasibility*
    Problem tree in, 46–7
    Problem analysis, *See Problem Analysis*
    Root cause analysis, 73–7
    Stakeholder analysis, *See Stakeholder analysis*
    When designing new entity, 77–80
    When improving existing entity, 71–7
Anecdotal evidence, Use of, 17, 33, 149
Applied sciences vs. Basic sciences; 38–9
Argumentation, 53, 61–2
    Types of arguments, 61
    When to argue for your choices, 60–1

Basic sciences, Use of, 38, 39
Body language, voice, and eye contact, 188-9

Causal analysis, *See Analysis*
Causal trajectory, 19, 55, 75, 158
Cause for problem, 25, 27–8, 45-8, 56, 73–75, 85, 157–9
    Actual versus generic (theoretically possible), 47
    Generic (theoretically possible), 45–7
    Identification of, 45–8, 56, 73–75
    One or multiple causes, 45, 56, 71, 73–4, 87
    Causes's relative impact on problem, 76–7
Cause-and-effect relationships, *See Causal trajectory*
CDIO (Conceive, Design, Implement, and Operate), 2, 4, 10
Choices, Unconscious, 61
Clarity, *See Language and Graphical Displays*
Coherence, 31, 41, 56–7, 61, 80, 120, 152, 157, 162, 174, 187–8, 197
Collaboration, 5, 109–21
    Building trust in your team, 113–15, 118
    Contract, 110–13, 115, 118
    Differences in effort, commitment and perception of objectives, 116–17

Differences in skill-level, 117
    Handling conflicts, 115–18
    Industrial partner collaboration, *See Industrial partner*
    Psycological safety, 113–15
    Team collaboration, *See Collaboration*
    Trust, *See Building trust in your team*
Communication within your team, 5, 104–5, 110–13
Communication in your report, *See Language and Graphical displays*
Complaint filing, *See Examination, Complaint*
Conclusion, 147, 157, 169–70
    Developing conclusions, 169
    Validity of, 169–70
Confidentiality agreement, 134–5
Conflicts, *See Collaboration, Handling conflicts*
Construction codes, 38–9, 48, 93, 152
Contract, *See Collaboration, Contract*
Contribution to knowledge, *See Knowledge, Contribution to*
Critical thinking, 5, 16, 30, 59, 90, 120–1, 134, 170, 197

Data, 66–83
    Collection of, 67–71
    Collection purpose, 67-9
    Data analysis, *See Analysis*
    Data type diversity, 66–7
    Generation of, 70, 72, 149
    Location of, 69–70
    Meaning of the term, 66
    Precision, *See Reliability*
    Relevance, *See Validity*
    Reliability, 80–3
    Top tips when data is not available, 70–1
    Trustworthiness, *See Reliability*
    Validity, 80–3
Deduction, 49–50
Deductive reasoning, *See Deduction*
Definitions, *See Variable, Definitions*
Delimitations, 27, 149–50, 205
    From problem statement, 27, 149–50, 205
    Local in particular report sections, 150
Design, *See Solution design*

Design requirements, 30, 55–9, 77–80, 85, 88–90, 92, 152–4, 161–4
 Absolute (must have) requirements, 78
 As good as possible requirements, 78
 Breaking down requirements, 79-80
 Description of, 152-4, 161–4
 Identification of, 78-9
 Most common requirement categories, 78
 Operationalization of, 79-80
 Specification of, 79
Diagrams, *See Graphical displays*
Discussion section, *See Project report, Discussion section*

Engineering research, *See Research*
Entity, *See Variable*
Equipment, *See Methodology, Methods and materials*
Errors in report, Dealing with, *See Group presentations*
Examination, 184-94
 Complaint, Formal, 120, 192–3
 Discussion at the exam table, 191–2
 Dissatisfaction, 192–3
 Oral, 191-2
 Resit (re-exam), 194
Executive summary, *See Project report, Executive summary*
Experimentation, 49, 70, 155–6, 209
External examiner, 134–5, 137, 174, 195–200
Extrapolation, *See Quantification*

Faculty, 14, 42, 119
Feasibility, *See Solution, Financial feasibility*
Financial feasibility, *See Solution, Financial feasibility*
Fishbone diagram, 74
Five-why method, 73–4
Focus, 15–16, 30–3, 124, 126, 131–133
Forming groups, *See Group formation*
Function, *See Subsystem*

Gantt chart, 62-4
Grammar, *See Language*
Graphical displays, 180–2
Group collaboration contract, *See Collaboration, Contract*
Group collaboration, *See Collaboration*

Group communication, *See Communication within your team*
Group discussions, 112–14, 117-18
Group dynamics, *See Group formation*
Group formation, 109
Group meetings, *See Collaboration*
Group meetings, Use of online platforms, *See Communication*
Group presentation, 184–90
Group presentations, Coherence in, 187
Group, Professional behavior, *See Collaboration*

Hypothesis, 18

Illustrations, *See Graphical displays*
Implementation, 91, 93–4, 101–5, 127, 165–6, 167–9, 189
Improvement opportunities, 45–7
IMRAD, 54, 144, 204–11
Induction, 49–50
Industrial partner, 2, 6, 14–18, 20, 26–7, 104–5, 122–35
 "Selling" project to, 123
 Agreeing on problem statement with, 125–6
 Breadth versus focus, 132–4
 Continuous involvement, 104–5, 126–7, 129
 Cooperation, 122-35
 Department head, *See Industrial partner, Managers*
 Ensuring available employee time, 128–9
 Getting data on time, 128–9
 Informal power structure, *See Stakeholder analysis*
 Initial conversations, Top tips for, 16
 Ownership of project, 104–5
 Pitfalls, 130–4
 Project portfolio, 20
 Search for, 123
 Unfolding circle of relevant persons, 123–5
 Use of workshops, 105, 126–9
 Wish for solution, 14–16
Information, *See Data*
International students, 109, 118
Interview, 18, 66, 69, 72, 83, 159, 181, 197, 210
 Bias, 83, 197
 Interview guide, 66
 Semi-structured, 18

Iterative design process, 57–9, 80, 88, 161–3
Iterative process for problem identification, 18–9

Journal, Scientific, 37, 86, 202

Knowledge, 13–14, 37–49, 52, 151
  Contribution to, 202–3, 205–6, 210
  Foundation, 37–49
  Level of, 13–14
  Review of, See Literature, Review of

Language, 173–4
Learning goals, See Learning objectives
Learning objectives, 13, 41
Literature review, 151, 207–9
Literature review, Documenting process for, 208–9
Literature, 14, 18, 37–45, 78–9, 151–4, 205–9, 209
  Operational, 48–9
  Relevant, 40–1, 75, 78–9
  Review of, See Literature review
  Search for, 41–2, 208–9
  Use of, 42–6
Logical reasoning, 47, 49–50, 57–9, 75, 96, 159, 161, 197

M.Sc. project, see Master of Science project
Master of Science project, 201–11
Metacommunication and metatexts, 174–6, 198
Methodology, 24–5, 29–30, 51–62, 154–7, 163, 166, 209–10
  Description, 154–7, 163, 166, 209–10
  Planning of project, 62–5
  Project structure, See Project structure
  Selecting methods, tools, and techniques, 59–60, 60–1
  Selection, 53–4, 60–2
  Timing of methodology selection, 60–1
  Typical structure of project, See Structure of project
  When developing of a new entity, 29–30
  When improving an existing entity, 24–5
Methods and materials, See Methodology
Milestones, See Gantt chart
Multi-criteria variables, 32–3

Need for solution, See Problem, Solution need
Nervousness, Managing, 172, 188–9, 192
Non-disclosure agreement, See Confidentiality agreement
Nontraditional choices, 62

Operationalization, See Theory operationalization or Design requirements, Operationalization of
Opportunities, Generic, See Improvement opportunities
Organizational politics, 136–42
Owning the stage, See Body language, voice, and eye contact

Paradigms, Selection of, See Philosophy of Science
Personal network, Use of, 14, 122
Personality tests, Use of, 109–10
Perspectives, Selection of, See Philosophy of Science
Philosophy of Science, 52–3
Positivism, See Philosophy of Science
Poster design, 190–1
Poster sessions, 190–1
PowerPoint presentations, See Group presentations
Practiced-oriented literature, 37–8
Preference test, See Role preference test
Presentation, See Group Presentation
Presentation, PowerPoint, 184–90
Problem, 8–9, 14–20, 22–4, See also Problem Statement
  Archetypes, 8–9, 34, 55
  Causes for, See Analysis
  Design new entity, 29–30
  Existence, 15–18
  Hierarchy, 19–20, 45–8, 73–5
  Identification of, 14–16
  Improve existing entity, 24–9
  Landscape, 14–16, 18–19, 68, 119, 123
  Measurement of, 17, 33, 71–2, 149
  Problem solving, 1, 7, 52, 202–3
  Problem tree, See Problem tree
  Size of, 15–18, 71–2, 149
  Solution need is problem, 18, 29–30, 57–8, 126
  Structuring, See Problem, Hierarchy
  Verification of, See Problem, Measurement of

Problem statement, 9, 14, 22–36, 40–1, 51,
  67–8, 119–21, 124–6, 149, 205
  Changes in, 27–9
  Characteristics of, 30–4
  Clarity, 25–7, 29–30
  Components of, 26
  Focus, 31-33
  Formulation of, 25–7, 29–30
  Need for solution, 29–30
  Quantifiability, 33–4
  Subquestions, 35–6
Problem structure, *See Problem tree*
Problem tree, 18–20, 31–2, 46–8, 73–5,
  158–9
  Generic (theoretical), 46–8
  Hierarchical, 46–8
  Actual, 75
Problem analysis, 14–20
Problem-based learning (PBL), 4
Process, The nature of a, 23–4
Professor, *See Supervisor and Faculty*
Project beginning, *See Project initiation*
Project initiation, 12–21, 123–6
Project methodology, *See Methodology*
Project problem, *See Problem*
Project report, 144–72
  Abstract, *See Project report, Executive
    summary*
  Analysis section, 157–62
  Appendices and data documentation,
    171–2
  Clarity, *See Language and Graphical Displays*
  Conclusion section, 169–70
  Delimitations, 149–50
  Discussion section, 170
  Executive summary, 147
  Front page, 145–7
  Implementation section, 167–9
  Introduction, 147–9
  Literature review, 151–4, 207–9
  Numbers and quantitative analyses in,
    179–82
  Problem statement in the report, 149
  Recommendations for industrial partner,
    169–70
  References, 171–1
  Solution description 161–6
  Title, 145–7
Project stakeholders, *See Stakeholders*
Project structure, 54–59

Project structure for traditional research, *See
  IMRAD*
Psycological safety, *See Collaboration,
  Psycological safety*

Qualitative data, 66–7, 71, 76, 97–8, 159–60,
  181, 209
Quantification, 98–9
Quantitative data, 66–7, 72, 97–8, 159–60,
  179–81

Re-exam, *See Resit*
Reliability, *See Data, Reliability*
Report, *See Project report*
Requirements, *See Design Requirements*
Research, 202–11
Research design, *See Methodology*
Research project, Structure of, *See IMRAD*
Research questions, Typical, 206–7
Research reports, *See Research and IMRAD*
Resit (re-exam), 194
Role preference test, 109–10
Root cause analysis, *See Analysis*
Root cause, *See Cause for problem*

Safe space, *See Collaboration, Psychological
  safety*
Semi-structured interviews, 18
Social constructivism, *See Philosophy of
  science*
Soft skills, 5
Solution, 84–99, 162–6
  Design of, 84–99
  Ease of implementation, 93–4, 165–6
  Effect of, 92–3, 165–6
  Financial feasibility, 95–6
  Implementation of, *See Implementation*
  Nature of engineering solution, 85
  Specifications (the "spec"), *See Design
    specifications*
  Test, *See Testing the solution*
Spec, *See Design requirement specification*
Spelling, *See Language*
Stakeholder analysis, 138–41
Stakeholders, Managing, 136–42
Stakeholders, Typical, 136–8
Standard methods, 59–60
Structure of project, 55–9
Subquestions to problem statement, *See
  Problem statement, Subquestions*

Subsystem, 57–59, 68, 77, 80–1, 85, 160–2
  Identification of, 80–1, 161–2
  Technical solutions for, 80–1
Success criteria, 58, 78, 88, 90, 197–8
Supervision, 14, 98–9, 115–8, 118–121
  Reflection on ideas and advice, 120–1
  Subjects for discussion, 120
  Supervisor as examiner, 121

Testing the solution, 100–1
Textbook references, 170–1, 178–9
Textbook, Use of, 14, 42
Theory, 37–50
  Choice, *See Theory, Selection*
  Location of, 41–2
  Operationalization, 48–9
    Selection, 40–1
    Use of, 42–50
Trust, *See Collaboration, Trust*

Unit of measurement, 33, 44, 165
User of solution, 59, 71, 77, 92, 104, 126,
    137, 153, 163, 167, 195

Validity, 54, 61, 80–3, 127, 169–70, 209–10
Variable, 25–9, 31–4, 43–4, 55–6, 125–6,
    151, 206
  Definitions, 43–4, 151
  Dependent and independent, 206–7
  Quantifying variables, *see Quantification*
  Relationships between variables, 26, 206–7
Variables, The central, 43–4, 151